REREADING
GERMAN HISTORY

In *Rereading German History*, Richard J. Evans draws together his seminal review essays on the political, economic, cultural and social history of Germany through war and reunification. This book provides a study of how and why historians – mainly German, American, British and French – have provided a series of differing and often conflicting readings of the German past. It also presents a reconsideration of German history in the light of the recent decline of the German Democratic Republic, collapse of the Berlin Wall and the reunification of Germany.

Rereading German History re-examines major controversies in modern German history, such as the debate over Germany's 'special path' to modernity in the nineteenth and twentieth centuries, and the discussions in the 1980s on the uniqueness or otherwise of Auschwitz. Richard J. Evans also analyses the arguments about the nature of German national identity, the recent debates over the extent of a national tradition of popular antisemitism and the recent re-emergence of the right-wing nationalist politics.

Rereading German History presents the collected reviews of one of the single most important historians of modern Germany. The book offers trenchant and important analytical insights into the history of Germany in the last two centuries.

Richard J. Evans is Professor of History and Vice-Master, Birkbeck College, University of London and author of many books, including *Rethinking German History* (1987).

REREADING GERMAN HISTORY

From unification to reunification
1800–1996

Richard J. Evans

London and New York

First published 1997
by Routledge
11 New Fetter Lane, London EC4P 4EE

Simultaneously published in the USA and Canada
by Routledge
29 West 35th Street, New York, NY 10001

Typeset in Garamond by LaserScript Limited, Mitcham, Surrey

Printed and bound in Great Britain by
TJ International, Padstow, Cornwall

British Library Cataloguing in Publication Data
A catalogue record for this book is available from the British Library

Library of Congress Cataloguing in Publication Data
A catalogue record for this book has been requested

ISBN 0–415–15899–0 (hbk)
ISBN 0–415–15900–8 (pbk)

CONTENTS

CONTENTS

Part IV Faces of the Third Reich

Part V Reunification and beyond

PREFACE

This book has a deliberately ambiguous title. *Rereading German History* means in the first place a study of how different historians – mainly German, but also American, British, and French – have provided a series of differing and often conflicting readings of the German past in recent years. In a previous collection of essays, *Rethinking German History*, published a decade ago, I presented a case for breaking away from the traditional concentration of historians of Germany on high politics, foreign affairs, parties, organizations and pressure-groups, and broadening out our view of the German past, taking an approach which included everyday life and experience, the social and cultural history of the mass of German men and women, and the subjective elements of people's perceptions of the times they lived through. This book does not abandon the arguments advanced in the earlier one, but rather pursues them through an examination of some of the most significant historical work of the intervening decade. The emphasis, as before, is on the arguments that have raged over the long-term continuities that some historians have detected in modern German history, and the extent to which the roots of Nazism can be traced deep into the German past. The essays collected here, most of them written in the late 1980s and early 1990s, ask how far historians of Germany have indeed broadened their approach in the past decade, and seek to determine how far they have defended, changed or abandoned the arguments discussed in the earlier book.

But *Rereading German History* has a second meaning. For the decade or so of historical writing which it covers saw the decline and fall of the German Democratic Republic, the collapse of the Berlin Wall, and the reunification of Germany. These were among the most dramatic of the events which marked the demise of Communism in Central and Eastern Europe in 1989/90. Few people were prepared for them – least of all, myself. In common with the great majority of commentators, I had assumed that the division of Germany would last a good while yet, and was quite unprepared for the speed at which events moved when the collapse finally began. The essays in this volume reflect on the extent to which reunification itself has forced everyone to reconsider the positions they took on German history in the 1980s and before. This, indeed, is the second meaning of the word 'rereading' used in the title to this book: it is about the ways in which the events of 1989/90 have led to widespread changes in historians' readings of the German past – or not, as the case may be.

In Germany, the events of 1989/90 led to a great deal of soul-searching. Reunification challenged the sense of identity that had been so carefully built up in West Germany over the decades since 1949. The right had seen anti-Communism as the defining element in this identity, while the left regarded the country's division as part of the price that had to be paid for the crimes of the Third Reich. Both were now faced with the task of having to rethink these definitions of German identity in the light of the end of Germany's division. History and historians have played a central role in this process. The essays collected in this book seek to examine that role. They are centred on two particular questions. First, they attempt to set German reunification in its longer-term historical context. Does reunification really mark the resurgence of an aggressive German nationalism, or are there many varieties of nationalist discourse in modern German history, and if so, to which of them, if any, does the debate over reunification in Germany itself most closely correspond? How can a rereading of the German past help us understand the dynamics of reunification and post-unification politics in the German present? Secondly, they try to discuss how reunification itself has affected the way German historians have written about their country's past – both about the first unification of Germany in the nineteenth century and about the subsequent course of German history, up to and including Hitler's 'Third Reich'. Has it led to a renewal of the attempt made in the mid-1980s, in the famous *Historikerstreit*, to relativize and gloss over the crimes of Nazism? Has it caused German historians, as some have argued, to retreat from their previous view of German history as taking a 'special route' to modernity, the famous *Sonderweg*, a view which located the origins of National Socialism deep in the German past? Is there a general trend away from the idea of German exceptionalism, and towards the view that there is nothing historically unusual about the Germans; that it was merely a matter of chance circumstance that the Third Reich happened in Germany and not in some different but closely related alternative version elsewhere?

What this book hopes to show is that while there are answers to all of these questions, none of them is particularly simple or clear-cut. That is partly because historians are all individuals, with their own particular ideas and interpretations which cannot easily be reduced to a simple political or methodological formula. But it is also because history is far more than merely a rereading of past politics in the light of present circumstances. As an academic discipline it has its own rules, its own methods, its own fashions and trends, its own history indeed, and all of these possess a distinct relative autonomy from the social and political milieu in which history is written and researched. The emergence of social history in Germany, for instance, cannot simply be reduced to a reflection of the emergence of a generation of liberal and Social Democratic historians in the 1970s. The two developments are clearly related, of course, but social history is also an international phenomenon, of which there are – in Germany as well as in other countries – conservative as well as liberal or left-wing variants. Professional historians not only write within the context of an academic discipline, they are also bound by the constraints of evidence, and they cross the line between reinterpretation and distortion, reasoned argument and special pleading, at their peril, as a number of the essays in this book demonstrate. It is precisely this interplay between the objective constraints of history, the disciplinary and methodological contexts of writing and research, and the political beliefs and perceptions of the historian living in a particular present-day context, which makes the study of how historians have dealt with the German past during the period of reunification so fascinating.

The book is divided into five roughly equal parts, each prefaced by a brief introduction. The first part looks at some major new syntheses of modern German history written during the late 1980s and 1990s, focusing particularly on Germany's first unification in the nineteenth century. Their approach varies considerably. The American historian James Sheehan placed the emphasis on contingency and chance circumstance in an attempt to undermine traditional nationalist accounts of the unification of Germany under Bismarck. The German historian Thomas Nipperdey, by contrast, sought to justify unification in the 1860s as a 'natural' and 'inevitable' historical process, while at the same time uncoupling its consequences from the coming of Hitler sixty years later, in an attempt to provide an historical legitimation for German unity. The once-dominant thesis that the roots of the Nazi dictatorship lay in the 'special path' or *Sonderweg* taken by Germany in the transition to modernity during the nineteenth century has now been effectively abandoned by its leading proponent, Hans-Ulrich Wehler, but, it will be argued, more for sound scholarly reasons than because of any alleged deference to the politics of reunification.

All the historians who have written about Bismarck, however, including the author of the latest survey of these events, Wolfgang J. Mommsen, are forced to agree, whatever their politics, that the 'Iron Chancellor' laid down what Nipperdey calls 'shadow-lines' in modern German history that were to have disastrous consequences for German political culture after his death. In France, by contrast, as the work of Joseph Rovan, the last to be discussed in Part I, indicates, there is in some quarters often a strong tendency to gloss over the unpleasant aspects of German history in the interests of European unity, in a manner that ultimately fails to carry conviction because of the scant regard it pays to the empirical imperatives of historical scholarship. All these different attempts to construct a grand narrative of German history in the nineteenth century (or, in Rovan's case the whole of German history) also have their own particular concept of historical method, and this too forms an important part of the discussion. Does writing a 'history' of a whole country mean including everything, as Nipperdey argued? Does it require a more precise, and therefore more restricted, organizing concept, such as the 'societal history' which Wehler offers? Or is it mainly important to concentrate on the detailed exposition of the course of domestic and foreign policy, as Mommsen does? Does it mean primarily writing a work of reference, such as Sheehan attempts, or does it demand a 'return to narrative', in which the historian tells a story that can be read with pleasure from beginning to end, as Nipperdey wanted his book to be? As the essays in Part I show, rereading German history is not only a matter of political agendas, it also involves a whole series of theoretical and methodological decisions before it can even begin.

The second part of the book turns to patterns of authority and revolt in modern German history and the way in which these have been dealt with by historians. Many historians have drawn attention to the tradition of the strong state in Germany, dating above all from the era of Absolutism in the late seventeenth and eighteenth centuries. It is a tradition, indeed, which the advocates of a 'new right' in Germany today would dearly like to revive, if indeed it has ever gone away. But a reading of recent histories of one of the main agencies of the strong state, the German police, while confirming the general impression of their wide-ranging powers and competencies, leads to a questioning of the role of Absolutism in the formation of this tradition. Here, too, the historian has to make crucial theoretical and methodological decisions before embarking on research; and it is striking how German work on the history of the police still relies on Weberian concepts and methods, while it takes a North American historian to apply the arguably more fruitful concepts developed by the French philosopher-historian Michel Foucault in this area.

The next chapter in Part II deals, more briefly, with Bismarckian Germany as a Protestant state, discriminating heavily against Catholics in the so-called *Kulturkampf*, a topic already dealt with in some of the essays in Part I. Here too, for all its limitations, the power of the strong state was much in evidence in the 1870s, backed, even more ominously, by the enthusiasm of liberals who were too eager to sacrifice civil liberties in the name of intellectual progress. Catholics, on the other hand, mounted a strong resistance to the disciplining initiatives of the state, and in discussing a study of one particular incident in their struggle, the chapter takes a close and critical look at the benefits and limitations of the recent trend in historical research towards 'microstudies' of particular events and localities. The last two chapters in Part II turn to the resistance offered by the other major objective of Bismarckian state discrimination: the labour movement. The first of them looks at the failure of the idea of producer co-operatives in the early German labour movement, and draws some parallels with developments within German consumerism at the time of writing. From the Bismarckian period onwards German Social Democracy focused on the political organization of the working class as the key to power. The final essay in Part II examines the failure of the German labour movement in the Weimar Republic, and in so doing offers a critique of the approach of historians who, like Heinrich August Winkler, whose massive three-volume history of the labour movement from 1918 to 1933 is at the centre of the picture here, stand close to the present-day German Social Democrats. Here the present-day concern to provide a legitimation for a flexible, non-Marxist form of democratic socialism which is concerned above all with the maintenance of political and social stability, has structured, and perhaps distorted, the historical assessment of a different Social Democratic Party operating under different political and social circumstances.

Part III turns to the intellectual origins of the Third Reich. The breakdown of public order in the early Weimar years was brought about not least by the activities of the paramilitary Free Corps. The first essay in Part III explores the ethos of these proto-Nazi bands and discusses the psychoanalytical reading of it put forward by Klaus Theweleit in his celebrated book *Male Fantasies*. Under the Third Reich, the visceral but unsystematic violence of the Free Corps was replaced by planned state violence directed against racial and other minorities. In recent years, the sterilization and murder of the handicapped undertaken by Nazi Germany in the name of racial progress, and the encouragement of medical experimentation on concentration camp inmates, have become the focus of a great deal of research. Two further chapters in Part III discuss the roots of these policies in the development of medical and biological science and the rise of Social Darwinism. Here too, there has been a marked shift in the focus of historical research in recent years. Marxist readings of the Third Reich have given way to a much greater emphasis on racism as that state's organizing principle; as Chapters 11 and 12 argue, the enterprise of tracing back Nazi policies and ideas to the late nineteenth century is a legitimate one, despite the fact that historians have so frequently become conceptually confused between the search for origins and the postulate of inevitability. Here too, concepts and definitions arrived at by historians at the outset of their work tend to shape the conclusions they reach at the end.

Finally, Chapter 13 takes a long and hard look at the history of German antisemitism, which has recently been the focus of a heated debate between the young American political scientist Daniel Jonah Goldhagen and professional historians in Germany and elsewhere. The chapter examines in detail Goldhagen's claim that 'eliminationist antisemitism' was deeply embedded in German political culture in the nineteenth century, and that Hitler's programme to exterminate the Jews was therefore extremely popular amongst Germans and found hundreds of thousands of willing and enthusiastic helpers keen to put it into action. The revival of this idea, first mooted in wartime propaganda, has come as a shock to many German commentators, who thought that reunification had drawn a line under the German past and brought the post-war era to an end; and the chapter investigates some of the reasons for the popularity of Goldhagen's book *Hitler's Willing Executioners* in Germany itself, as well as in Britain and the United States, and explores the motives of its many critics.

Part IV asks some controversial questions about key figures in the history of Nazi Germany, focusing on the vexed question of resistance and accommodation. Was the conductor Wilhelm Furtwängler a Nazi cultural icon, a hero of the resistance, or just a naive conservative collaborator? Were the plotters behind Claus von Stauffenberg, the man who almost succeeded in blowing up Hitler on 20 July 1944, democrats or reactionaries, and how representative were they of the German resistance as a whole? Did Hitler's favourite architect and wartime Minister of Armaments, Albert Speer, know about Auschwitz; was he just a politically neutral technocrat or did his involvement in the regime go deeper? Did he ever admit his true part in the crimes of Nazism? And was it likely that Hitler would have concluded a separate peace with Britain in 1941 if a more flexible figure than Churchill had been Prime Minister of Britain at the time? In answering all these questions, historians, as Chapters 14–17 show, have, perhaps more than usually, provided a reading of German history based on present-day concerns, whether these have reflected admiration for a great musician, family piety and conservative politics, retrospective self-justification, or right-wing Euroscepticism. All the essays in Part IV suggest that such agendas, when applied without regard to the complexities of the historical circumstances involved, obscure the contours of the past rather than throwing them into the kind of sharp relief that is needed.

The final part of the book takes the story up to the present. Chapter 18 sets the events of reunification in their historical context and warns against the temptation, to which a good number of politicians and journalists on the left as well as the right outside Germany have succumbed, of simply equating them with a revival of German nationalism or the 'rise of the Fourth Reich'. Chapter 19 looks at the famous (or notorious) *Historikerstreit* – the very acrimonious public dispute which took place in the second half of the 1980s over the attempt of some conservative German historians to relativize the Nazi past – in the light of reunification, and deals with the parallels which some have tried to draw between the aftermath of Communism and the aftermath of Nazism – parallels which have involved, it is argued, a forced rereading of denazification in the interests of the plea for a comprehensive process of destalinization. Such a plea has been one of the major demands of the German right in the 1990s; yet, as Chapter 20 argues, disorientation and a feeling of resentment have characterized the

PREFACE

German right in this period rather than a rampant sense of triumphalism
after the collapse of Communism. Finally, the book concludes with a brief
general look at the relationship between reunification and German
historical writing, and argues against those who have seen a wholesale
revival of nationalistic history, accompanied by the craven capitulation of
those one might have expected to resist it. This ties up the arguments put
forward in many other chapters in the book, and suggests that historical
writing develops in response to a multiplicity of influences, disciplinary as
well as political, international as well as domestic. The passage of time may
mean that the Nazi experience will become less central to the study of
modern German history, but explaining the Third Reich will always pose a
challenge to historians in the future, as it has done in the present and the
past.

The twenty-one chapters in this book were all written as extended book
reviews or review articles. All except three of them date from the 1990s.
They have mostly been reprinted as they were first published. However, in
some cases, where they were cut by newspaper editors for reasons of space,
the passages omitted from the original articles have been restored, while
some contemporary references in the more journalistic pieces have been
excised. Inevitably, too, there are some overlaps between the different
chapters, and while some passages have been deleted to reduce the amount
of repetition, it has not been possible to do this in every case without
damaging the article in question beyond repair. Chapter 21 was written
specially for the book; Chapter 13 began life as a contribution to an ongoing
debate in the German weekly *Die Zeit*, but was axed when the series was
brought to an end; it also incorporates an earlier book review and a lecture
delivered in Jerusalem in November 1996.

I am grateful to all the editors concerned for having commissioned the
essays in the first place, and for permission to reprint them here. Thanks are
also due to the various archives and libraries where the research was carried
out, in the case of chapters which incorporate work on primary and
secondary sources. Many colleagues and friends have supplied me with
material, read and commented on and discussed the merits or otherwise of
many of the articles and the arguments in them, and given encouragement
and criticism of particular chapters. I am particularly grateful to Manfred
Berg, Michael Burleigh, Norbert Frei, Geoffrey Cocks, Martin Jaques, Robert
Gellately, Heinrich Senfft, Volker Ullrich, Hans-Ulrich Wehler, and the
members of London University's Research Seminar in Modern German
Social History. Heather McCallum has been a helpful and enthusiastic editor
at Routledge; Stephanie Rogers and the production and design teams have
done a splendid job in putting the book together. To all of them my thanks.

Richard J. Evans, London, November 1996

ACKNOWLEDGEMENTS

The author and publisher would like to thank the following for permission to reproduce material published elsewhere as follows:

Chapter 1. 'Towards Unification', *The Times Literary Supplement*, 4–10 May 1990, pp. 463–4. Chapter 2. 'Bürgerliche Gesellschaft und charismatische Herrschaft', *Die Zeit*, 13 October 1995, pp. 32–3. Chapter 3. 'Nipperdeys Neunzehntes Jahrhundert: Eine kritische Auseinandersetzung', *Geschichte und Gesellschaft*, 20 (1994), pp. 119–39. Chapter 4. Review of Wolfgang J. Mommsen, *Das Ringen um den nationalen Staat* and *Bürgerstolz und Weltmachtstreben* (Propyläen Geschichte Deutschlands, Vol. 7/I and 7/II, 1993, 1995), in *Bulletin of the German Historical Institute London*, 18 (1996), pp. 15–26. Chapter 5. 'Jenseits der Schattenlinien', *Die Zeit* (7 April 1995), p. 30. Chapter 6. 'Polizei und Gesellschaft in Deutschland von der Aufklärung bis zum Dritten Reich', *Geschichte und Gesellschaft*, March 1996; and review of Robert Gellately, *The Gestapo and German Society* (Oxford University Press, 1990), in *Vierteljahreshefte für Zeitgeschichte*, 39 (July 1991), pp. 485–8. Chapter 7. Review of David Blackbourn, *Marpingen. Apparitions of the Virgin Mary in Bismarckian Germany* (Oxford University Press, 1994), in *German History*, 13 (1995), pp. 121–5. Chapter 8. Review of Christiane Eisenberg, *Frühe Arbeiterbewegung und Genossenschaften* (Verlag Neue Gesellschaft, 1985), in *New German Critique* 42 (1987), pp. 188–92. Chapter 9. Reviews of Heinrich August Winkler, *Von der Revolution zur Stabilisierung, Der Schein der Normalität* and *Der Weg in die Katastrophe* (Vols 1–3 of *Arbeiter und Arbeiterbewegung in der Weimarer Republik*, Verlag J.H.W. Dietz Nachf., Berlin, 1984–7), in *Journal of Modern History*, 58 (June 1986), pp. 572–4 and *American Historical Review*, 92 (1987), pp. 443–4 and 95 (1990), pp. 195–6. Chapter 10. 'Weimarama', *The London Review of Books*, 8 November 1990, p. 27. Chapter 11. 'In Search of German Social Darwinism', in Manfred Berg and Geoffrey Cocks (eds), *Medicine and Modernity* (Cambridge University Press, 1996). Chapter 12. 'From Racial Hygiene to Auschwitz', *The Times Higher Education Supplement*, 19 January 1990, pp. 18–19. Chapter 13. Review of Rosemarie Leuschen-Seppel, *Sozialdemokratie und Antisemitismus im Kaiserreich* (Verlag Neue Gesellschaft, 1978), in *Social History* 5 (1980) 2, pp. 330–3. Chapter 14. 'Playing for the Devil', in *The Times Literary Supplement*, 13 November 1992, pp. 3–4. Chapter 15. 'The Bomb that Failed', *The Times Literary Supplement*, 25 September 1992, p. 33. Chapter 16. 'The Deceptions of Albert Speer', *The Times Literary Supplement*, 29 September 1995, pp. 4–6. Chapter 17. 'Das Empire verspielt? "Ende des Ruhms". Eine neue Churchill-Biographie sorgt in England für Aufregung', *Die Zeit*, 22 January 1993, p. 16. Chapter 18. 'Promised Land', *Marxism Today*, April 1990, pp. 18–21. Chapter 19. 'Beyond the *Historikerstreit*', *Patterns of Prejudice*, 28 (1994), pp. 83–6. Chapter 20. 'Prisoners of the German Past?', *Patterns of Prejudice* 30 (1996), pp. 73–82. Chapter 21. 'German History: Past, Present, and Future', in Gordon Martel (ed.), *Modern Germany Reconsidered 1870–1945* (Routledge, 1992), pp. 237–54.

Every effort has been made to obtain permission to reproduce material throughout this book. If any proper acknowledgement has not been made the holder should contact the publishers.

Part I

PARADE OF THE GRAND NARRATIVES

The five essays grouped together in Part I all deal with attempts by established historians to write synthetic narratives of long stretches of German history, concentrating above all on the nineteenth century. The first of them discusses the volume in the *Oxford History of Modern Europe* covering German history from 1770 to 1866, written by the American historian James J. Sheehan. At the time the essay was published, the process of German reunification had only recently begun. The tone of the review reflects above all the concerns which that process was arousing early in 1990 in Britain and the USA, where worried commentators were raising the spectre of a resurgence of German nationalism and the rise of a 'Fourth Reich'. British Prime Minister Margaret Thatcher invited a group of eminent specialists in German history to a meeting at Chequers, her official country residence, where there was wild talk of the Germans' historic ruthlessness, aggressiveness and unreliability and the threat that reunification posed to the future stability of Europe. One of Thatcher's most trusted Ministers, Nicholas Ridley, subsequently went on record comparing Chancellor Helmut Kohl to his predecessor Adolf Hitler. Although the historians at the Chequers meeting subsequently claimed they had been misrepresented, and Ridley was forced to resign his office because of the uproar that greeted his remarks, there was no doubt that apprehensions about the re-emergence of a united German state in Central Europe were widespread among Conservatives. On the left, too, reunification rekindled historic fears of fascism and great-power politics, while on the right it revived the myth of a Britain standing alone against the might of Europe in 1940, a myth which remains central to the ideology of the 'Eurosceptic' wing of the Conservative Party. An invitation to review a new history of Germany leading up to the first unification of the 1860s offered the opportunity to reflect on these fears, and to see what light the study of Otto von Bismarck cast on the rather different figure of Helmut Kohl. *German History 1770–1866* emphasized the role of chance

1

circumstance in the process. Its sceptical view of grand theories and doctrines of historical inevitability was characteristic of much American scholarship as postmodernism, with its frontal assault on all forms of 'grand narrative' and overarching historical interpretation, made its influence felt on intellectual life in the United States.

In sharp contrast to Sheehan, the German historian Hans-Ulrich Wehler has devoted many of his writings to developing a structural theory of modern German history, the so-called *Sonderweg* argument, emphasizing Germany's unique – and uniquely damaging and destructive – path to modernity between the mid-nineteenth century and the mid-twentieth. Chapter 2, dealing with the third volume of Wehler's enormous 'societal history' of modern Germany, covering the years 1849–1918, takes a close look at how this argument has been modified and qualified in the light of research, and asks whether indeed it has not been so badly damaged that, even on Wehler's own account, it no longer holds together. Wehler's work also embodies a very partiular approach to the past, based on the application of neo-Weberian sociology to historical subjects. This approach has been very influential among German scholars in the last couple of decades, and Chapter 2 takes the opportunity to examine some of the advantages and disadvantages it brings with it. Wehler began his great work well before German reunification, and the implicit argument of Chapter 2 is that the modifications it has made to the original *Sonderweg* thesis put forward in the early 1970s owe more to the progress of historical research and debate than to the changing political circumstances in which it was written.

A very different kind of historical theory stands at the centre of the work of Thomas Nipperdey, discussed in Chapter 3 – not 'historical social science' and the search for structural causes of Nazism in German history, but 'historicism', reading the past as it was written and not in the light of what happened in the fateful years between 1933 and 1945. Here too, it is argued, is a position which involves theoretical contradictions which, in the end, their author was unable to resolve. Nipperdey too began writing before the reunification of Germany seemed even a remote possibility; yet he placed the doctrine of the historical inevitability of German unification and German nationhood at the very centre of his work. Retrospectively, therefore, he assumes something of the aura of a prophet. In the last volume of his great work, written while reunification was taking place, his drive to provide historical support for the legitimacy of German nationhood led him, Chapter 3 argues, to gloss over too many of the problematical aspects of the Bismarckian and Wilhelmine eras, and in his treatment of the First World War his concern to redress the balance against what he saw as the excessively negative picture of German history in this period painted by Wehler and others too often degenerated into special pleading. Moreover, Nipperdey's belief in the inevitability of German nationhood contradicted his desire to avoid the teleological approach which he so criticized in the work of the 'critical' historians.

As a self-confessed 'historicist', Nipperdey sought to reconstruct the past as it happened, in all its aspects. Chapter 3 asks whether such an ambition is really capable of fulfilment any more, at a time when professional historians, especially in Germany, eschew many of the narrative techniques, such as character sketching, the provision of local, 'atmospheric' colour, and so on, which adorned the work of the true historicists of a century ago. In its immense breadth of coverage, Nipperdey's project sought to encompass almost every aspect of German life in the nineteenth century, and in this respect is closer to 'historical social science' than the work discussed in Chapter 4, Wolfgang J. Mommsen's massive two-volume history of Germany from 1850 to 1918. Ironically, perhaps, for an historian whose career has been closely focused on the work of the great German sociologist Max Weber, Mommsen follows the example of the nineteenth-century historians in concentrating heavily on a narrative of foreign and domestic politics at the centre and in making ample use of contemporary quotation and detail in doing so. The view he gives of German history is very much the view from Berlin. Written after reunification had been achieved, Mommsen's immensely detailed account of the creation and subsequent travails of the German nation-state in the nineteenth century returns continually to the question of comparing the two processes, and is constantly alive to the possible alternative histories that might have occurred had things been different in 1866 or 1888 or 1914. Above all, he is concerned to draw a sharp contrast between the Bismarckian unification process and the events of 1989/90; yet, in the end, he is still forced to confess that reunification has made the history of the German Empire created in 1871 more relevant than ever.

If Mommsen's view of Bismarck is overwhelmingly negative, then the interpretation advanced by the French historian Joseph Rovan goes very much to the other extreme. Covering the whole sweep of German history from the beginning to the present, Rovan's purpose is to interpret the German past for a French readership in order to overcome many of the prejudices and misconceptions under which the French, like the British, evidently continue to labour. Yet, as Chapter 5 argues, the result is an account which glosses over too many of the difficulties of German history in the interests of present-day international harmony and European integration. At many points in the narrative, Rovan's work illustrates only too clearly the perils of an excessive subordination of historical scholarship to political ends. A foreign perspective on the history of a nation can be fruitful and illuminating, as Rovan's indeed is in a number of respects; but true understanding and respect can only be based on clarity of vision, not on whitewashing. Moreover, as with Mommsen's work, Rovan offers a vision of the past which privileges high politics and powerful individuals. As with all the other studies discussed in Part I of this book, his attempt to write a grand narrative of German history runs into the inevitable problem of what to include and what to leave out, and how to weave the many different and sometimes divergent strands of the story together. It raises not only the question of how historical knowledge can be conveyed, but also the far more fundamental problem of what historical knowledge actually is.

1

TOWARDS UNIFICATION

As German unification proceeded on its apparently inevitable course in 1989/90, and Chancellor Kohl scrambled with almost indecent haste to write his name into the history books as the second Bismarck, images sprang to mind of that previous unification, over a century and a quarter ago, and the consequences it brought to Europe and the world in the following decades. After Charlemagne's First Reich, Bismarck's Second and Hitler's Third, were we now seeing the rise of a Fourth Reich of equally imposing dimensions and equally uncertain duration? Did the new and seemingly unstoppable drive to reunify Germany in our own day mark the resumption of a submerged but ultimately ineradicable tradition of German national feeling and identity? Or did it merely register a stampede for material goods by the East Germans, their consumerist appetites whetted by years of watching West German television advertisements?

Those who seek an answer to these important questions could do worse than turn to James J. Sheehan's contribution to the *Oxford History of Modern Europe*,[1] a series whose own origins are themselves now virtually lost in the mists of time. His is the seventh volume to appear in the series since the publication of *The Struggle for Mastery in Europe* by A.J.P. Taylor, way back in 1954. The series editors, advertised on the jacket as Alan Bullock and F.W.D. Deakin, have since become Lord Bullock and Sir William Deakin, and their task is beginning to look as endless as that of painting the Forth Bridge; if the current rate of appearance – at two volumes a decade, leisurely even by Oxford standards – fails to speed up, so much more modern European history will have happened by the time it is complete that a whole new set of books will have to be commissioned to bring the story up to date.

Part of the trouble is surely that the standard set by those authors who have so far managed to complete their task has been so formidably high. But Sheehan, although he appears to have been at work on *German History 1770–1866* (1989) for only a decade or so, triumphantly maintains it. His book can easily stand comparison with Theodore Zeldin's on France, Raymond Carr's on Spain, or Hugh Seton-Watson's on Russia. The range and depth of his scholarship are tremendously impressive. Although the book is very long, it is a pleasure to read. Sheehan writes with elegance and clarity and enlivens his narrative with plenty of interesting detail and the occasional flash of scholarly wit. This is historical writing of the highest order. It deserves to be judged as such.

Sheehan had to compete not only with an intimidating array of distinguished predecessors in the same series, but also with a deeply entrenched tradition of writing about the process of German unification in the nineteenth century under Prussian leadership as if it were inevitable. This tradition has left is mark even on the most recent syntheses of German history in this period. German historians have a habit of reading back the *kleindeutsch* version of a united Germany, without Austria and under the domination of Prussia, into the early and mid-nineteenth century and even further, as if there was never any really serious alternative to it.

Sheehan's book can be read as a sustained attempt to undermine this tradition of German historical writing. At every step, he emphasizes the contingency and uncertainty of the unification process. If the opening of the Berlin Wall in November 1989 and the East German vote for unity with the West in March 1990 both came as more or less complete surprises in our own day, then, Sheehan reminds us, the same was no less true of the Prussian military victory over Austria in 1866, which marked the most crucial step towards the unification of Germany completed by the war with France in 1870. Most people expected the Austrians to win. And indeed they very nearly did. Far from being the perfectly planned and executed operation of Prussian historical legend, Moltke's victory at Königgrätz was, like most battles, a tale of muddle and confusion, in which the great general was only saved from humiliation by the opportune arrival of the Prussian Second Army led by the heir to the Prussian throne. 'You are now a great man', someone told Bismarck as the Austrians retreated, 'but if the Crown Prince had arrived too late, you would be the greatest scoundrel in the world.'

It is to indicate the role of individual personality and historical chance in the process of German unification that Sheehan concludes by asking rhetorically, 'Is it a mistake to end this book with Bismarck and the Prussian victories of 1866?' In asserting that it is not, Sheehan is also paying homage to his colleague at Stanford, Gordon A. Craig, the author of the succeeding volume in the *Oxford History*, who opens his account of *Germany 1866–1945* by asking, 'Is it a mistake to begin with Bismarck?' But when it comes to defining his approach at the beginning of the book, Sheehan takes a rather different point of view. Thomas Nipperdey started his magisterial account of German history in the nineteenth century by declaring: 'In the beginning was Napoleon.' Sheehan, commencing his narrative in the eighteenth century, feels constrained to warn the reader that modern German history did not begin with Frederick the Great. Modern German history, in other words, amounts to a lot more than the rise of Prussia.

Instead, Sheehan organizes his account around three rather more wide-ranging developments: the rise of sovereign territorial states, the growth of economic activity and social mobility, and the emergence of a literary culture. Each of the book's four chronologically defined sections is thus divided roughly into three parts, dealing separately with politics, society and culture.

The advantage of this procedure is that it enables Sheehan to deal from a variety of perspectives with the central question of the emergence of a German national identity. He is sceptical of the idea that it had anything much to do with economy or society. The Prussian historians of the late nineteenth and early twentieth century, writing with the false wisdom of hindsight, thought that the creation of the German Customs Union, the *Zollverein*, under Prussian leadership, uniting a large number of German states in a single market from the 1830s onwards, paved the way for political union under Prussian leadership in the 1860s. But as Sheehan points out, most of the member states actually fought against Prussia in the war of 1866, although their principal ally, Austria, was not a member. Indeed, the Customs Union did not even create a unified economy; as late as the 1860s there were still numerous different systems of currency, weights and measures in operation, and different parts of Germany were sometimes more closely linked to other economies than they were to each other. Sheehan is equally sceptical of the notion, popularized by the novelist Wilhelm Raabe, that 'The German Empire was founded with the construction of the first railway.' 'If one studies a map of the central European rail system in 1860', Sheehan remarks, 'any number of political, social, economic and cultural connections seem possible.'

The political importance of such economic developments, Sheehan argues, lay in their contribution to the strengthening not of the nation, but of the state; and in so far as they benefited Prussia more than other states, they did indeed pave the way for Bismarck's victory in 1866. But that victory did not mark the realization of any deep-rooted concept of national identity. Many Austrians and South Germans, indeed, felt thoroughly alienated by it. 'You claim that you have founded a *Reich*', the Austrian poet Franz Grillparzer told Bismarck, 'but all you have done is to destroy a *Volk*.' The nationalist historians created the seductive legend of a Germany united by historical necessity. But Germany was not united in 1866, nor was it in 1871. Millions of Germans remained outside the Reich, not only in Austria but also further afield, in areas of settlement all over East-Central Europe. Yet many more millions of people belonging to other ethnic groups also lived in these areas in a tangle of different nationalities. As Sheehan remarks, the nationalist writer Ernst Moritz Arndt's 'famous declaration that the fatherland extended "as far as the German tongue is heard" was stirring poetry but woefully inadequate political geography'.

The German Reich, then, really was created by 'Blood and Iron'. It was the product of violence, not of any natural process. It is widely believed, says Sheehan, that nations and nationalism are natural phenomena. But, he goes on:

> That this belief has no historical basis should be peculiarly apparent in the German case, where geography, language, culture, and politics combine to confound attempts to find a natural, objectively defined nation. Nations are inventions, the products of particular historical circumstances and movements.

In 1848 German nationalism was a predominantly liberal force. Writers and politicians saw the creation of a constitutional nation-state as the quickest way to achieve the civil freedoms and human rights which they felt the small, often semi-absolutist states of the German Confederation were denying them. It was only after unification that a more sinister variant of nationalism, based on the creation of negative stereotypes such as Slavs or Jews, and dedicated to solving the continuing dilemmas of German national identity through the conquest and subjugation of further territory beyond the borders of the Reich, gradually gained ascendancy.

If there was nothing natural or inevitable about the Bismarckian version of national unification and national identity, then there was nothing natural or inevitable about what followed it either. Nations remake themselves in every generation, and of no nation has this been more true than the Germans. The process which we are witnessing in Central Europe today represents another twist in the tale. German reunification in our own time has nothing to do with blood and iron. It was accomplished peacefully and without bloodshed. It brought together two states which occupied only two-thirds of the area of the old Bismarckian Reich. But it did so without any serious claim to territories beyond, where there are now very few ethnic Germans indeed. And it has taken place in the name not – as in 1866 – of Prussian militarism and authoritarianism, but of freedom, democracy and prosperity. Chancellor Kohl never really looked like a second Bismarck. It is simply impossible to imagine him appearing in the spurred and jackbooted military uniform that the Iron Chancellor used to wear.

Sheehan does a good job of disposing of the myths of nationalist historiography, whether on a large scale, in his account of the origins of the Bismarckian Reich, or in a smaller compass, as in his assessment of the Austro-Prussian agreement at Olmütz in 1850 to share responsibility for Schleswig-Holstein, an agreement traditionally regarded by nationalist historians as a humiliation for the Prussians. But he is less successful in finding something coherent to put in its place. This is partly because he rejects – not without good reason – the related myth of the German Sonderweg or 'special path' to modernity, which gives just as much prominence to broader historical forces in the unification of Germany under Prussia, but sees them in much more negative terms. Sheehan concedes, of course, that the liberals did not succeed in assuming political hegemony in

1848 or afterwards. But while illiberal political forces remained strong, this did not in his view reflect any peculiar weakness of the middle class in German culture and society. On the contrary, the German bourgeoisie, he says, were dynamic and modern, far from being the weak-kneed and politically apathetic creatures that many historians suppose them to have been. If they had a weakness, it lay in the fact that they were deeply divided by region, religion and relationship to the state (a large proportion of them being state servants of one kind or another). Nor did they confront a rampant neo-feudal aristocracy hell-bent on resisting the forces of modernity. 'The nineteenth-century nobility', says Sheehan, 'were a product of their age, not the residue of pre-modern times.'

Sheehan makes these points with a wealth of convincing detail. But the book's lack of a coherent overall interpretation is compounded by his decision to give equal weight to his three chosen historical dimensions of politics, culture and society, and by the ambition – appropriate perhaps to the series of which the book forms a part – to be comprehensive and definitive. This wreaks particular havoc in the realm of culture, where Sheehan seems to find it necessary to give an account of the life, works and thought of every second-rate philosopher and third-rate novelist Germany managed to produce during the period about which he is writing. In Chapter 3, for example, we get not only Goethe, Schiller, Lessing, Klopstock and Herder, but also Wolff, Moses Mendelssohn, Hamann, Febronius and the Mosers, while in Chapter 6 we move on to the Romantics (Schlegel, Novalis, Kleist, Hölderlin, etc.), and thence to philosophers such as Hegel and Schleiermacher, but also including Baader and Bolzano. By the time we get to the mid-nineteenth century Sheehan is giving the full treatment – character sketch, life, works, thought – to realist writers such as Gutzkow, Freytag, Raabe, Keller and Hebbel (before devoting a brief section to discussing the problem of why there were no great German realist writers in the period). The problem is not that this is not well done – it is very well done – but that it makes whole sections of the book read like little more than a high-class biographical dictionary, and we end up not being able to see the wood for the trees. Goethe may indeed have remarked on one occasion that the Germans were admirable as individuals but miserable as a group, but was there any real need to take this comment so much to heart?

It is hard to feel that this biographical comprehensiveness is really necessary, especially when it spills over into the chapters on politics – as in the discussion of national identity towards the end of the book, which is taken as the cue for portraits of Wagner, Droysen, Sybel, Treitschke, Mommsen, Klopp, Frantz, Gervinus and Giesebrecht, or the section, earlier in the volume, on 'Participatory Politics 1830–1848', where we are treated to sketches of Haller, Stahl, Dahlmann, Rottek, Welcker, Pfizer, Fröbel, Blum, Schön, Jacoby and others. Sheehan devotes so much space to individual thinkers and writers that he loses the thread at numerous points in the book and leaves himself too little room for describing and analysing the course that politics actually took. His account of 1848 and of the events of the 1860s is much briefer than it really should be in a book such as this. And the contrast with the rather abstract, statistic-laden sections on society and the economy, where all too few real ordinary people manage to put in an appearance, could not be more striking. Moreover, Germany's real contribution to world culture in the nineteenth century lay above all in the realm of music, and it is disappointing to find neither an attempt to explain why this should be so, nor any mention at all of great composers such as Mozart, Haydn, Beethoven, Schubert, Schumann, Mendelssohn or Brahms.

Sheehan's concentration on writers and thinkers, and his emphasis on chance and contingency, also suggests that he likes his history taken from the top down. In one sense, of course, it is currently fashionable to treat what people thought was happening as more important than what actually did happen, and to regard politics as a virtually autonomous sphere determined by nothing much except its own symbolism and discourse. But *German History 1770–1866* is very far from being a work of postmodernist historiography. It says much more about the ideas of great (and not-so-great) thinkers than about their wider representation and dissemination, for example, and it hardly troubles to make even a token gesture towards women and the role of gender. Its concept of culture is resolutely elitist. The mass of ordinary Germans spend most of the time off-stage, and even at the moments when they play a role in the central political drama, it is, in Sheehan's presentation, only a bit part (even in 1848). Ultimately, therefore, this represents a rather traditional approach to its subject, for all its tilting at long-established orthodoxies.

Nevertheless, its range and scope, and the consummate ease and skill with which it is written, mean that Sheehan's book has no serious rival as an account of German history in the century before unification, and is likely to remain a standard work of reference and teaching for a long time to come. All the more pity, then, that its production at the Clarendon Press should have been so slipshod. I soon gave up any attempt to find a rationale for the use of italics, for example – frequently the same German word appears in roman and italic type on the same page – and I lost count equally quickly of the number of pages on which the print was wrongly aligned, both horizontally, with uneven gaps between lines, lines set at an angle instead of running straight across, and lines bending in the middle, and vertically, with untidy and uneven margins in the index. There is no consistency about the anglicization of German names (the King of Hanover appears in the text as Ernst August and the index as Ernest August, for example). The bibliographical references are full of errors, and there are too few maps. On page 456 one line is printed twice and others are evidently missing. Worst of all from the point of view of the book's use as a teaching aid, the text is full of untranslated German, from innumerable individual words up to great chunks of poetry. Most students will only be able to get through this book with the aid of a German dictionary. At least the succeeding volume in the series, by Gordon A. Craig, provided an appendix with English translations of the German poetry quoted. Any future editions of Sheehan's book should do the same, and add a glossary of individual German words as well.

Meanwhile, however, those who are worried about Germany's future can take some comfort from this book. If the scores of short biographies which it contains do nothing else, at least they give a final and definitive burial to all those histories of ideas so common in the post-war decades that attempted to construct a 'German Mind' from selected elements of the thought of writers and thinkers from the mid-eighteenth to the mid-twentieth century. And the broader analysis is almost equally destructive – perhaps too destructive – of the political and economic teleologies that have dominated the historiography of modern Germany for so long. No one looking for alarming parallels between the Bismarckian unification of Germany and the unification process of the early 1990s will find them here. In place of violence we have peace; in place of authoritarianism, democracy; in place of elitist ideologies and practices we have a genuinely popular, grass-roots movement that forced on politicians in East and West something scarcely any of them were seriously willing to consider at the beginning of 1989. Chancellor Kohl may be driving the bandwagon of German unification at present, but he was not the one who got it moving in the first place. The way ahead may be fraught with difficulties and dangers but it scarcely seems likely to lead to another Königgrätz or Sedan, let alone another Verdun or another Auschwitz.

NOTES

1 James J. Sheehan, *German History, 1770–1866* (Oxford, Clarendon Press, 1989).

2

WHATEVER BECAME OF THE SONDERWEG?[1]

Historians, it has been said, spend the first third of their career attacking the errors of their elders, the second third putting forward their own, more convincing interpretations to replace them, and the last third defending historical truth against the misguided iconoclasm of their younger colleagues. But it has also been said that as historians get older, the firm, clear-cut views with which they begin their career become fuzzier and more complex in the light of their increasing knowledge, until they are so nuanced that scarcely anything is left of the grand simplicities with which they set out. This, no doubt, is what gives each new generation of historians its opportunity to challenge existing ways of looking at the past. But it is also how historical understanding advances over time.

Comparing Hans-Ulrich Wehler's major new book on Germany from 1849 to 1914 (1995) with his brief but epoch-making study of *The German Empire 1871–1918* (1985), first published in German in 1973,[2] in many ways illustrates the truth of these observations. In his earlier book, and in many other works, Wehler and his associates, in what has come to be known as the 'Bielefeld school' of historians, criticized an older German historiography which denied the long-term roots of Nazism in German history and, under the sign of the 'primacy of foreign policy', insisted on the 'encirclement' of Germany before 1914 and the iniquities of the Treaty of Versailles as the root causes of the collapse of civilized standards in the age of mass democracy under the Weimar Republic. In its place, Wehler advanced a new theory of German history, based on a fusion of Marxism and Weberian modernization theory. The sources of Germany's descent into barbarism in 1933 were to be sought, he insisted, not in its geopolitical predicament in the middle of Europe, but in the 'special path' or *Sonderweg* taken by German society to modernity between the middle of the nineteenth century and the middle of the twentieth. In 1848, so the argument went, the German bourgeoisie failed in its attempt to wrest power from the aristocracy in the way that its counterparts in other countries had done; in England in 1640 for example, or France in 1789. As a result, the Prussian aristocracy was able to preserve its sociopolitical hegemony. It cemented it through the conservative 'revolution from above' which united Germany under Prussian domination from 1866–71. Continuing industrialization and social change increasingly threatened its position, but it was able to maintain it through its monopolization of key positions of power in the army, the civil service and the Reich leadership. To bolster this, it engaged in a successful 'feudalization of the bourgeoisie' into aristocratic modes of behaviour and value-orientations (such as duelling, deference to inherited status, the hunt for decorations and titles, the scramble for the position of reserve officer, the adoption of an authoritarian and paternalistic attitude towards employees in industry, and, crucially, the rejection of democracy and parliamentarism), a process made easier by the replacement in Germany of liberal competitive capitalism by a state-oriented, oligopolistic 'organized capitalism' as a result of the 'great depression' of 1873–96, which left big industrialists heavily dependent on the interventionism of the undemocratic state.

Thus, while in other European countries industrialization was accompanied by social mobility and opportunity and political parliamentarization and democratization, in Germany the social and political clocks were held back. Social hierarchies and values remained premodern. Under the 'Bonapartist' political system established by Bismarck, the Reichstag was emasculated and elections were turned into plebiscites on issues drummed up by the leadership of the Reich. But as economic modernization continued apace, so the ruling Junker elite had to reach for increasingly desperate means of staving off its inevitable social and political consequences. It attempted to divert the popular demand for political equality into support for the status quo by the arousal of nationalist, imperialist and, fatally, antisemitic enthusiasms, in the Agrarian League and the nationalist pressure-groups. With the collapse of the monarchy in 1918 the old elites grew even more desperate, and as the right-wing forces they had manipulated into being re-formed themselves into the Nazi party with the votes of the feudalized bourgeoisie and the manipulated petty bourgeoisie, the large landowners, heavy industrialists, top civil servants, army officers and aristocratic politicians manoeuvred them into power in January 1933, when Hitler was appointed Chancellor.

This interpretation – presented here in an inevitably abbreviated form – was provocative in the best sense of the word. Over the last quarter of a century or so, it has inspired a vast amount of questioning and contradiction, and almost every aspect of it has been attacked in one way or another. To the late Munich historian Thomas Nipperdey, for example, it presented a one-sidedly negative picture of modern German history, which he proceeded to counterbalance in his own, great, three-volume account covering the years 1800–1918. And to some English historians (including myself), it seemed strange that a German colleague was holding up Britain's political development as normal, at a time when a heated debate was in progress on the left about the long-term backwardness of the British social and political system, with its snobbish social hierarchies and its seemingly immovable 'Establishment', and when the continued dominance of aristocratic, rural values and aspirations was being made widely responsible for Britain's long-term relative economic decline. In the early 1980s, David Blackbourn and Geoff Eley, two British colleagues, now, like many of the best British historians of their generation, teaching in the United States, launched a full-scale attack on the *Sonderweg* thesis which attracted vehement opposition from Wehler in particular. They argued that there was no general path to 'modernity'; each nation had its own peculiar experience based on a particular mix of factors. What distinguished the German experience was the way in which it represented an intensified and extreme variant of patterns which could in one form or another be found in other European countries as well. As the ensuing debate began to ebb, polemic was replaced by research, especially by a massive research project on the history of the German middle classes, centred on Bielefeld; in contrast, say, to the *Historikerstreit,* the furious debate about the uniqueness of Auschwitz which engulfed German historians in the 1980s, generating in the process rather more heat than light, this was an encouraging example of how fruitful historical controversy can sometimes be. Knowledge of all these subjects in the mid-1990s is thus far greater and more sophisticated than it was two decades ago.

In the meantime, Wehler has embarked on his 'German societal history' (*Deutsche Gesellschaftsgeschichte)*, of which this is the third volume to appear; a fourth, covering the twentieth century, is still to come. There is no doubt that this is a major achievement, one of the great works of twentieth-century German historical scholarship. It impresses by the clarity of its structure, the precision of its conceptualization, the breadth and thoroughness of its bibliographical reference, the fullness of its statistical detail, and – despite its very great length – the consistency of its arguments. Wehler's tone here is measured rather than polemical, and he takes full account of the almost unmanageable mass of research that has appeared on the subjects with which he deals over the last few decades. This makes it less entertaining to read than some of his more argumentative texts, but it also makes it much more persuasive. It is not a book to read through from beginning to end; unlike Nipperdey, Wehler has not written a narrative history but a structural one. His analysis also assumes a certain degree of existing knowledge of the subject, and in many places his drive for precision leads him to clog the text with masses of statistics which render it virtually unreadable. Instead of presenting the quantitative material in easily digestible graphic form, he prints it in large and forbidding statistical tables. There is not a single map in the book. All this reflects the striking lack of visual imagination shown by German historians in contrast for example to their French colleagues.

For many people this will be a work to consult rather than to read from end to end (and it is sure to be used in this way as a standard work by students for years to come). Frequent brief, or not-so-brief, summaries of chapters and sections ease the task of the reader who does not wish to plunge into the detailed exposition. Yet the subtlety and power of the argument go a long way towards carrying the reader along. How does this argument look in comparison to Wehler's views of the early 1970s? One of the most deeply impressive aspects of this book is the author's willingness to jettison old views in the light of new research. And a lot has been thrown overboard. Gone, for example, is the 'great depression' of 1873–96, to be replaced by the 'great deflation', a much weaker concept with correspondingly much less explanatory power. Gone is 'organized capitalism', a concept which Wehler now agrees was misleading because it implied capitalism was previously unorganized, unhelpful because it could not account for change over time, and one-dimensional because it understated the autonomy of political developments. In its place comes 'corporativism', another weaker concept denoting merely the growing influence of economic interest groups on the state, and the growing intervention of the state in the economy. Gone is the manipulative model of politics in the German Empire, with Wehler now rightly according a high degree of autonomy to the extreme nationalist and other political movements which mobilized themselves from below in the years before the First World War. Gone is the 'primacy of domestic politics', to be replaced by a much more convincing recognition of the interdependence of domestic and foreign policy.

All these revisions weaken the original *Sonderweg* thesis, but they do not fundamentally undermine it. However, much more serious for the continued viability of the thesis are three more far-reaching changes which Wehler has made to his original views. First, as the second volume of Wehler's 'societal history' already made clear, he no longer regards 1848 as the failed bourgeois revolution which marked the turning-point at which German history failed to turn. Wehler still believes that a successful revolution 'is a good thing for the political culture of any nation', a view which fails to convince in view of the deep and often violently resolved divisions which plagued French political culture in the century and a half after 1789, or the paralysis which adherence to a revolutionary constitution written in the eighteenth century has meant recently for policy-making in the USA. But he now accepts that 1848 in Germany was not a failed revolution in the Marxist sense. While of course its immediate political ambition of German unification on a liberal, parliamentary basis was frustrated, it did bring about major reforms which constituted a huge step towards the formation of a viable civil society in Germany, including the establishment of legislative assemblies, the extension of civil rights under the law, and so on. And, crucially, liberal nationalism underwent a tremendous revival in Germany at the end of the 1850s following on its great triumph in the unification of Italy. All was not lost in 1849, therefore; everything remained for bourgeois liberalism to play for; and with the Prussian constitutional conflict that began in 1862, and a liberal majority in the Prussian Chamber of Deputies pushing for the effective destruction of the traditional structure of the Prussian army, victory seemed in sight.

This concession leads to a second respect in which Wehler's revised views undermine the concept of the *Sonderweg*. By dating the beginning of the *Sonderweg* to the unification process in the 1860s, Wehler inevitably places Bismarck far more at the centre of the picture than he did when his argument was based on the structural deformations of German history brought about by the failure of 1848. This turn from a structural to a personalistic interpretation of the origns of the *Sonderweg* is strengthened by Wehler's abandonment of his previous characterization of Bismarck's rule as a plebiscitary, Bonapartist regime appropriate to a certain phase in the development of capitalism. While he rightly insists on the numerous ways in which the founding Reich Chancellor learned from the experience of Napoleon III, Wehler now accepts that it is going too far to elevate this into a theory. Elections in the German Empire were not comparable to the single-issue plebiscites of the French Second Empire. Bismarck did not usurp power like Louis Napoleon, and he did not wield power in order to defend the interests of the bourgeoisie in a situation of political equilibrium between the conficting interests of aristocracy, bourgeoisie and proletariat such as that posited by Marx for France in the years 1848–51. What does Wehler come up with to replace Bonapartism as a characterization of the Bismarckian regime? He turns his Weberian prayer-wheel and comes up with a new paradigmatic super-weapon: charisma. Bismarck, argues Wehler, was a classic example of the charismatic leader in the Weberian sense: he was extra-historical and unforeseeable, he depended on a 'charismatic community' of devoted followers, he inspired fanatical enthusiasm on a more general level, he gained power in a major crisis, retained power through solving further major crises (some of them, like the 'war-in-sight' crisis of 1875, manufactured by himself), and he lost power in 1890 when he was prevented from manufacturing a further crisis which might have stopped the degeneration of his rule into a humdrum matter of everyday politics.

The concept of charisma is used to interpret, or reinterpret, many aspects of Bismarck's policy, including for example his colonial policy, which is now portrayed as less an 'anticyclical therapy' designed to combat economic depression at home (never a very plausible idea) than a device intended to combat the erosion of Bismarck's charisma (we are now asked to believe that this was the true meaning of Bismarck's statement that the colonial question was 'a matter of life or death' for him!). Wehler concedes, as he must, that Bismarck's rule deviated in a number of respects from this ideal type, but insists none the less that the charismatic elements were dominant. But this is in the end not very convincing. Bismarck's power was institutional; it depended neither on a 'charismatic community' (which did not really exist in the Weberian sense) nor on popular acclamation (which was not important to his remaining in office), but on the Kaiser, the political parties, the bureaucracy and the army. As a radical-conservative modernizer he was not extra-historical but had clear contemporary parallels in other European countries, such as Disraeli in Britain or Cavour in Italy. He left office not because his charisma failed, but because a pliant, mediocre Kaiser was replaced by a self-willed, ambitious one, and because the parties were proving more difficult than before to manage. Of course Bismarck had enormous prestige, but to describe it as charisma elevates it to the super-historical and implies the abandonment of a structural explanation for the *Sonderweg* in favour of a personalistic one.

Thirdly, Wehler now abandons the theory of the feudalization of the bourgeoisie, and accepts that there was no 'deficit of middle-classness' in the German Empire; the evidence, much of it gathered by the Bielefeld research project on the history of the German middle classes, is against it. Few of the wealthiest bourgeois possessed or sought titles, and some, like Albert Ballin, Emil Kirdorf and Max Warburg, refused them when offered. Few bought major landed estates, those who did continued to get most of their wealth from industry and commerce, and there was nothing 'feudal' about the mostly small country seats which many wealthy commoners purchased as a refuge from the noise and dirt of the city. There was relatively little intermarriage with the aristocracy, and the social gap between the two classes remained wide. Titles such as 'commercial counsellor' *(Kommerzienrat)* were specifically bourgeois and mainly reflected a need for influence in high places, as did the reserve officer's commission. Wehler is not entirely consistent in his arguments, to be sure, for he still suggests at more than one point that the nobility remained a 'socially normative model' for the middle classes. His main illustrations of this point are duelling (despite the work of the Bielefeld historian Ute Frevert, who has argued powerfully that it represented a specifically bourgeois form of self-assertion for its middle-class exponents) and the authoritarian mentality of many big employers, which he suggests was economically irrational while in fact providing a number of examples of its economic benefits for employers and no evidence at all to the contrary. Yet in general he concedes that recent research has underscored the huge cultural influence of the bourgeoisie and the successful achievement of bourgeois hegemony in the civil society of Wilhelmine Germany. Where the bourgeoisie failed, he says, was in the fight for political power. Its peculiarity in Germany was its high degree of subordination to and dependence on the state. Thus he abandons a central element of the *Sonderweg* thesis – namely, the argument that society as well as politics failed to modernize. The entire thesis is now concentrated in the political sphere.

Wehler lists twelve respects in which the German Reich's experience was unique among that of Western European states: the dominance of a charismatic ruler in its formation, the direct control of its army by the sovereign, the key role played by the military and by militarism, the power of the nobility, the toothlessness of legislative assemblies, the failure of liberalism, the rule of the civil service, the limits placed on bourgeois hegemony by all of this plus the existence of a massive, highly organized and politically radical labour movement, the trend of nationalism towards right-wing extremism, the legitimation of the regime by external success (social imperialism), the willingness after the heady victories of 1866 and 1871 to risk war at any time, and the fact that the creation of the nation-state coincided with industrialization and the creation of a class society. He also adds, as an afterthought, the depth of the conflict with the Catholic Church, the strength of antisemitism and anti-socialism, and the presence of the educated, university-trained segment of the middle class, the so-called *Bildungsbürgertum*. No theory any more; just a list.

In fact, it is easy enough to point to the existence of one or more of these supposedly German peculiarities in quite a number of European countries in the late nineteenth century and the early twentieth. In Italy, the genuinely charismatic figure of Garibaldi provided a fatal model for Mussolini, the King remained head of the army, imperialism was used to legitimate the political system, and nationalism, above all after the defeat of the army in Abyssinia in 1896, moved to the extreme right. In Spain the army was every bit as independent and central a political institution as in Germany and the landed aristocracy every bit as powerful, while in Austria-Hungary the same two conditions applied, and in addition parliamentary institutions were just as toothless and the bureaucracy was just as strong. The limits of bourgeois hegemony in civil society were even more apparent in Spain, the strength of antisemitism even more obvious in France. In France, too, as in Germany, conflict with the Catholic church was the most important issue in politics in the 1870s but in addition continued up to disestablishment in 1906, the legacy of the violent Church–state conflict of the Revolution. The educated middle class had its equivalent in the French intelligentsia. And Germany was not the only European country prepared to risk war in a crisis, as 1914 only too clearly showed.

Of course, there were crucial differences; most obviously, other European nation-states were formed before industrialization, whereas Germany became a nation-state not just coincidentally with it but, more importantly, well after the process had actually begun. Gemany was also a far larger entity and a far greater economic and military power than other European states, with correspondingly greater ambitions. The German nation-state was only a partial creation, leaving millions of ethnic Germans outside its boundaries and nursing in extreme nationalists the ambition of completing Bismarck's work through a policy of conquest and expansion.

Most vital of all, it was only in Germany that all of Wehler's twelve or fifteen conditions were present. This may suggest that the German experience did indeed represent an intensified version of structures and processes at work in Western and Central Europe as a whole. But it does not suggest that there was a 'special path' taken by Germany to 'modernity' over a long period of time. To say that this was not the case is not to deny that National Socialism and its triumph in Germany had long-term roots. But it is to conclude that these cannot be understood by the *Sonderweg* theory as it was originally propounded.

What is left after the effective abandonment of this argument is a general history rather than a book with an overarching central thesis. Wehler divides his subject-matter into four main headings – economic development, social inequality, political rule, and culture. This basic pattern is repeated across the different time-periods covered by the project as a whole. In the last section of the volume under review, he reverses the usual order of the sections and places culture before politics in order to put his overall argument more clearly, and it would perhaps have made sense had he followed this pattern throughout; the basic purpose of structuring the book this way, after all, is to show how the economy and society related to, and provided the structural context for, politics, so that the political section appears as the culmination of the analysis, and culture appears rather as an afterthought. The clarity and transparency of this structure are bought at a price. In the first place, the coverage of each aspect is as complete as possible, so that, for example, if one takes the various sections on the economy, every boom and every slump is analysed in depth, and a virtually complete economic history of the whole period is delivered; but much of this is not necessary to explain the social and political developments covered in subsequent sections, so that the mass of detail threatens at many places to explode the structure of linkages implied by the concept of 'societal history' that underlies the book as a whole.

Secondly, Wehler builds his societal history on a model of society that is precisely delineated but in many ways incomplete. Economic sectors, social classes and sub-classes, institutions and organizations are carefully defined, and then quantitative data are assembled to indicate the objective dimensions and performance of each entity. The subjective aspects of human behaviour are left out of account, so that for topics like sexuality, eating and drinking, clothing, sickness and health, leisure, sport, travel, attitudes to nature, and mentalities in general – all of them the subject of a mass of scholarly research in recent years – the interested reader will have to turn to Nipperdey's rival volumes. In particular, this is basically a history of the male half of German society in the period in question, since classes – the fundamental category of social analysis – are defined according to the socioeconomic position of the male breadwinner, and the public, political sphere was an all-male affair, with the exception of the women's movement, which duly gets a short section to itself. Apart from this, there are a few brief mentions of women, for example at work or in education, but they do not add up to very much. Even more conspicuously absent are science, literature, culture and the arts, because Wehler's definition of 'culture' only encompasses those aspects of culture which are either quantifiable or relate directly to politics: religion, education, and publishing. A history of nineteenth-century Germany without a coverage of these topics – for example, without Wagner – is a very partial history indeed. Here again, the interested reader will have to turn to Nipperdey for enlightenment.

Thirdly, in concentrating so much on what is quantifiable about the social constructs he discusses, Wehler also concentrates time and again on what is typical: his history is a history of averages, in which the individual all but disappears. The absence of a human dimension to this book serves among other things to increase still further the overwhelming prominence of Bismarck, the only individual whose life-history is recounted and whose character is analysed in all its 1,500-odd pages. Ordinary Germans are completely absent from the scene except as statistics. But concentrating so much on global averages – average wages, average cost of living, average birth rates, and so on – is sometimes unhelpful in understanding the subjective side of history. For example, Wehler refutes contemporary antiurbanist charges that the big cities were havens of immorality by pointing to their average illegitimacy rates, whereas it was not the average (across all social classes, in other words) that worried critics, but the far higher figures in some of the poorer urban districts (in the slums of late nineteenth-century Hamburg, for example, there were nearly five times as many illegitimate births per 100 live births as there were in the villa quarter). Wehler's exclusive interest in the 'structural outcome' of social-historical studies is also bought at a price, therefore.

Finally, in judging the past according to whether or not it conformed to his *ex-post-facto* definition of modernity, Wehler makes it more difficult for himself to understand the behaviour and mentality of whole sections of the German population in the period under consideration. Typical for instance is his treatment of Catholicism, with its unthinking condemnation of the 'archaic mother-cult' of the Virgin Mary, its sniffiness about the supposedly 'ancient forms of superstition' present in popular religiosity, its contempt for the 'anachronistic dogmatism' of the Church hierarchy and its snobbism about the 'deficit of modernity' in the Catholic community as a whole. Among other things – a small point perhaps, but symptomatic – this uncomprehending attitude leads Wehler to explain lower infant mortality in Protestant rural areas to 'the more active relationship of Protestantism to the world, its positive attitude to modernity, its appeal to individuals' responsibility for their own lives', instead of looking to factors made responsible by demographic historians, such as the reluctance of mothers in some parts of rural Catholic Germany to breast-feed their infants. More importantly, it leads Wehler to portray the *Kulturkampf*, the Church–state struggle of the 1870s, in a distorted fashion as a simple conflict between religious fundamentalism and secular modernity, in which the liberals, to be sure, violated their own standards of liberality but were still in principle doing the right thing.

Thus, despite the weakening, modification or abandonment of many of his earlier theses, Wehler has lost none of his old ability to challenge and provoke. This does not prevent him from delivering clear and thorough accounts of many aspects of German history in the 'long nineteenth century' which are not to be found in comparable fullness or precision elsewhere, including Nipperdey's three volumes. His coverage of education, for example, in its nuance and detail, is a world removed from the sloganizing of his treatment of the same subject as an aspect of the 'matrix of the authoritarian society' in his earlier book of 1973; the same can be said of many other sections of this volume, for example social policy, which he now sees in far more positive terms than in 1973. Everywhere the book combines solid and detailed empirical coverage based on an enviable command of the literature, with theses and judgements that are as exciting and controversial as ever. Even the bibliographical notes, all 200 pages of them, in fine print, are not free from controversial judgements, as Wehler delivers his usual waspish comments on work of which he disapproves. One book or article after another is written off as 'antiquated', 'useless and unreliable in every respect', 'a collection of glaring false judgements', 'dyed-in-the-wool orthodoxy', 'outdated', 'colourless invention', 'useless', 'much too sweeping', 'dogmatically restricted', 'as usual, superficial and uncritical', or 'pretentious and inexact' (that last comment refers to an article by myself – ouch!). One wonders why, if they are so useless, these works have been listed at all.

Despite these blemishes, there can be no doubt that this book will be used as a work of reference, a source of interpretations and a stimulus to controversy and research for many years to come. Like so many of his contemporaries among German historians, Wehler is laying down a markstone for eternity in a multi-volume work of history that, if not quite Rankean in its dimensions, is none the less deeply impressive, even awe-inspiring, in the thoroughness of its coverage, the sharpness and decisiveness of its judgements, the clarity of its structure and exposition, and above all perhaps the sheer energy and stamina that have gone into its preparation. In an implicit criticism of the late Thomas Nipperdey, Wehler asks at one point: 'Who indeed is supposed to regard as credible the emphatic assertion that modern German history of all things can only be written in innumerable tones of grey?' If his tones in this book are somewhat more nuanced than previously, and if the human side of history has largely been excluded in favour of grey, impersonal averages, there are still plenty of black-and-white judgements here, as well as intellectual excitement and colourful language. It is not just a great book by a great historian, it also sums up the work of a whole generation of social-liberal German historians, a generation which believed that modernity was an unmitigated good and anything that resisted its advent was lamentable obscurantism.

NOTES

1 Hans-Ulrich Wehler, *Deutsche Gesellschaftsgeschichte, Dritter Band: Von der 'Deutschen Doppelrevolution' bis zum Beginn des Ersten Weltkrieges 1849–1914* (Munich, Verlag C.H. Beck, 1995).
2 Hans-Ulrich Wehler, *Das deutsche Kaiserreich 1871–1918* (Göttingen: Vandenhoeck & Ruprecht, 1973); idem, *The German Empire 1871–1918*, trans. Kim Traynor (Leamington Spa, Berg Publishers, 1985).

3

NIPPERDEY'S NINETEENTH CENTURY[1]

For many years, Thomas Nipperdey was a leading opponent of the 'critical school' of German historians, who have seen the nineteenth century above all as the period in which the foundations were laid for the triumph of Nazism in 1933. The upheavals of the early part of the century, the Napoleonic Wars and the reforms they brought about, only served, in this view, to strengthen the structures of absolutism and underpin the dominance of aristocratic elites in German society. The 1848 Revolution failed to pave the way for a bourgeois society such as had been ushered in by the 1789 Revolution in France. Instead, German society diverged from the normal path towards modernity taken by the other Western nations. The unification of Germany under Bismarck created a German Empire that was dominated by the authoritarian, backward-looking values of its ruling caste, the Prussian military and landowning aristocracy. Despite its booming industrial economy, the Empire's social and political structures were in many ways 'feudalized', its middle classes cowed and deferential to the state and the titled nobility, its urban and rural masses regimented into loyalty and obedience by the disciplining influence of the army, the police, the judiciary and the educational system, all of which were geared to producing not independent, thinking citizens but supine, unquestioning subjects. Bismarck, as Gladstone once observed, may have made Germany great, but he made the Germans small; and in the view of the 'critical' historians it was hardly surprising, therefore, that after the collapse of the Empire in the Revolution of 1918 that followed Germany's defeat in the First World War, so many millions of Germans were unable to come to terms with the uncertainties of democracy and fell prey to the demagogic authoritarianism of the National Socialists.

This 'critical' view of the German past, which located the roots of Nazism in the structural flaws of German history in the nineteenth century, was not, of course, shared by everyone who wrote on the subject, perhaps not even by a majority; but it was propounded in a wide range of general surveys, textbooks, essays and reviews from the mid-1960s onwards, and, just as important, it permeated a great deal of the monographic research published in the 1970s and 1980s. In many ways it may be said to have set the research agenda and dominated debate on the period ever since. It is this view that Nipperdey sought to demolish. In a number of essays and reviews, he castigated the 'critical' approach as one-sidedly negative. Rather than being viewed merely as the antechamber of the Third Reich, nineteenth-century Germany should be seen in its own terms. Every epoch had its own meaning and value, and it was wrong to reduce a particular period to the status of a mere precursor of what came later. By doing so, the historian distorted the complexity of historical reality and robbed the past of its integrity:

> Everything that is admittedly a prehistory from the perspective of 1933 is a prehistory of many other things, and has many other post-histories . . . Every historical period . . . stands in a network of prehistories, and in this way these prehistories undergo a mutual relativization. The greater the distance in time from a period, the clearer it becomes that no one of them has priority. One must learn to live with the multiplicity of continuities and discontinuities. An historical epoch . . . is more than an ensemble of prehistories. It is itself. That is what Ranke meant with the old-fashioned and for us no longer directly accessible formula that every epoch was direct to God . . . The historian and his readers must give back to the past what it once had, what every period has, our own included, namely an open future.
>
> (Vol. III: pp. 880–1)

This meant, among other things, taking a balanced and fair-minded approach to the past. It meant, indeed, trying to be 'objective': 'We live', he wrote, 'from the hope . . ., that there is something objective beyond the subjectivity of our own perspective, namely the truth, towards which we are approaching, and which relieves us of the burden of our subjectivities' (Vol. I: p. 805).

It was in pursuit of this ideal that Nipperdey began his great history of the 'long nineteenth century' from 1800 to 1918 in the late 1970s and finished it, fifteen years, three volumes, 2,669 pages and over a million words later, in 1992. The vast length of the work reflects not only the scale of his ambition, to rival, indeed to replace, the classic, unfinished, and now hopelessly outdated multi-volume survey completed many years ago by the late Franz Schnabel, but also his conviction that doing justice to the past means much more than writing a balanced political history. The first volume, *Deutsche Geschichte 1800–1866* (1983), deals not only with German politics in the years from the beginning of the nineteenth century to the Prussian victory over Austria in the war of 1866, but also with daily life, religion, education, science and scholarship, music, the visual arts and literature. It is intended to

24

stand on its own. For the following period, Nipperdey divides his account into two volumes, which in turn form a separate study. But in fact the three books belong together, and it does not really make much sense to treat them as two separate entities. Indeed, the nature and significance of the whole enterprise can only be fully grasped if all three volumes are taken as a whole: it is only then, as we shall see, that some of the flaws and contradictions of Nipperdey's approach really become apparent in practice.

In Volume II, subtitled *Arbeitswelt und Bürgergeist* ('the world of work and the civic spirit of the bourgeoisie') (1990) the enormous scale and ambition of Nipperdey's project become fully apparent. Here, he seeks

> to offer a history which grasps the totality of the milieux of life, which covers the many possible histories of the economy, classes and class struggle, industrialization, everyday life and mentalities, and high culture. This all-encompassing vision, and the relaxed approach necessary to achieve it, requires an amplitude of coverage . . . The truth is the whole truth, and it needs patience to tell it.
>
> (Vol. II: pp. 837–8)

And indeed, the scope of this volume is simply astonishing. All the subjects mentioned above are given a full treatment for the period 1866 to 1918, but there are also substantial sections on women, sexuality, youth, eating and drinking, dress, housing, sickness and health, leisure, sport and tourism, nature, transport, theatre, the press, and a host of other subjects. In the final volume, *Machtstaat vor der Demokratie* ('the powerful state before democracy') (1992), the range is hardly less impressive, with finance and administration, law and justice, policing and crime receiving full treatment alongside political parties and ideologies, national minorities, constitutional questions, the role of the federated states, and detailed narratives of the internal and external politics of the German Empire and its forerunner the North German Confederation from 1866 all the way through to 1918. It is hard to imagine any other historian writing a general history of the period with such a breadth of sympathy and range of subject matter. Certainly no one else has yet done so.

Nipperdey's command of the relevant scholarly literature in all the areas he covers is little short of awe-inspiring. His book provides a sovereign synthesis of the vast amount of research carried out on this period of German history over the last few decades. It will not easily be superseded. It is accurate and reliable, and there are very few mistakes (a confusion of the percentage poll figures on pages 731 and 746 of Volume III, a misprint on page 902 and a wrongly attributed book in the Bibliography on page 928 of the same volume are rare exceptions). The three volumes are all written clearly and unpretentiously, and the arguments put forward are easy to follow. The work is on the whole sensibly structured, with one or two exceptions, especially near the end.[2] Nipperdey says he hesitated before carrying on the narrative to 1918, instead of stopping, as he might have done, in 1914, but although the First World War did indeed represent a new experience for Europeans and mark the beginning of a troubled new era in more than one respect, it also saw the fall of the German Empire which is the subject of the second and third volumes of his work, and a concentration of all the problems that had dogged it through its history that proved fatal in the end. The decision to include it was surely justified.

The comparison with Schnabel, or indeed with Treitschke and the other great German historians of the nineteenth century, is invited not merely by the scope and subject-matter of Nipperdey's work, nor simply by the fact of his explicit appeal to the tradition of historicism, the doctrine that one has to understand the past in its own terms, but it is also suggested by the project's style and form. Nipperdey's three volumes are not written as a textbook or a handbook, for reference only, nor are they written as an interpretative essay or series of reflections. They are intended, in the style of the great historical works of the period which is their subject, to be read from end to end; they are written in a literary tradition of historical scholarship, as 'the history of a world', a 'panorama', 'an ensemble of histories which we narrate, of realities which we describe and analyse' (Vol. III: p. 877). For the most part, the text does indeed manage to hold the reader's attention. Nipperdey falters only in the middle volume, where in his anxiety to get everything in, he clogs many paragraphs with dense masses of statistics and endless lists of names, rendering whole passages virtually unreadable in the process. This does indeed lend it in part the character of a handbook, for consultation rather than for continuous reading, though that characteristic failing of modern German works of historical scholarship, the absence of a proper subject index, makes consultation difficult too. On the whole, however, the books are mercifully free of the jargon, specialized terms, abbreviations and acronyms, and the many other things that make so much modern German historical scholarship so difficult to read with pleasure. The writing flows easily, and the reader is carried along effortlessly by the artfully constructed mixture of narrative, description and argument. This is indeed history in the grand tradition of German historicism.

II

Nipperdey's volumes owe their allegiance to the traditions of German historicism in another respect too. For underneath the surface flow of the narrative, the brilliant analyses of particular areas, the subtle syntheses of modern scholarship, and the many-sided portrayal of an epoch, this is a history that is at heart nationalist in inspiration. It delivers a modernized, cautious, but yet undeniably National Liberal version of events. In the first volume, for instance, Nipperdey seems to me to exaggerate the coherence of the nationalist 'movement' in the Napoleonic, Restoration and *Vormärz* periods (Vol. I: pp. 300–13), and does not pay enough attention to the diverging and often contradictory principles which animated its leading figures. In his political interpretation of the 1848 Revolution he does the same thing, overestimating the significance of nationalism in his treatment of the Revolution and Counter-Revolution in the Habsburg domains, and underestimating the diversity of approaches that existed in the Frankfurt Parliament to the Schleswig-Holstein question. He puts the national question at the heart of his account of the Revolution, devoting well over half the chapter on 1848 to this subject, and relegating social aspects to the sidelines (Vol. I: pp. 595–673). Moreover, in his coverage of the various states within the German Confederation, he generally devotes the lion's share to Prussia, which gets thirty-eight pages in the section on the great reforms of the early nineteenth century, for example, in contrast to only two for 'a glance at Austria' (Vol. I: pp. 33–69, 80–2). In describing the building of the alliance that eventually defeated Napoleon, Nipperdey similarly draws too sharp a contrast between what he sees as the dynastic motives behind Metternich's policies and the national interests behind Prussia's (Vol. I: pp. 82–101).

All this goes to underpin one of the central arguments of the whole enterprise, namely that the growth of German national identity and its eventual expression in a 'little German' or *kleindeutsch* state without Austria was historically natural and inevitable, and would have happened even without Bismarck. There were, says Nipperdey in the third volume, no realistic alternatives to the way in which the German Empire was founded in 1871, neither a 'big German' or *grossdeutsch* alternative including Austria nor a radical-democratic alternative based on parliamentary sovereignty and popular participation. A liberal–conservative unification without war and without Bismarck would not have changed the course of history very much; developments such as the Church–state struggle of the 1870s, the *Kulturkampf*, the introduction of antisocialist legislation, the further growth of German nationalism, and so on, would still have taken place. Nationalism is presented as a natural development, which continued on its way under the Empire as the nation gradually became more integrated and cohesive. And its eventual expression in the rise of Wilhelmine overseas ambitions under the slogan of *Weltpolitik* and the challenge to the maritime and imperial hegemony of England was equally natural and inevitable. All this culminates in a concluding analysis of the German national character, and the author's confession of gratitude in the Afterword, dated '3rd October 1991, the day of German unity', that he has lived in times 'which have allowed me in these years of my life to have experienced the unhoped-for happiness of the unification of Germany' (Vol. III: pp. 904–5, 909). Thus the creation of German nationhood as it happened in the nineteenth century was a natural and largely inevitable process, which had parallels everywhere in Europe. It gives historical legitimacy to the reunification of Germany in the form which it took in 1989/90.

This argument certainly helps bind the whole narrative together. But it also brings problems with it. In the first place, it runs sharply counter to Nipperdey's declared intention of giving an open future back to German history. Putting it polemically, one might say that Nipperdey argues for historical inevitability when this unburdens German history of some of the load of guilt heaped on it by the 'critical' historians and legitimates the creation of the German Empire and the basic features of its foreign policy, but opts for openness, chance and circumstance when it comes to linking nineteenth-century German history to the later development of the Third Reich. Yet it is possible, of course, to redistribute chance and determinacy very differently through German history. The 'critical' historians have done it one way, by arguing that things could have been different at a number of points, above all in 1848 but also in the 1860s, or between 1912 and 1914, and that had they turned out otherwise, German history could have developed in a more democratic, less authoritarian, less militaristic direction and so have avoided visiting upon the rest of Europe and the world the terrible trauma of the Third Reich. But one could do it differently again, for example by recognizing that the Battle of Königgrätz in 1866 could easily have gone the other way, or by accepting that the recovery of the Habsburg monarchy in 1848/49 was by no means preordained. The creation of a German national identity, and the shape and form eventually taken by the German nation-state, were far from inevitable. Ultimately, indeed, the adherence to an essentially 'little German' view of German national identity and an exaggerated concentration on interpreting nineteenth-century German history in terms of its origins and development are two more things that Nipperdey and the 'critical' historians have in common. Yet it is in the end highly questionable whether the settlement reached in 1866 and 1871 did represent the coherent expression of the national principle in Germany, based as they were on the exclusion of millions of people who had previously considered themselves German from the creation of what was supposed to be the German nation-state. There are good reasons for arguing, indeed, that this fact (which one could with equal justification see as more or less inevitable) stored up a problematical legacy for the development of German nationalism in the future, though it is one to which Nipperdey, in his eagerness to provide a historical justification for the foundation of the German Empire, does not pay much attention.

This brings us to a second problem which the nationalist thrust of Nipperdey's history creates – namely, the fact that it does in the end fail to interpret the past in its own terms. We have already seen, for example, that he pays far more attention to Prussia and the Prussian reforms in his account of the early nineteenth century than he does to Austria, or for that matter to the states of the Rhenish Confederation. This cannot really be justified in terms of a balanced treatment of the German history of the period; it can only be justified in terms of what came after – namely, the unification of Germany under Prussian domination. One can certainly make out a case for selecting and analysing the material relating to the 1800s and 1810s in this way, not because of its contemporary significance but because of its eventual impact on what happened fifty or sixty years later in the 1860s and 1870s. However, this essentially ideological procedure cannot be justified when one is simultaneously arguing that it is wrong to select and analyse material about the 1860s and 1870s, not to mention the following decades, principally on the basis of its eventual impact on what happened after a similar, or indeed in some ways rather shorter gap, in the 1920s and 1930s. Here again, it looks suspiciously as if Nipperdey is trying to have his cake and eat it.

The third and perhaps most serious problem to which the underlying nationalist thrust of Nipperdey's work gives rise only fully emerges towards the end of the final volume, which is indeed in some places not quite up to the very high standard of the work as a whole. In his account of the genesis and course of the First World War, his desire to redress the balance of historical opinion and to give 'justice' to contemporaries leads him perilously close to the apologetic stance from which he goes to such pains to dissociate himself on a more general level. Bethmann Hollweg is portrayed as a man of peace, whose acceptance of the risk of war only grew slowly during the crisis of 1914. Even Tirpitz, Moltke and the Kaiser were only in favour of a war that was preventive and defensive, not aggressive and expansionist. What counted above all was the growing might of Russia. This is what impelled the German leadership to issue the famous 'blank cheque' to Austria. But this and its deafness to appeals for a peaceful mediation of the Balkan conflict constitute the only two respects in which it was to blame for the outbreak of war:

> The leadership of the German Reich was not the sole originator of the First World War; it did not even bear the principal responsibility. The Russian mobilization was just as decisive as the bank cheque. In the German case, as in that of the other powers, guilt and fate were mixed. It is important to focus on the motives of German policy. German security was seriously threatened; above all, Germany's status as a great power was seriously threatened. The Germans felt themselves to be 'encircled' and thus to be on the defensive – and they were, too.
>
> (Vol. III: p. 695)

Of course, Nipperdey realizes that the Reich leadership had brought this encirclement on itself by the foreign policy it had pursued since the end of the 1890s. He is right, too, to emphasize the general European dimensions of the war, and to cast doubt on the wilder excesses of the Fischer school, who have sometimes seen the events of July 1914 too exclusively in terms of the internal mechanisms of German politics. Yet when all is said and done, it is really casuistical to see the German actions in the crisis as 'defensive' or 'preventive'.

The Schlieffen Plan was not immutable, and there was nothing inevitable about the invasion of France and Belgium to which it gave rise. Everyone knew, too, that Russian mobilization would take six weeks to achieve, so there was plenty of room for manoeuvre even after it commenced; it was by no means the decisive action that Nipperdey says it was, and there is every reason to believe that the Reich leadership was using it mainly as an excuse to present the Russians as the aggressor, above all to the Social Democrats, for whom this was a key factor bringing about support for war credits. Nipperdey's presentation of the war of 1914 as in essence preventive requires, of course, a dismissal of the vast ambitions of the September Programme as the product of the war itself, speculative, unofficial and quickly discarded (Vol. III: p. 803). But again, it is hard to believe that such ambitions were not current in the Reich leadership before the war broke out. Time and again in the course of the war, as Fischer showed over thirty years ago, debate about various annexationist and hegemonial schemes left no doubt that it was from the beginning a 'bid for world power'; not only in Europe but also in Africa and overseas (and here Nipperdey altogether fails to mention the course of the war in the colonies). Nipperdey goes on to claim that all the belligerents had annexationist and hyperannexationist war aims (Vol. III: p. 802). Not only is this misleading when contrasted with what he says was the need for 'security' which the 'central geographical position' imposed on Germany and which was the fundamental factor in determining German war aims, it is also simply factually incorrect, as a whole series of monographs on the war aims of the various belligerent countries has long since demonstrated. In the end, only Germany (and to some extent Austria) actively planned and fostered the outbreak of war, and only they harboured extensively annexationist war aims from the beginning to the end.

In describing the course of the war, too, Nipperdey's desire to redress the balance against the 'critical' school leads him to overstep the line between even-handedness and apologetics in more than one way. Thus on the one hand, he is at pains to play down German war crimes in occupied Belgium as temporary excesses exaggerated by propaganda, (Vol. III: p. 760), although the systematic shooting of civilians has long been known to have been part of German military ocupation policy, and recent research is revealing it to have been even more widespread than previously thought. On the other hand, he repeatedly refers to the British violation of the law of the sea in actions such as carrying supplies under a false neutral flag (Vol. III: p. 821), hoping by so doing to 'balance' his account of the German decision to begin unrestricted submarine warfare. The contrast between his speculations on Bethmann Hollweg's willingness to sue for a peace without annexations (Vol. III: p. 827) and his allusion to the 'wild drive to continue the war until victory of the governments' in London, Paris and Petrograd in 1917 (Vol. III: p. 817), does not convince, and again comes uncomfortably close to an apologetic stance. Finally, to describe Wilson's armistice terms as amounting to 'unconditional surrender' (Vol. III: p. 865) is a piece of rhetorical overkill that goes far beyond any kind of balanced approach.

Obviously, all the major European powers before 1914 shared a common, positive attitude towards war, coupled with a facile belief in quick victory, an imperialist, racist, Social Darwinist attitude towards international relations, and a willingness to take huge risks in pursuit of international prestige that seems extremely irresponsible in retrospect. Austria-Hungary and Russia in particular played a part in bringing the war about that has often been underestimated by German historians obsessively concerned with their own country's policies. The crucial role played by the British Empire's desire to retain naval and colonial supremacy should not be overlooked. But when all is said and done, Nipperdey's account is too exculpatory. It has the effect of severing the continuities that Fischer drew so carefully between Wilhelmine and National Socialist foreign policy, and the First World War and the Second. And it implicitly casts the Treaty of Versailles in the role of an unfair and arbitrarily imposed *Diktat* that threw a pall over Weimar democracy far blacker than that cast by the 'shadow-lines' left by the Wilhelmine era.

There is some justification, therefore, in the charge levelled at Nipperdey's work by some critics: that this is a history written for the new national mood of Germany in the 1990s, smoothing over and relativizing the problematic aspects of Germany's past, providing the new German nationalism with historical legitimation, and above all dissociating the contingent excesses of individuals like Wilhelm II from the broader and deeper currents of policy based on a justifiable sense of national identity and self-assertion. Despite his claim that the past should be studied in its own terms and for its own sake, Nipperdey is not really consigning history to the dustheap of political irrelevance. On the contrary, he is saying that history shows that 'normal' German nationalism is historically justified, no exception from the European norm, and therefore nothing for Germans in the present day to be ashamed of. This is an argument, it should be emphasized, that is developed in the course of his three volumes with immense subtlety and power; but it is an argument that is led from the present as much as are those of the 'critical' historians whose present-mindedness Nipperdey so scorns in his text.

III

For all his self-confessed allegiance to the principles of 'historicism', Nipperdey is also a very modern historian. His modernity is apparent not only in his inclusion of a whole range of subjects which the followers of

Ranke would have considered unworthy of treatment, but also in the perspective he adopts on the problem of causation. Three aspects stand out here. The first is his insistence on the importance of influences operating on the course of events not only 'from above' but also 'from below'. In discussing the development of Wilhelmine imperialism and *Weltpolitik*, for example, he writes:

> Imperialism was not simply a method by which the ruling classes diverted pressure from below in order to retain their power and their system of rule. Nor was it a 'method' by which they sought to gain legitimation. It was not a means to an end but an end in itself . . . Imperialism was not an artificial product, initiated and driven on from above, but a mass phenomenon, as the resonance and popular successes of the first initiatives in this direction show. The Navy League corresponded to a general atmosphere in German society, as evidenced for example by the popularity of sailor-suits and naval clothing . . . *Weltpolitik* was not just the policy of the Kaiser or of the 'ruling cartel', it was the policy of the Germans; the fleet was the Kaiser's fleet, to be sure, but it was also the fleet of the Germans. The German middle classes became imperialistic voluntarily and of their own free will, and allowed themselves to be gripped by a lust for power and space . . .
>
> (Vol. III: p. 885)

Not quite 'the Germans', therefore, but implicitly only 'some Germans'. Still, the historian has to take into account both 'politics from above' and 'politics from below' (Vol. III: p. 885) when considering such matters.

Time and again in these volumes, Nipperdey puts this insight to good use. He persuasively identifies the emergence of the notorious, right-wing Agrarian League in 1893, for instance, as an example of protest 'from below' rather than manipulation from above, and points to its status as a mass movement, with major peasant support west of the Elbe, as evidence for his rejection of the argument that it was merely a tool of the Junkers (Vol. III: p. 527). An approach of this kind also enables him to distinguish plausibly between attempts at manipulation and popular mobilization from below, as in his illuminating description of the contrast between the officially sponsored monuments to Kaiser Wilhelm I and the mass movement to erect monuments to Bismarck (Vol. III: p. 599). It helps him weigh up the relative importance of Bismarck's political manoeuvrings and wider, more general historical developments in bringing about the decline of liberalism from the 1880s onwards (Vol. III: pp. 314–31, 521–35). It enables him to give due weight to the liberals' real enthusiasm for the anti-Catholic policies of the *Kulturkampf*, which he rightly portrays as far more than a mere piece of Bismarckian manipulation (Vol. III: p. 362). The advantages of such a perspective are seen at their best, perhaps, in Nipperdey's account of the origins of the Revolution of 1918, which is portrayed as the outcome above all of drastic changes in the 'world of experience' of the mass of ordinary people during the war and the failure of the Wilhelmine regime, even in the belated constitutional reforms of October 1918, to take account of them (Vol. III: pp. 850–8, 869–70). In many places in these volumes, therefore, Nipperdey is able to give a subtle and more persuasive account of political developments that owes a good deal to his determination to keep both perspectives, 'above' and 'below', in mind.

Secondly, Nipperdey warns against assuming a one-way relationship between internal and external politics:

> There is domestic policy and there is foreign policy, and in both cases, autonomous developments and decision-making processes are involved. Contemporaries knew this. So do historians. Any hasty or sophistical admixing of these spheres, whether it is the old-fashioned, specifically German view of the 'primacy of foreign policy', the dependence of the constitution and of the basic contours of domestic politics on foreign policy, or the new-fangled reverse theory of a 'primacy of domestic politics', of socio-economic structures and of the power-politics of whatever elites were in power at the time, leads to terribly one-sided judgements or to absolute chaos.
>
> (Vol. III: p. 993)

Only by recognizing the fundamental autonomy of the two spheres, he says, is it possible to reach a balanced view of the ways in which they affected each other. Thus, for example, Nipperdey portrays the notorious 'Hottentot elections' of 1907 as 'a classic example of the successful instrumentalization of imperialism for domestic politics' but points out at the same time that *Weltpolitik* on a wider scale had its own roots in the international imperialist culture of the time, in the international situation, and in the aspirations and desires of social and political groupings such as the left-liberals which were otherwise highly critical of the Wilhelmine political system (Vol. III: p. 647). Once again, this flexibility enables Nipperdey to disentangle a number of complicated foreign policy problems which refuse to yield to a more simplistic, more dogmatic approach. On the other hand, of course, as we have seen, it also enables him to legitimize developments such as the 'little German' unification of Germany or the rise of *Weltpolitik* as the product of the inevitable growth of a broad-based German national consciousness rather than the outcome of conservative manipulation from above.

Part of Nipperdey's concern in these volumes is to rehabilitate the German bourgeoisie, that social stratum that has come in for so much criticism from historians over the years. Much of the time, as the subtitles to his first two volumes suggest, he is writing about the world and spirit of the bourgeoisie, and he argues plausibly that by the end of the nineteenth century bourgeois values dominated German culture and society. While the bourgeoisie features as the subject of more than one section of Nipperdey's work, however, the aristocracy, which he is so anxious to dethrone from the central position accorded to it in modern German history by the 'critical' historians, nowhere receives separate or extended treatment, surely a deficiency in a history that claims to be comprehensive. The rise of bourgeois society is equated by Nipperdey largely with the process of 'modernization', and the centrality of this concept to his narrative forms a third important respect in which he is, in the end, a very modern historian. For in the end, just like the 'critical' historians, Nipperdey interprets the history of Germany from 1800 to 1918 in terms of 'retarded and contradictory modernization', though unlike them he argues that both economy and society were fully modernized, and sees the retardation mainly in terms of attitudes and mentalities rather than social and political structures (Vol. III: p. 881). In a key passage towards the end of the book, he concedes that

> the question of the conditions for the rise of Hitler does not, as is well known, lead to the contradictions of capitalism, but to the persistence of the power of preindustrial, traditional elites and mentalities in Germany, and of the fears of modernization which derived from the lack of bourgeois liberality. The discrepancy between a modern economy and a more premodern system of rule was basic, it leaps to our attention as we look back. Our survey has not refuted this model, but it has amended it and reshaped it.
>
> (Vol. III: p. 903)

Nipperdey's modification lies in his (rather Marxist-sounding) insistence that the bourgeoisie and the proletariat came to dominate society, rather than the traditional elites; but the tempo of modernization was such that its costs were higher than elsewhere, and its destabilizing effects on emerging 'modern' social groups and institutions were more severe than they might have been had the pace of change been slower. At the same time, the rapidity of change delivered into the hands of premodern ruling structures and groups modern instruments of control and mobilization which they used to prolong their power. Much of what 'critical' historians have described as 'premodern', from sociocultural mores to the policies of imperialism, Nipperdey thus interprets, with good reason, as essentially modern, or at least typical for the advanced states and societies of the day. In these various nuances and qualifications which he brings to the well-known thesis of Germany's uneven development, there is much to ponder over and discuss. Yet in the end, he only modifies it, he does not succeed in overthrowing it; he stands on the same interpretative ground as the 'critical' school, and maps it out in a rather similar way, simply changing some of the negative signs into positive ones. So his account is open to many of the same objections that have been raised against theirs, from the vague and protean nature of the concept of modernization itself, through its unhistorical and normative basis, to the arbitrariness of its application in the case of German history.

IV

At the end of his book, after having consciously avoided such questions for the best part of three volumes of text, Nipperdey comes to the problem of the relationship of the Kaiserreich to what came after. 'Did not the German Empire', he asks,

> lay the foundations for the collapse of the Weimar Republic, indeed for the rise of National Socialism and its seizure of power? Was not the Second World War a new version of the German struggle for world power and hegemony? Hitler, with his monstrous crimes the curse of our century, our world, rose to power in Germany, under German circumstances and preconditions, and not somewhere else. Is Hitler not the unavoidable fact with which all our historical retrospectives on modern German history must begin? Is that not the legacy of the era of the German Empire, put together from guilt and fate, the legacy of its 'shadow-lines'? Must this not determine our perspective?
>
> (Vol. III: p. 880)

Such a perspective, Nipperdey concedes, is legitimate, even necessary. But it is 'misleading' if it is adopted as the only way of seeing the past. 'I have consciously and emphatically', he confesses, 'kept it subordinate, and explicitly rejected it in its biases' (Vol. III: p. 880). Thus his history is intended not as an exercise in even-handedness, but rather to *redress* the balance against the 'biases' of the 'critical' school. The impressive bibliographies are full of adverse comments on works Nipperdey considers excessively 'critical' or ' biased', but there is scarcely a word of criticism of publications which have been widely regarded by others as 'apologetic'. And at a number of points in the text he seems to me to lean too far towards the positive.

For example, in Volume II, Nipperdey succinctly summarizes research on workers' savings and on the organized working-class leisure activities of the labour movement. While he certainly pays due attention to the deep class antagonisms and inequalities that divided German society at this period, and provides plenty of detail on poverty, slums, and other aspects of the working-class predicament in the Kaiserreich, he places his main emphasis on what he sees as the gradual embourgeoisement of the proletariat. He repeats the now discredited legend, on which the cultural aspects of this argument largely rest, that 'workers' culture' was 'largely identical with labour movement culture, in other words with Social Democratic culture' (Vol. III: p. 562). He does no more than mention the rough and disorderly side of working-class life, and he does not touch at all on the proletarian passion for gambling and lotteries, or the role of the pawnbroker on the proletarian family economy. Similarly, there is very little in his portrayal of the Kaiserreich on the subjects of crime and protest – just three pages (Vol. III: pp. 185–7), and these appear in a section on law and justice, where his main concern is to demonstrate that Imperial Germany was a state which kept to the law in its methods of rule, a *Rechtsstaat*. Thus by a classificatory device he removes the question of relations with the police, of 'class justice' in everyday life, and of the petty crimes and misdemeanours which were so important a part of proletarian existence, from consideration in the context of the thesis of the embourgeoisement of the working class.

More serious than this, however, is the fact that this attempt at a balance ignores most of the arguments that have been put forward by the historians who have produced the research on which Nipperdey relies. The point of arguing that the working class was becoming more prosperous and respectable, or of suggesting on the contrary that this view has been exaggerated, or takes too undifferentiated a view of the working class as a whole, or ignores major aspects of everyday life, has never been simply to argue for a rosy or a gloomy view of proletarian existence in this period, or to emphasize its plus or minus side in drawing up some kind of historical balance-sheet. The point has been, rather, to try and explain things like the support of some kinds of workers for a Marxist-oriented labour movement, or the alienation of many workers from the institutions of the Wilhelmine state, or the attitudes which surfaced in the working class in 1914 or four years later, in the Revolution of 1918. In so far as political attitudes are rooted in the experiences of everyday life, they have to be accounted for by research into social history. For much of the time in Volume II, what Nipperdey seems to be offering is social history as 'history with the politics left out'.

Yet in his pursuit of justice, Nipperdey throws overboard much of the conceptual apparatus of the social sciences which informed the research of the 'critical' historians. The result is, especially in Volume II, in many places a basically descriptive account. Time and again, Nipperdey fails to make connections between the different subjects with which he deals, even where other historians have made them before him. One example of this is in his section on the rise of bacteriology and the discovery of the cell (Vol. II: pp. 615–17). Both of these had important consequences for the emergence of new, biologistic ways of understanding state and society which were to have fateful consequences in the interwar period, and both also reflected important social and political currents at the time. But Nipperdey treats them in largely scientific terms and fails to bring out these wider resonances. In Volumes I and II, the account of economic history is equally descriptive, and the theories and explanations put forward by economic historians are not really discussed, perhaps because Nipperdey's main concern is simply to put economic growth forward as one of the 'positive' aspects of German history in the period he is surveying. In Volume III, his account of the wartime economy from 1914 to 1918 says too little about the deficiencies of resources and management which were so decisive in determining the war's eventual outcome, and confines himself too much to a description of the popular experience of wartime hardship.

Perhaps it is inevitable that in such a vast undertaking, the effort of imposing a structure on the subject-matter has taken precedence over establishing connections between its different aspects. One must remember, too, that Nipperdey is reacting against what he regards as simplistic and reductionist accounts of these connections by insisting over and again on the autonomy of different areas of human life. Nevertheless, this insistence does have unfortunate consequences for some of his interpretations. In his account of the 1848 Revolution, for example, he argues for a radical separation of social issues, which he suggests were quickly settled, from political ones, which he says were largely autonomous, and which dominated the action once the initial upheaval was over. Eighteen forty-eight, in other words, was a political revolution, not a social one. In arguing this, Nipperdey seeks to undermine the social interpretation of 1848 as a failed bourgeois revolution, centring on class antagonisms that ultimately worked out to the advantage of the feudal order (a view deriving ultimately from Marx and Engels, and occupying a central position in the 'critical' historians' account of the 'divergent path' (*Sonderweg*) taken by Germany from the mid-nineteenth century to the Third Reich). But his radical separation of the social from the political does not really convince. Social issues such as the emancipation of the peasants carried as much political significance in 1848 as they did in 1789 or 1917, even if the consequences were different in each case. Similarly, it is taking too narrow a view of the political to define it simply in terms of who controlled and ran the state. The social aspirations and demands of the peasantry, some of whom supported the Revolution and some of whom did not, need to be linked to the programmes and actions of the liberal and conservative elites in order to understand why the Revolution failed. It simply isn't good enough to assert, as Nipperdey does, that the revolution failed for political reasons, and because 'the people' were in the end too conservative (Vol. I: pp. 667–70). Here again he presents too undifferentiated a picture of 'the people' and says too little about the connections between society, economy and politics.

V

Despite the many ways in which Nipperdey's great work consciously reflects and embodies the principles of German historicism, one may express a degree of scepticism as to whether it is really possible in the end to write a book reflecting traditions of historical scholarship established in the nineteenth century but based on the knowledge and experience of the twentieth. The historians of a hundred years ago, for example, had no problem in writing about great men in history, or in ascribing to them an autonomous, sometimes almost elemental power to shape events. But the perversion of this view in the leadership cult developed under National Socialism, which included not only the ascription of world-historical status to Hitler himself but also a tendency to reinterpret the whole of history as the result of the personal leadership exercised by great men, from Arminius to Frederick the Great, has rendered German historians highly allergic to any attempt to revive it, even in a modified form. Moreover, the degeneration of the historicist tradition under National Socialism has had the further effect of causing German historians to fight very shy of any kind of historical judgement that could run the risk of being labelled subjective. It has also caused German historians to avoid as far as possible any confession of personal motives in their writing, a point that does not trouble their English or American colleagues, as can easily be seen by any comparison of the Prefaces which they attach to their books. The rhetorical strategies which German historians adopt to persuade their readers that they are writing 'objective' history, free from any subjective element, are many and varied, and have left their trace in Nipperdey's work too – for example, in his use of the word 'we' instead of 'I' when giving a personal judgement or a cross-reference ('we have spoken of this' instead of 'I have spoken of this'). Judgements on individual historical personalities are more subjective than most, so German historians have been extremely reluctant to make them; this accounts for the relative weakness of the tradition of political biography in postwar Germany, for example. Here too, Nipperdey is no exception.

Despite the ringing declarations with which he begins the first and last volumes of the trilogy ('In the beginning was Napoleon' – 'In the beginning was Bismarck'), Nipperdey thus stoutly denies any desire to revive a 'personalistic view of history', which is indeed 'really untenable'. It was only in exceptional times, he says, that individuals such as Bismarck and Napoleon were able to put their stamp on history (Vol. III: p. 11). So Nipperdey includes them only as historical forces, not as real human beings. Nowhere does he make any attempt to tell us what they were like as people. They are individuals with a name and an identity but without character or individuality. This is very different to the way that the original historicists treated the great men of the past, as Nipperdey himself confesses:

> In the way in which we tell our history and our histories, the individuality of personalities doubtless gets too little attention, as well as the colourful and the characteristic and the chance circumstance in the interlacing of structures; that is a consequence of our ideal of totality and of the overall perspective we adopt in traversing the history of half a century.
>
> (Vol. III: p. 418)

The only real exception is Wilhelm II, whose personal foibles had a real effect on the politics of the day, and are therefore described in a biting *vignette*:

gifted, with a quick understanding, sometimes brilliant, with a taste for the modern, – technology, industry, science – but at the same time superficial, hasty, restless, unable to relax, without any deeper level of seriousness, without any desire for hard work or drive to see things through to the end, without any sense of sobriety, for balance and boundaries, or even for reality and real problems, uncontrollable and scarcely capable of learning from experience, desperate for applause and success, – as Bismarck said early on in his life, he wanted every day to be his birthday – romantic, sentimental and theatrical, unsure and arrogant, with an immeasurably exaggerated self-confidence and desire to show off, a juvenile cadet, who never took the tone of the officers' mess out of his voice, and brashly wanted to play the part of the supreme warlord, full of panicky fear of a monotonous life without any diversions, and yet aimless, pathological in his hatred against his English mother . . .

(Vol. III: p. 421)

Later, with perhaps rather less justification, particularly in the absence of any comparable account of Bismarck, there are also brief character sketches of Wilhelm II's Reich Chancellors Caprivi, Hohenlohe and Bülow (Vol. III: pp. 699, 709, 724). It is disappointing, therefore, that virtually none of the many other figures whose social, intellectual or political impact is discussed in these volumes receives similar treatment. Personal quirks and foibles played a role in German history long before the advent of Wilhelm II, after all.

The reasons for this lie deeper than the exaggerated fear of 'personalizing' and of subjective character judgements so common among German historians in recent decades. At the root of the problem is Nipperdey's conviction, which pervades the book, that the historian's task is above all to *judge* the past. He thinks the 'critical school' has been too eager to convict, too reluctant to find mitigating or extenuating circumstances, too neglectful of evidence in favour of the accused. The declared aim of Volume I, acording to the dust-jacket, is to give 'justice' to the Germans of the nineteenth century (in the blurb for Volume II these are 'our grandfathers'; by the end of Volume III they have become 'great-grandparents' (Vol. III: p. 880)). But are the language and the conceptual apparatus of a court of law really what the historian should be using in dealing with the past? Should the historian be a judge? The point of studying the past, surely, is not to judge it, but to understand and explain it. In exercising his judgement, too, Nipperdey constantly obtrudes himself in a way that ultimately, long before the end of the book, becomes extremely tiresome. At every point he is there, usually in the plural form, directing his readership, the jury, on what verdict should be reached. There are hardly any quotations from contemporaries in any of the three volumes – none at all in Volume II, perhaps half a dozen (ignoring remembered phrases like 'blood and iron') in Volume III, just a handful in Volume I. There are no case-studies to point up the generalized judgements. There is not one description of a town, a village, or a landed estate, scarcely a single anecdote or story. The people who lived in the period hardly get a word in edgeways. All we hear instead is the voice of Nipperdey, weighing up, balancing out, judging them. Is this really doing justice to the people of the time?

The trilogy, in other words, does very little to bring the past alive. Its discussion of social history in particular is extremely generalized: synthesizing history seen as a history of averages. Nor does it make much of an attempt to entertain the reader. Doing justice to the past evidently means, for Nipperdey, taking it *seriously*. In 2,669 pages of text there is not a single joke, not even a faint flash of scholarly wit. The nearest thing to either of these can be found in a rare quotation, on page 498 of Volume III; but the wit lies in the quotation, not with the historian. Moreover, like most German historians, Nipperdey seems to have no interest in presenting information visually. There are two maps, on pages 761 and 763 of Volume III, illustrating the progress of the First World War on the Western and Eastern Fronts respectively; and two graphs, on pages 505 and 507 of the same volume, conveying the results of Reichstag elections under the Empire. These rather arbitrarily selected visual aids are all that enliven the acres of words. One can respect the decision to attempt a literary narrative without accepting that it necessarily implied a total renunciation of maps and graphics. Vast and complicated statistical tables are no substitute for easily digested graphs, histograms and pie-charts; if maps are deemed necessary for the narrative of the First World War, then why not of the Austro-Prussian War, the Schleswig-Holstein question, or the founding of the Bismarckian Empire? Why not, indeed, as a means of conveying the regional dimension of German social history in Volume I or Volume II? This is not necessarily Nipperdey's own fault; one only has to compare the use of maps and graphics in French historical scholarship with their absence from most comparable German works to realize that this is a cultural rather than an individual deficiency. A deficiency it is, none the less.

Such deficiencies are compensated for to some extent by Nipperdey's skilful use of illuminating detail, from his story of how the wood from the scaffold on which the assassin Karl Ludwig Sand was executed was taken by the hangman, who had democratic sympathies, to a Heidelberg vineyard and used to build a summer house in which the *Burschenschaften* subsequently held their meetings (Vol. I: p. 282), to his illustration of the nature of everyday nationalism in the Empire by references to the singing of

German nationalist songs at the dynastic festivals of the Bavarian dynasty of the Wittelsbachs, and the replacement of 'three cheers for the Pope!' at the annual congress of the Roman Catholics (*Katholikentag*) by 'three cheers for the Kaiser!' from 1887 onwards (Vol. III: p. 596). At his best, Nipperdey can be wonderfully interesting and full of absorbing detail. But ultimately, one feels, this is secondary to his main purpose, of reaching a balanced judgement. Nipperdey does not really, in the end, try to understand the past from the inside, in the manner of a true historicist, because this involves an element of subjective judgement which the modern German historical profession finds unacceptable. Rather, he judges it from the outside, without any attempt to allow it its own voice. The result is a book whose overall impression is rather colourless. 'The basic colours of history are not black and white,' Nipperdey says at the very end of his book, 'its basic pattern not the contrast of a chess-board; the basic colour of history is grey, in endless degrees' (Vol. III: p. 905). But history is not really grey at all: it is colourful and varied in hue. To do it justice, the historian needs to employ the full range of his palette. Nipperdey has given us German history in monochrome: he has not sought to bring it to life in all its colourful variety, but by the unremitting application of his judgement to reduce it all to an exercise in chiaroscuro.

Yet it would be wrong to end on a negative note. Taken as a whole, there can be no doubt that Nipperdey's three volumes represent historical scholarship of the very highest order. Nipperdey's rhetorical gesture of beginning the first and third volumes, as we have seen, with an adaptation of the opening phrase of the Gospel according to St John ('In the beginning was Napoleon' – 'In the beginning was Bismarck') is bold, not only in its affirmation of the importance of the individual in history but also in its implicit claim of biblical status for the text. Yet in a mundane sense this claim is surely justified. These three volumes sum up, clearly, accurately and on the whole fairly, the research of recent generations on nineteenth-century German history and will surely establish themselves as the standard work on the period for generations to come. They are filled with subtle analyses, challenging interpretations and masterly syntheses of a mass of disparate and often difficult material. All this is done without bombast or pretentiousness. One of the most attractive features of Nipperdey's approach is his modesty. In the competitive, achievement-oriented world of the professional historian in the late twentieth century, too many works of historical scholarship begin with a small-minded denigration of their predecessors and rivals, and too many historians, obsessed with delivering a new theory, a new approach or a new interpretation, summarily dismiss as useless or misguided the work of those who have gone before them. How refreshing it is, therefore, to find a historian with the humility and generosity of spirit to recognize, as Nipperdey does, that

> We stand in a continuity and community of historians, our predecessors, our teachers, our colleagues, our pupils, who have worked before us and taught us, who stimulate and provoke us, criticize and revise . . . We are dwarfs on the shoulders of giants.
>
> (Vol. II: p. 805, Vol. III: p. 838)

Certainly, with the last sentence, Nipperdey was being too modest. With these volumes, he has written a work which can easily stand comparison with the great monuments of historical scholarship of the past.

Despite his disclaimers, it *is* a work with a thesis, and one that invites contradiction as well as recognition. In the Afterword to the first of these volumes, Nipperdey thanked his scholarly opponents and critics for their contribution to his own thinking, and he certainly would not have expected these three volumes to go uncriticized themselves. But they in their turn provoke readers to consider how they themselves would interpret the period and the subject with which they deal; more than this, they force one to reflect on how history should be written, and what it is ultimately about. This is no small achievement for a general historical synthesis. For a decade and a half, Nipperdey worked to produce a general history of Germany from 1800 to 1918 that is readable, masterly, provocative and profound. He demonstrated extraordinary energy, assiduity and perseverance. He showed staggering and unflagging erudition over a vast historical canvas, controlling it all with a seeming effortlessness that must have belied a great deal of hard and careful thought. Most astonishingly of all, he did all this, towards the end, in the face of a serious and ultimately fatal illness which must have required a tremendous effort of will to overcome. It is good to know that he was able to see the finished version of the final volume in his hands before he died.

NOTES

1 Thomas Nipperdey, *Deutsche Geschichte 1800–1866: Bürgerwelt und starker Staat* (Munich, C.H. Beck Verlag, 1983); *Deutsche Geschichte 1866–1918, Band I: Arbeitswelt und Bürgergeist* (Munich, C.H. Beck Verlag, 1990); *Deutsche Geschichte 1866–1918, Band II: Machtstaat vor der Demokratie* (Munich, C.H. Beck Verlag, 1992). For ease of reference, *Deutsche Geschichte 1800–1866* will be referred to as Volume I, *Deutsche Geschichte 1866–1918, Band I: Arbeitswelt und Bürgergeist* as Volume II, and *Deutsche Geschichte 1866–1918, Band II: Machtstaat vor der Demokratie* as Volume III.

2 In Volume I, the sections on population, the family, and everyday life in Chapter III would have been better placed after the sections on the agrarian and industrial economy, which would then have provided the necessary background against which the changes described had to be seen. In Volume II, there is sometimes a confusing tendency to repeat the same information where it falls under more than one heading, as in the account of the life and work of the Darwinist Ernst Haeckel, which appears both in the section on religion and in the section on

science (Vol. II: pp. 509–11, pp. 627–8), or in the treatment of Heinrich Hertz's discovery of electromagnetic waves, which is repeated in almost identical phrasing twice in three pages (II/607, 609). In Volume III, it would surely have made more sense to have placed all or part of the section on foreign policy at the end of Chapter V, leading directly on to the account of the First World War in Chapter VI. As it is, the fact that this section comes at the beginning, even though it includes a narrative of the events of July 1914, and is followed by a lengthy account of the development of the internal politics of the Kaiserreich from 1890 to the outbreak of the war, creates an unfortunate hiatus. It is arguable, too, that the forty pages of narrative of the military conduct of the war and its internal political ramifications which open Chapter VI would have been easier to follow had they been preceded by the section on German war aims instead of having been followed by it. But otherwise the structure is admirably clear and straightforward.

4

FROM UNIFICATION TO WORLD WAR[1]

Even today, after reunification, Wolfgang Mommsen points out, the German Empire created by Bismarck forms a central point of orientation for the national identity of the Germans. It was created not by an act of free will on the part of its citizens but rather by a 'revolution from above'. It was forged in the heat of battle, and imposed by force. It was incomplete, excluding many ethnic Germans from its boundaries, and it was divided, including many people of other nationalities as well as different confessions, classes and regional groups. Yet, says Mommsen, it soon came to incorporate in the eyes of the majority of its inhabitants the historic dream of a German nation-state. It continued to do so long after its formal collapse in the revolution of 1918. From today's point of view, indeed, the Weimar Republic of 1918–33 looks more like the last phase of the Imperial period than any kind of genuinely new beginning. Its institutions were, broadly speaking, continuations of those which had existed under Wilhelm II, from the Reichstag and the central government ministries to the provincial legislatures and federated administrations. The legal system remained the same as under the Empire, as did, by and large, those who ran it. The political parties renamed themselves but were still in effect the same parties which had existed for decades under the Empire. Even the President, elected in a separate national vote, and armed with extensive legal and administrative powers, above all in time of emergency, was a kind of substitute Kaiser. To symbolize the continuity, the Weimar Republic referred to itself as the German *Reich* rather than trying to invent a nomenclature that was fundamentally new.

The basic structures of the Bismarckian Empire were swept away only after 1933 – first (and partially) by the Nazis, then more completely by defeat and occupation in 1945. Mommsen sees the division of Germany at the end of the Second World War as part of the price Germans had to pay for Weimar's failure to free itself from the historical burden imposed on it by the Bismarckian Empire. The problems which that Empire left unsolved were compounded by the disasters of Weimar. Democracy was too widely identified with defeat in war for it to stand much of a chance of surviving the social and economic upheavals of inflation and depression. Hitler's Third Reich represented a radical attempt to solve these problems by violence. The drastic boundary changes which followed its defeat, the westward movement of Poland, and the vast and bloody forced repatriation of millions of ethnic Germans from East-Central and Eastern Europe, altered the situation almost beyond recognition, and make it absurd in Mommsen's view for anyone to claim that the reunification of 1989/90 involved, or implied, any kind of return to the Bismarckian nation-state. Not only is the territory of the present-day reunited Germany very different from that of the German Empire of a century ago, but reunification itself was achieved through a process of democratic self-determination that was very different from the authoritarian violence in which the original Empire itself was born.

Nevertheless, as the first and historically most powerful modern incorporation of German national identity, the Empire created by Bismarck remains a source of enduring importance for the ongoing German quest for self-definition. This is a powerful reason for its continuing fascination for historians. Recently the leading representatives of the generation of German scholars born around the year 1930 have turned their attention to writing major syntheses incorporating the decades of research which they themselves have done so much to inspire. Wolfgang J. Mommsen's two enormous volumes, dealing respectively with the years 1850 to 1890 (1993) and 1890 to 1918 (1993), come after the late Thomas Nipperdey's massive three-part history, covering the 'long nineteenth century' from 1800 to 1918, and the three equally lengthy instalments of Hans-Ulrich Wehler's *Deutsche Gesellschaftsgeschichte* covering the period from 1849 to 1914. If Wehler was the counsel for the prosecution, and Nipperdey the counsel for the defence, Mommsen, as one would expect from his previous writings, stands somewhere in between, and does his best to achieve a balanced view. On the whole, however, again as one might expect, he takes a markedly more critical view of the Bismarckian Empire than Nipperdey did.

For, Mommsen argues, that Empire was a flawed creation from the very outset. It excluded the Catholics and degraded them to the status of second-class citizens, while it included many national minorities, storing up trouble for the future. Mommsen backs this up by devoting a great deal of space to the *Kulturkampf*, delivering in the process the fullest narrative of Bismarck's struggle with the Catholic Church now available in any general survey. He makes clear the sheer scale and variety of government anti-Catholic measures taken during the 1870s up to the death of the reactionary Pope Pius IX and the era of conciliation which began with his successor Leo XIII. In a number of particularly impressive sections (Vol. I: pp. 595ff., Vol. II: pp. 214ff and 424ff.) Mommsen also details the many and varied forms of discrimination to which the Polish citizens of Prussia were subjected from the 1880s to the First World War. Religious and racial discrimination were built into the fabric of the Empire from the very beginning. Founded on power and force, the Empire not only stigmatized those whom it conceived to be its internal enemies, it also created a myth of external power and force by the very fact of its existence. The temptation to prioritize these factors in foreign policy in pursuit of this myth was eventually to prove too strong to resist.

Mommsen emphasizes, however, that the Empire was not simply the creation of Bismarck and the Prussian army, but also involved the essential collaboration of the German liberals. Bismarck's whole policy was in part dictated by his desire to find a way around the Prussian constitutional struggle which had begun in 1862, when the liberals had started to try to get control over the Prussian army by refusing to pass the budget. Moreover, without the head of steam for it built up by the *Nationalverein* and the liberal nationalists in the early-to-mid-1860s, the process of unification would never have come to the boil at all. All the same, the liberals made too many compromises in this process. Their elitism and distrust of democracy, their acceptance, however grudging, of a semi-constitutional system in which ministers lacked all parliamentary responsibility, and their negative tactics in the Reichstag, all undermined the reputation of democratic parliamentarianism and prepared the way for the rise of independent pressure-groups of various kinds in the 1890s. Nationalism became a substitute for political participation, and the rule of the bureaucracy encouraged political irresponsibility and demagoguery. Clinging to power in the municipalities, the liberals showed an irremediable disdain for the masses which contributed much to the growing isolation of the elites to which they belonged from the rest of German society. All this stored up a fatal political legacy for the future.

Like other historians of this period, Mommsen feels obliged in making such criticisms to ask whether there was any real alternative to the course that German unification eventually took. Nipperdey, famously, argued that there was not. Wehler thought that at least the constitutional system might have been different. Mommsen reveals himself as an adherent of the 'big German' idea of national unity, and suggests that the German Confederation, destroyed by Bismarck in 1866, could have provided the basis for the creation of a nation-state which included Austria. This, he thinks, would have created a more even balance between Protestants and Catholics in the population, and softened the baleful hegemony of Prussia. A nation-state created on the basis of the German Confederation would have been a far more decentralized state than the Bismarckian Empire. Created by peaceful means rather than by military action, it would have posed no real threat to the rest of Europe. It would have been spared the great-power dreams which haunted the Wilhelmine era. Thus German cultural hegemony in Central and Eastern Europe would have been preserved and the First World War would never have happened.

But all this is wishful thinking. Eighteen forty-eight had already revealed the impossible obstacle posed to a unification on the basis of the territory of the Confederation by the understandable insistence of the Habsburg monarchy on preserving its own integrity. The emergence of strong nationalist movements in parts of the Confederation such as Bohemia, where the Czechs were reluctant in the extreme to participate in a 'big German' nation-state, and the vitriolic reaction to this of many German nationalists in the Frankfurt Parliament, suggested that tensions between the majority and the minority would have been even greater in a 'big Germany' than they eventually were in the Bismarckian Empire. Equally untenable was the exclusion of a large part of Prussia from the Confederation. Neither the Austrians nor the Prussians were going to allow major chunks of their states to be sliced off to form part of a united Germany without a struggle. If a German nation-state was going to be established at all – and the process was virtually unstoppable after the dramatic unification of Italy in 1859/60 had shown the way – then it was going to be on a 'little-German' basis, and it was going to be at least in part by force, just as happened with the unification of other European states, including that of Britain in the seventeenth and eighteenth centuries.

Mommsen's penchant for speculation – and there are plenty of other 'what if?' discussions in these volumes – reflects his refreshing awareness that things could easily have gone in another direction at any number of points from the battle of Königgrätz onwards. Bismarck himself was well aware of the precariousness of Germany's international situation, and his dizzying sequence of European alliances and alignments during the 1870s and 1880s, described by Mommsen in great detail, was a stark reflection of this sense of insecurity. Bismarck helped to give the newly founded Reich a breathing-space of two decades by this policy. Overall, however, the picture Mommsen paints of his rule in the first of these two volumes is overwhelmingly negative. He drove the Social Democrats to the left by unnecessary repressive measures and drastically reduced their fitness to participate in the political process. His constitutional arrangements for the Empire amounted to a 'system of evaded decisions' in which the lines of responsibility were left fatally unclear, and proper arrangements for financing the running of the Reich were never made. He left a bourgeoisie unused to political responsibility, an upper class reluctant to modernize, a lower middle class hostile to liberal constitutional values, and a proletariat alienated from the mainstream of society and politics. His pursuit of cabinet politics in international affairs, irrespective of the dictates of public opinion, cut off potential links between government and people in this sphere and opened the way for the populist demagoguery of the radical nationalists after he had gone. His attempt to forge an alliance involving Russia and Austria was doomed from the start, given the increasingly antagonistic interests of those two powers in the Balkans. Even before he was forced to resign in 1890, the elaborate system of international security he had built up over the years was in tatters.

Bismarck's long-term influence on Germany, therefore, was a negative one. Whether these arguments amount to a reassertion of the much-vaunted idea of a German *Sonderweg*, a 'special path' to modernity, however, must be doubted. As might be expected from a specialist on Max Weber and one of the principal editors of the great sociologist's collected works, Mommsen quotes frequently from Weber's commentaries on the events of his times, often to good effect. In some respects, however, theories and interpretations which have their origins in Weber's incisive commentaries on the society he lived in have been overtaken by subsequent historical research. The once-popular idea that the Wilhelmine economy was a kind of 'organized capitalism', for instance, now seems to be untenable (Vol. II: pp. 19–20). The role of the state in the economy remained relatively insignificant, and there was no thought of establishing any kind of systematic economic management on the part of the bureaucrats in Berlin.

Similarly, the theory of the 'feudalization of the bourgeoisie', Mommsen concedes, also has to be abandoned (Vol. II: p. 72), Despite the persistent influence of aristocratic ideals and values in Wilhelmine society, conveyed through institutions such as the reserve officer system and the student duelling corps, the Prussian nobility lost steadily in influence through this period and gave way increasingly to the social hegemony of the upper middle class. There was no effective merger between the old and new elites to form a broad new ruling class (a process which, Mommsen claims, happened in Britain, but which the work of Lawrence Stone showed some years ago to have been in fact something of a myth). Instead – and here Weber's influence on Mommsen's interpretation is perhaps at its strongest – Wilhelmine Germany was a bureaucratic state in which the higher civil service ran everything and indeed exercised so much power that they alone can be made responsible for the fact that the creation of a civil society, dominated by modern bourgeois-capitalist values, remained only partial and incomplete.

This view, however, does not really convince. The high Prussian and Imperial bureaucracy certainly was powerful, but it was also very small, and it had to operate in a much wider social and political context. Power comes in many different forms and operates at many different levels, and if there was a deficit of 'bourgeois values' in Imperial Germany – something which other historians, such as Wehler, have recently doubted, and which Mommsen, in so far as he analyses it at all, certainly exaggerates – then its causes were far more wide-ranging and complex than the simple domination of a handful of highly placed officials. The problem is that Mommsen does not really allow himself the space to develop these interesting arguments properly. Out of a total of roughly 1,800 pages, fewer than 200 are devoted to social and economic history, and that includes separate sections on women in society, and on the social and economic aspects of the First World War. The overwhelming bulk of these two volumes is devoted to a minutely detailed narrative of high politics. So elaborate is it, indeed, that structural factors inevitably fade into the background and lose all explanatory power. It is here, of course, that high officialdom comes into its own – not as a social institution, but as a collection of named individuals whose particular actions are depicted as largely shaping the course of events. But if this is all that Mommsen means by bureaucratic hegemony, then it is not very convincing.

All this, surprisingly for a historian whose intellectual career has been so closely bound up with the work of Max Weber, gives these volumes an extremely old-fashioned look. In the first volume, Bismarck dominates everything, and the narrative is largely an account of his actions and policies at home and abroad. In the second volume, the action becomes more complex, largely because Mommsen argues (convincingly) that Wilhelm II was too erratic to provide any consistent leadership from the top, except in the brief period of 'personal rule' from 1894 to 1897, a period so littered with failed political initiatives and legislative fiascos that it is hardly surprising that it soon came to an end. Because the focus of these two volumes is so heavily concentrated on high politics, individuals loom far larger than they would have done had Mommsen taken a broader approach. A characteristic example of the weight given to personal factors in this account of German history between 1850 and 1918 can be found in one of Mommsen's counterfactual speculations, delivered towards the end of Volume I, when he comes to discuss the brief reign of Kaiser Friedrich III, who succeeded Bismarck's protector the aged Kaiser Wilhelm I in 1888. As is well known, Friedrich III was already terminally ill when he came to the throne, and never had a chance to show whether or not his widespread reputation as a liberal was justified. After 100 days of rule, he was succeeded by his bombastic, authoritarian and unstable son Wilhelm II.

Mommsen uses these events to speculate on what might have happened had German custom allowed a woman to succeed to the throne. He suggests that Kaiser Friedrich's widow Victoria, daughter of the British queen of the same name, would then have succeeded, and declares that she would undoubtedly have made a good Empress. 'One suspects', he writes (Vol. I: p. 681) 'that an Empress Viktoria would have saved the German nation from a great deal of the misfortune that overtook it, and Europe, during the reign of her son.' But this is based on a complete misunderstanding of the rules of succession. In no monarchy has the widow of a deceased monarch taken precedence over that monarch's children; royal succession always follows in the blood-line, and judged by this criterion, Victoria's claim was really too remote to be taken seriously. As someone who lived in Britain for many years, Mommsen ought to know this; but his grasp of English forms is surprisingly shaky (he consistently gets the titles of British statesmen wrong, for instance, calling the late Victorian Prime Minister 'Lord Robert Cecil Salisbury' on p. 280 of Vol. II, for instance, instead of the correct Robert Cecil, Lord Salisbury). In any case, whatever the details, Mommsen only slips into such implausible speculations because his gaze is so unwaveringly focused on the actions of the Kaiser and the Chancellor and their immediate entourages. When he occasionally takes the broader view, he makes it clear that he knows this kind of thing is nonsense, and recognizes explicitly that the Bismarckian system was too well established by 1888 for Friedrich III to have made any difference to it even had he been capable of it (Vol. I: p. 679). Given this undoubted truth, it is extremely unclear how Victoria could have made a difference even had she by some bizarre chance been heir to her husband's throne, for all the undoubted strength of her personality.

Mommsen's account of politics at the top is often compelling, full of lively detail, cogent and clear narration, and carefully balanced historical judgement. He is very good on the miscalculations of Wilhelmine foreign policy, its lack of realism and its self-fulfilling nightmare of the encirclement of Germany by mistrustful and finally hostile foreign powers. The narrative of the drift into war from 1912 to 1914 is masterly. Mommsen makes short shrift of the argument that the 'war council' of December 1912 forged permanent, long-term plans of which the events of July–August 1914 were the more or less inevitable outcome, showing convincingly that it was a short-term, panic reaction to a temporary though serious crisis in Anglo-German relations. The confusion and indecision of the Reich leadership in 1914, the vacillations of men like Wilhelm II and Bethmann Hollweg, and the underlying, half-aggressive, half-fatalistic belief of the ruling group in Berlin that war was inevitable at some time and worth the risk anyway – all this has seldom been better recounted. At the same time, however, Mommsen is at a loss as to how to explain it all. He is unable to deliver any convincing reasons for the unreality of Wilhelmine *Weltpolitik* (Vol. II: p. 320), and his reference to the decision to go to war in August 1914 as a 'flight to the front' (Vol. II: p. 449) is not backed up by an appropriate depth of evidence or analysis.

Where Mommsen provides a good alternative to the rival accounts of Nipperdey and Wehler is therefore in the clarity and detail of his political narrative. In contrast to his two rivals, Mommsen has a sharp eye for the telling quote, and lets the people of the past speak for themselves in a way that Nipperdey never does, and Wehler does only intermittently. He is not afraid of repeating well-known quotations, such as Bismarck's 'blood and iron' speech, but there are plenty of less familiar ones as well. They are particularly telling, for example, in Mommsen's account of Tirpitz and the Navy Laws, where they provide a sharp insight into the motivation and intentions behind the construction of a big German navy at the turn of the century. On the other hand, like Wehler and Nipperdey, Mommsen has no interest in any of the individuals that people his book. For him, and therefore for the reader, they are just names; they never emerge as personalities. Not even Bismarck comes alive in these pages. As for Wilhelm II, Mommsen is so uninterested in him as a person that he seems to think that the Kaiser was crippled in his right hand, not his left (Vol. 1: p. 680). Similarly, Mommsen describes Bismarck's successor as Reich Chancellor, the hapless Leo von Caprivi, as an admiral (Vol. II: p. 90), presumably because he was in charge of the navy during the 1880s; but he was, of course, a Prussian general, and his appointment to the Navy Office was a characteristic sign of the subordination of that service to the military in the days before Tirpitz took over. This lack of attention to personal detail is unfortunate, and deprives Mommsen of much of the kind of significant colour that is needed to enliven a narrative such as this.

In contrast to other modern German historians, Mommsen goes to some lengths to put statistical information in graphical form, and the reader can usually identify the trends he is presenting at a glance, instead of having to plough through the massed lines and columns of figures which modern German historiography customarily prefers. This is all to the good, and goes with the generally lavish production of the volumes, which have a good number of illustrations to enliven the text. Mommsen shares in full measure, however, the strange aversion of modern German historians to maps. The only maps he provides are three each of Africa and the Balkans, and one each of the Eastern and Western fronts during the war. There is not a single map of Germany in all 1,800 pages; not even a map to illustrate the boundaries of the German Confederation or the division of forces in the wars of unification, let alone any indicating the geographical structure of social and economic factors. Moreover, the illustrations are poorly chosen, and in keeping with the overall focus of the book, concentrate heavily on scenes from high politics, such as photographs of Reichstag debates or group portraits of leading political figures.

Perhaps the most original parts of these two volumes are the sections on culture, which occupy 100 pages at the end of Volume I and another seventy at the end of Volume II (the latter devoted exclusively to the cultural history of the First World War). Mommsen writes interestingly about the artistic scene, and takes issue with Nipperdey's thesis that the emergence of a modernist avant-garde before the First World War demonstrated that the German bourgeoisie had found its way into the modern cultural world. The individualism of the avant-garde certainly found its echoes in the bourgeois cultivation of the autonomous personality, especially in phenomena such as the *Wandervögel*, the emergent German youth movement. But little else in the culture of modernism found much sympathy among the German middle classes. Mommsen argues plausibly that the spread of abstract and expressionist art, atonal music, symbolist literature, and other aspects of modernism before the First World War, signified the cultural dissolution of the bourgeoisie. Bourgeois culture, which had sustained the lifestyle and aspirations of generations of middle-class Germans since before the foundation of the Empire, fragmented into a mass of competing subjectivities. Here too was a process whose fateful consequences were to work themselves out in the increasingly bitter cultural confrontations of the Weimar years.

Interesting and original though this argument is, however, it demonstrates once more Mommsen's largely traditional view of German history and culture during this period. The concept of culture with which he operates is an old-fashioned, elitist one which confines itself to socially recognized artistic production. He equates working-class culture (*Arbeiterkultur*) with the aesthetic dimension of Social Democracy – its cultural appropriation of art, music, theatre and literature – and so it is hardly surprising that he concludes that is was largely *embourgeoisé*. His promising analysis of culture in terms of four different milieux (aristocratic/court culture, bourgeois culture, petty-bourgeois/Catholic culture, and workers' culture) is never pursued systematically and falls victim in the end to the narrow and outmoded concept of culture with which he operates.

In the end, therefore, it is difficult not to feel a certain disappointment about these two volumes, despite their many virtues and despite the tremendous achievement which they represent in terms of the sheer scale, detail and thoroughness of their coverage. Over the years, and particularly during his tenure of the Directorship of the German Historical Institute in London from 1977 to 1985, Wolfgang Mommsen did an enormous amount to encourage younger scholars attempting to develop new approaches to German history, and left a lasting impression with his breadth of intellectual sympathy and taste for theoretical and methodological innovation. Of all this, however, there is scarcely a trace in these two volumes. The extreme imbalance between the coverage of high politics which takes up over three-quarters of the book, and the all-too-brief treatment of social, economic and cultural history which takes up the rest, gives a totally misleading impression of the direction and distribution of research on the history of the German Empire over the last quarter of a century. Anyone who wants a well-informed overview of the many subjects with which it has dealt, from the everyday life, housing conditions, work and leisure pursuits of the working class to marriage and sexuality among the bourgeoisie, from the social history of sickness and health to crime, policing and the law, and a host of other topics, will have to turn to Thomas Nipperdey's panoramic depiction of Imperial Germany for enlightenment. The brief sections in Mommsen's volumes on women, the family, and gender, with their heavy concentration on the public activities of the women's movement, are little more than a gesture in the direction of all the work that has been done in the field in recent years. The enormous weight placed on the narration of the day-to-day events of domestic and foreign policy takes them effectively out of the only briefly sketched-in context of economy and society. Moreover, by treating domestic and foreign policy in entirely different sections throughout the book, Mommsen further undermines any possibility of delivering a coherent interpretation of the period he is covering. Nor is there any general conclusion to tie the whole survey together.

The same problem which affected Nipperdey's attempt to write a narrative history in an age where historians are all trained to prioritize argument and analysis affects Mommsen's two volumes to an even greater degree: traditional historical narrative technique, as practised by the great historians of the nineteenth century, always involved a generous amount of personal detail, character sketching and colourful anecdote, not least because, unlike their modern successors, they had no doubts about the paramount influence of personalities on history. By leaving all this out, without at the same time incorporating a structural analysis into the narrative, both these historians deliver a history which, however detailed and convincing in itself, remains largely colourless and not infrequently degenerates into a mechanical chronicling of events.

NOTES

1 Wolfgang J. Mommsen, *Das Ringen um den nationalen Staat. Die Gründung und der innere Ausbau des Deutschen Reiches unter Otto von Bismarck 1850 bis 1890*, (Propyläen Geschichte Deutschlands, Vol. 7, Part 1 (Berlin, Propyläen Verlag, 1993); *Bürgerstolz und Weltmachtstreben. Deutschland unter Wilhelm II. 1890 bis 1918*, Propyläen Geschichte Deutschlands, Vol. 7, Part 2 (Berlin, Propyläen Verlag, 1993).

5

THE VIEW FROM FRANCE[1]

The French do not have a very good track record when it comes to writing German history. Over the decades, relatively few historians in France have concerned themselves with the internal history of their neighbours across the Rhine, and the contribution of the French historical profession to modern research on the German past has been disappointing in comparison to that of its British and American counterparts. Those Frenchmen who did attempt to tackle the subject generally took a strongly anti-German line, from writers like Camille Bloch, who devoted themselves between the wars to trying to pin the exclusive blame for the outbreak of hostilities in August 1914 onto the Central Powers, to historians such as Edmond Vermeil, who thought Nazism was a degenerate form of a specifically German intellectual tradition, and sought the ultimate roots of Hitler's dictatorship in what he regarded as Germany's unfortunate abandonment of Western, Catholic ways of thinking for Lutheran doctrines of subordination to secular authority in the Reformation.

On the other hand, those French historians who were committed to Franco-German reconciliation in the 1950s often went to the opposite extreme, and sacrificed historical accuracy to political correctness. In 1951, for example, a delegation of French historians headed by Pierre Renouvin met with a group of German colleagues to hammer out an agreed version of the origins of the First World War for incorporation into the two countries' school textbooks, and concluded, unsurprisingly, that no country was to blame for the débâcle of August 1914; it was all a big mistake. Balanced and well-informed treatments of German history, such as can be found in Georges Castellan's *L'Allemagne du Weimar*, for instance, or the more detailed researches of younger historians such as Etienne François, are still regrettably uncommon.

If anybody of the older generation in France is in a position to deliver such a balanced treatment, it must surely be Joseph Rovan. Born into a German-Jewish family in Bavaria in 1918, he emigrated to France with his parents on the Nazi seizure of power in 1933 and became a French citizen. He returned to Germany in 1942 under an assumed name, which he has retained ever since, to devote himself to the struggle against National Socialism on its home ground. Captured and interned in the Dachau concentration camp, he managed to conceal his Jewish ancestry and survived the war to become an ardent advocate of Franco-German reconciliation. Already in 1945 he conceived the idea of writing a history of Germany that would overcome the hostile clichés then current in French historical writing on his native land and present a picture that would contribute to understanding instead of hatred. Over the following decades, through his activities in adult education in the French zone of occupation after the war, in the Franco-German Youth Association, in numerous articles and broadcasts, as a university professor in Paris, and as adviser to several French governments, Rovan devoted himself to the day-to-day problems of overcoming old animosities, and left his projected history book to one side.

Now, however, in his mid-seventies, he has finally completed it. Published in France last year, it has been swiftly and effectively translated into German by Enrico Heinemann, Reiner Pfeiderer and Reinhard Tiffert (1995). Is it a balanced treatment? Or has Rovan, like his predecessors in 1951, glossed over the difficulties of the past in the interests of the politics of the present? Certainly, the publisher's advertisements for the book cause one to fear the worst. Flanking a picture of the book on two sides are Barbarossa, Frederick the Great, Bismarck, and . . . Roman Herzog! It is no insult to the current President of the Federal Republic to say that he really doesn't belong in this company. More important, however, somebody else is clearly missing. Indeed, in the book itself Rovan even gets the absent Hitler's appearance wrong ('with a lock of black hair falling across his brow *to the right*', p. 564, my italics). The chapter devoted to the National Socialist period presents the dictator as someone not only outside German history – the product essentially of racial tensions within pre-1914 Austria – but even outside the Nazi movement. Most people in the 1930s, writes Rovan, regarded National Socialism as a national-conservative, restorative force, and ignored the fact that Hitler was something quite different – a radical nihilist who wanted only destruction. History books, he says, are useless as an aid to understanding him: he was the incorporation of pure evil, to which only the Bible can be a guide.

On the origins of the First World War, that touchstone of Franco-German historical relations for so long, Rovan is predictably bland. The Kaiser and his cronies, he says, 'did not unleash this conflict irresponsibly. Rather, they slid into it . . . As with almost all historical tragedies, the responsibility lay on many sides' (pp. 514–15). How comforting for all concerned! Rovan in fact is generally weak on the Empire, which receives only thirty pages in his book compared to fifty on the Weimar Republic. 'All in all', he writes by way of excuse (p. 525), 'very little happened between 1871 and 1914.' Anyone who has read even a fraction of the vast scholarly literature on this period, or tried to tackle either of the massive two-volume surveys by Thomas

Nipperdey and Wolfgang Mommsen, may be permitted a moment's doubt. The real reason for Rovan's cursory treatment of the Imperial period, one suspects, is that he is aware that if he went into it too deeply, he would begin to find too many 'shadow-lines', as Nipperdey called them, leading in the direction of 1933, and this would undermine his portrayal of Hitler's regime as coming essentially from outside the mainstream of German history.

Thus Rovan mainly exhausts the topic of the Kaiserreich by heaping praise upon Bismarck, a moderate, modern conservative, as he describes him, a kind of nineteenth-century Charles de Gaulle. Of course, it is true that, at least after 1871 and in comparison to Kaiser Wilhelm II, Bismarck was indeed moderate in his foreign policy. Nevertheless, insists Rovan, 'he also showed himself to be moderate in domestic politics' (pp. 492–3). There is little trace here of Bismarck's deformation of German political culture through the creation of 'enemies of the Reich' in his ruthless persecution of Catholics, Social Democrats and ethnic minorities, his use of police spies, *agents provocateurs* and the death penalty, or his suppression of press freedom (in the Empire, writes Rovan, unbelievably in view of the Anti-Socialist Law and the subsequent innumerable prosecutions of Social Democratic and other radical editors and writers for offences ranging from insulting officials, and *lèse-majesté* to high treason, 'there was extensive, if not unlimited, freedom of the press', p. 492). Surprisingly for a Catholic, Rovan even defends Bismarck's conduct in the *Kulturkampf* (a 'really great policy'), and compares his policy of binding German Catholics into the newly forged nation-state in the 1870s with Adenauer's policy of binding Germany into the newly created European Community in the 1950s. Bismarck, says Rovan improbably, limited religious freedom in order to preserve what could be preserved of the Christian faith in an increasingly atheistic age (p. 495). How the mass arrest of bishops and priests, the maltreatment of the faithful by police and the military, and the year-long deprivation of Catholic parishes of the services of their clergy were supposed to achieve this, he does not say.

This, then, is a book that smooths over many of the rough patches of German history. It is also a resolutely traditional history, which sees the German past as 'stamped by a few important historical personalities' (p. 492), and leaves the masses largely out of account: small wonder, therefore, that the author objects in his Foreword to the publisher's insistence on calling the book a *History of the Germans* instead of directly translating his original French title, *History of Germany*. Social history, women, peasant society, workers' culture, all these subjects on which so much research has been lavished by professional historians in Germany over the past quarter of a century, are barely alluded to, unless, in a rare exception such as the Peasant War of 1525, they make an entry onto the stage of grand politics. The 1848 Revolution is described in purely political terms (and once more, the misleading cliché of the 'Parliament of Professors' is trotted out to describe the Frankfurt National Assembly). Witchcraft, the subject of so many excellent books by younger historians in recent years, doesn't even get a mention. This is by and large a history of kings and battles, an impression confirmed by the maps which precede each chapter, which consist not only of boundaries but also of the carefully marked sites of major military engagements (one notable absence, however, is a map of Hitler's 'Greater German Reich' at its fullest extent during the Second World War). Rovan fails to take account of recent research, and trots out innumerable old clichés which have long since been disposed of by professional historians, from Germany's allegedly unique lack of clear geographical boundaries ('England is an island', he writes quaintly (p. 13), forgetting the problems caused by Ireland, and the fact that *British* national consciousness was only forged gradually in the century following the union of the English and Scottish crowns in 1707, and above all in the wake of the French Revolution) to the supposed responsibility of proportional representation for the coalition problems of Weimar's multi-party governments (forgetting that the Weimar six-party system was essentially a continuation of the five-party system that had existed under the Empire, with the addition of the Communists). In detail, as well as in approach, Rovan's *History of the Germans* has a very old-fashioned look about it.

There is, therefore, much to criticize in this book. But of what general survey of German history could this not be said? Writing in London at a time when leading intellectuals in the Conservative Party are bemoaning the absence of a historian capable of showing us how a 'reunited Germany' is once more trying to conquer us through its 'drive for "European unity"' (the concept itself is so distasteful to them that they have to surround it with the cordon sanitaire of inverted commas), I am all too conscious of the fact that complaining about a French book which tries to play down the negative aspects of the German past in the interests of what its author calls 'a future united Europe' can easily make me sound like one of those terrible Eurosceptics who made Mr. Major's life such a misery. For it would in truth be unjust to dismiss this book as merely another attempt to present the German past in a favourable light. Despite the many passages where one wishes the author had been more critical, Rovan's history is more complicated than that.

To begin with, he deals in a challenging way with the problem of German national consciousness and identity. Unlike many modern German historians, who identify Bismarck's small-German Reich as the core area of 'Germany' in the remote as well as the recent past, Rovan is very much aware of the shifting relationships between 'people, nation, territory and state' over the centuries. He may date the origins of German 'national consciousness' to the eleventh century, but he also declares that the Oder–Neisse line became the eastern boundary of Germany in the thirteenth (pp. 12–15). He is good at puncturing treasured nationalist myths, making it clear, for example, that the so-called 'war of liberation' of 1813 was not a 'popular uprising' borne on a wave of nationalist enthusiasm, but a cabinet war carried out by professional armies, with the assistance of no more than a few thousand genuine volunteers at best (p. 393).

Rovan's Franco-European perspective frequently makes for unpredictable judgements. He is, for example, determinedly 'big German' in his sympathies, describing the exclusion of Austria from the Reich as Bismarck's biggest mistake (not least because it drove the German-Austrians in on themselves and bred among them the racism that was later to give rise to Hitler). He covers the development of Austrian politics not only in the early nineteenth century but after 1866 as well, and in his account of Weimar culture Austrians like Schoenberg and Hofmannsthal feature just as prominently as their German counterparts. Rovan will have no truck with the present-day Austrian myth that most people resisted the German troops as they entered the country in March 1938, declaring roundly: 'the great majority of the population greeted them as liberators' (p. 606). The author's background as a Catholic who grew up as a member of a Jewish-Protestant family gives him a similarly unusual perspective on German religious history. All this makes his book a good deal more stimulating than the average overview of German history.

On the period through which he himself has lived, Rovan also has ideas which run counter to mainstream conservative historiography in the Federal Republic. He declares, for example, that the conspiracy to assassinate Hitler on 20 July 1944 was only an act of 'opposition' carried out by men who still sympathized with at least some of the regime's aims. True 'resistance', he says, was carried out mainly by the Communist Party, to which he devotes a correspondingly greater amount of space. Moreover, although he provides an extremely uncritical account of the political history of the Federal Republic, he is far from uncritical in his concluding reflections on the state of Germany today. 'The improvised structures flung together with the best of intentions in Germany between 1945 and 1949, partly after the example of the Western powers,' he says, 'are gradually becoming weak through old age' (p. 800). They do not offer much promise of taking Germany successfully into the next millennium. The best hope for the future, he declares in the final, and perhaps most surprising passage of the book, lies with the Greens, and he sees the ecological movement, which is undoubtedly stronger in the Federal Republic than anywhere else, as one of Germany's most important contributions to the welfare of humankind in the twenty-first century (p. 814).

Idiosyncratic views such as these make this, in the end, an unusual and individual view of German history which everyone can read with some profit. As befits a book written by a man with long experience of journalism, it reads easily and is entirely free from the deforming linguistic influence of academic jargon. As a non-German historian about to embark on a similar project myself – a history of the Germans written for an Anglo-American readership – I do not think it is necessary to gloss over the difficult aspects of Germany's past, or to go quite so far in detaching Hitler from the mainstream of German history. Those of us who believe that Britain's future lies in Europe have enough difficulty in battling anti-German prejudice in the present without opening ourselves up to the accusation of white-washing Germany's past. True mutual understanding between European nations will not be achieved on the basis of sweeping historical problems under the carpet. Nevertheless, flawed though it is, Rovan's *Geschichte der Deutschen* does make a contribution to that understanding, as much by the objections it arouses in the reader as by the thought-provoking and individual judgements which it presents. The more we Europeans can research and write about each other's history, the closer we will come together. Let us hope that Rovan's contribution to this process will stimulate more French historians to concern themselves with Germany – and more German publishers to translate them.

NOTES

1 Joseph Rovan, *Geschichte der Deutschen. Von ihren Ursprüngen bis heute*. Aus dem Französischen von Enrico Heinemann, Reiner Pfeiderer und Reinhard Tiffert (Munich, Carl Hanser Verlag, 1995).

Part II

PATTERNS OF
AUTHORITY AND
REVOLT

In Part II we turn from grand surveys of German history to the more particular problem of patterns of authority and revolt in modern German history. Many commentators have sought to account for the Germans' abandonment of democracy and their turn to dictatorship in the early 1930s with the argument that patterns of authority and obedience were deeply embedded in the German psyche. Some have looked to the tradition of the strong state in German history to explain the voters' dissatisfaction with the weakness and ineffectiveness of the Weimar Republic: a strong state not only in terms of its relations with other European states, but also in terms of its relationship with its own citizens. The great sociologist Norbert Elias, for instance, detected in the Germans a longing for authority which derived ultimately from the collective memory of the Absolutism of 'Enlightened' monarchs such as Frederick the Great in the eighteenth century. The 'Enlightened Despots' of this era sought to establish what contemporaries referred to as a 'well-ordered police state', in which everything was subject to regulation and control from above, and the ordinary subject was left with little room for individual initiative. From this period, it is often argued, dated the intrusive habits and powers of the German police. Their survival into the twentieth century made it easy for the Nazis to erect their own, radicalized version of the police state, based on the all-powerful, all-pervasive presence of the feared secret state police, the Gestapo. Chapter 6 takes a close look at the history of policing in Germany, charting the growth of research in recent years, and suggesting that it is time not only to paint a more complex and nuanced picture, but also, perhaps, to adopt a different approach from the neo-Weberian theories and methods which have characterized German work in this field so far. The fall of East Germany has opened up a whole new set of questions about compliance and control, which demand the application of

61

more differentiated theories of power and domination than those which have held the field to date.

Next in Part II, we turn to another crucial area in which patterns of authority established and exerted themselves in the course of the nineteenth century: religion and belief. David Blackbourn's sensitive exploration of the nature of popular Catholicism during the *Kulturkampf* shows how ordinary villagers in a Catholic region of the recently united German Empire turned to the cult of the Virgin Mary as a form of self-assertion in the face of massive discrimination by the Bismarckian state. The repressive response of the Prussian authorities inevitably had its effect. Inept though it was in many ways, the conduct of the Prussian police and army eventually succeeded in distancing both the villagers and, crucially, the Catholic Church, from the cult. What Blackbourn's study shows, almost depite itself, is that the Prussian state was strong enough to suppress major popular movements of this kind. From its own perspective, the *Kulturkampf* was a success; but as many historians, including some of those whose work we surveyed in Part I, have concluded, the tactic of creating 'enemies of the Reich' and denying them fundamental civil rights, such as freedom of worship, set a dangerous precedent for the future.

Chapters 8 and 9 turn to another disadvantaged organization in Bismarckian and Wilhelmine Germany, the labour movement. The proud, predominantly Marxist tradition of the Social Democratic and Communist parties was used by the East German regime as its primary source of historical legitimation. From the very beginning, workers' organizations looked to the creation of a future society that would do away with the evils of capitalism, inequality and exploitation. The German Democratic Republic regarded itself as that future society for which these organizations had been striving. Yet in the end, the planned economy and the 'dictatorship of the proletariat' in the 'workers' and peasants' state' delivered only spiritual oppressiveness, material deprivation and grey mediocrity. Chapter 8 explores an alternative socialist tradition in Germany, submerged for much of the late nineteenth and twentieth centuries, but enjoying a new lease of life from the 1980s: the co-operative tradition. If producer co-operatives, an early ideal of the labour movement in the mid-nineteenth century, never stood much chance of success in competition with the big battalions of capitalism, then consumer co-operatives were a different matter, and in new and often imaginative forms they have re-emerged in the wake of the 'green' and 'alternative' movements in our own time.

Chapter 9 moves to the other end of German labour history and tackles the problem of the failure of German labour in the Weimar Republic. In 1918 the overthrow of the Kaiser brought German Social Democrats to power. Yet only a few years later in 1933 the German labour movement was suppressed, its leading politicians and trade unionists silenced by the Nazis, forced into exile, gaoled, or murdered. The history of these fateful years was the subject of a major, three-volume study completed by the German historian Heinrich August Winkler in the 1980s, one of the great monuments of postwar German historical scholarship. Winkler has always been close to the present-day German Social Democrats, and his approach is deeply indebted to the doctrine, paramount in the party since its rejection of its Marxist heritage at the Bad Godesberg Party Congress in 1959, that collaboration with other, non-socialist political groupings and the recruitment of members and supporters outside its traditional basis of support in the working class, is essential for its success. In a way, Winkler is therefore criticizing the German Social Democrats of the 1920s and 1930s for not being the German Social Democrats of the 1960s and 1970s. But this, as the chapter argues, involves some violation of the actual historical context within which the labour movement of the Weimar Republic had to operate. Moreover, Winkler's treatment of the German Communist Party of the day shows a lack of sympathy all too common amongst West Germans in the decade before reunification, which has, if anything, deepened since 1990. Finally, an approach dominated by political questions such as these is almost bound to underplay social and economic factors, which German labour historians have all too often consigned to the politically irrrelevant category of 'the history of everyday life' (*Alltagsgeschichte*). The chapter argues in contrast that this dimension of labour history is essential if the failure of the labour movement in the Weimar Republic is to be fully understood.

6

POLICE AND SOCIETY FROM ABSOLUTISM TO DICTATORSHIP[1]

I

'The German policeman', complained the English humorist Jerome K. Jerome in 1900, 'does not understand a joke.' Perhaps, he went on, this was just as well, 'for I believe there is a heavy fine for joking with any German uniform; they call it "treating an official with contumely"'. Like many other foreign visitors to Germany both before and since, Jerome was struck by the omnipresence and omnipotence of the German police. 'To any young Englishman yearning to get himself into a scrape, and finding himself hampered in his own country', Jerome continued ironically, 'I would advise a single ticket to Germany . . . In the Police Guide of the Fatherland he will find set forth a list of the things the doing of which will bring to him interest and excitement.' Unlike in Britain, the police in Germany had independent powers of fining and punishing misdemeanours, and used them according to a fixed scale published in advance. Thus, Jerome advised his readers,

> You know exactly what your fun is going to cost you, You can spread out your money on the table, open your Police Guide, and plan out your holiday to a fifty pfennig piece. For a really cheap evening, I would recommend walking on the wrong side of the pavement after being cautioned not to do so. I calculate that by choosing your district and keeping to the quiet side-streets you could walk for a whole evening on the wrong side of the pavement at a cost of little over three marks.[2]

Other foreign visitors agreed. The American Ray Stannard Baker, visiting Germany the next year, found the constant police presence on the streets suffocating.[3] His compatriot the social investigator Raymond B. Fosdick, writing in 1914, was struck by 'the army of *Verboten* signs' and the fact that 'on every side and at every turn, the German citizen is confronted by newly adopted police regulations'.[4]

Anglo-American observers of the German scene were not wholly mistaken when they noticed major differences between the traditions of policing which existed in Germany and the traditions they were used to at home. The differences were most noticeable, perhaps, in three particular respects. First of all, there was the breadth of competence of the German police. As Peter Nitschke notes in his introductory survey of the question – his book (1990), in a manner all too familiar with German doctoral dissertations, does not reach its actual subject, the emergence of the police in the County of Lippe, until well over half-way through – *'Policey'* originally meant simply the internal civil government of the state. It emerged in the era of Absolutism and signified the determination of the Absolutist state to regulate society for the good order and prosperity of its subjects.[5] In the course of time, there emerged from this 'broad' definition of 'police' a narrower definition, according to which the police were especially concerned with the maintenance of internal security. In England and America, where the introduction of a formally organized police force was successfully resisted during the eighteenth century and into the nineteenth as a threat to the liberties of the free-born individual, only the narrow concept of police was imported from the European Continent when the need for a professional body of men dedicated to fighting crime and civil disorder was finally accepted in the 1830s.[6] Hence the repeated surprise of commentators such as Fosdick when they discovered entities in Germany such as the Buildings Police, the Market Police and even the Morals Police, all unknown in their own countries.

The survival of the broad concept of policing parallel to the narrow one meant that the breadth of competence of police forces in Germany was indeed significant, and involved a survival of the Absolutist, authoritarian regulation of many areas of society throughout the nineteenth century and well into the twentieth. At the same time, it is important not to assume – as the American historian Marc Raeff did in his comparative study of *The Well-Ordered Police State* (1986) – that this regulation was necessarily effective.[7] On the contrary, as historians have moved from the legal and conceptual history of policing to its social history, it has become increasingly clear that the grand ambitions of the Absolutist state were seldom realized in this respect. To write the history of policing, one also needs to write the history of crime; and it is one of the hazards of this enterprise, that writing it from the perspective of the police, using sources mainly generated by the police themselves, may all too easily lead to an exaggeratedly optimistic assessment of the success of police forces in fighting crime. It is the great service of Nitschke to set the emergence of the police in Lippe in the broad context of criminality, which he shows was particularly widespread and severe in the late eighteenth century. Poaching, wood theft, and above all violence, fighting and assault in everyday life seemed impervious to the flood of edicts sent down from the central authorities in a vain effort to control them. Organized banditry found a secure haven in the less populated south-east of the territory, while the proximity of state boundaries across which to flee made the county a tempting target for bands of robbers from outside. Neither rural nor urban militia forces nor the state military could do much about this dire situation. The rulers of this small territory shared the ambitions of many others in Germany to establish a 'well-ordered police state', but like many others too, altogether lacked the means by which it could be realized.

What finally prompted the creation of a professional police force in Lippe was the impact and example of the French during the Napoleonic Wars. During these years, armies of several nationalities repeatedly tramped across Germany, living off the land and causing considerable destruction as they went. The defeat of many German states by the French in battle, the redrawing of boundaries and the reorganization of administrations under French rule, destabilized law enforcement institutions and offered fresh opportunities to criminals. The economic problems of Central Europe in this period, exacerbated by Britain's blockade and Napoleon's Continental System, provided the incentive to many to embark on a life of crime.[8] This was the era of bandits such as Schinderhannes, a time when the slowly forming bourgeois public sphere took new and shocked cognizance of the prevalence of crime and violence amongst the common people and resolved to do something about it.[9] The superior legitimacy and apparently greater effectiveness of French administrative models at this time prompted the authorities in Lippe to introduce a French-style *Gendarmerie* in 1808 to deal with these problems: the first fully professional police force in the territory. Not the persistence of an Absolutist model of the police state, therefore, but the recognition of its ineffectiveness and its supersession by a new concept of policing under the impact of, and following the administrative example of, the French Revolution and the Napoleonic Empire was what provided the decisive impetus in the creation of a true police force.

Although the nineteenth-century German model of policing differed strongly from its Anglo-American counterparts, therefore, it did not differ so very greatly from the model of policing that evolved in France, and indeed owed a good deal to it. Similar things could be said of much larger German states at this time, including for example Prussia, where a *Gendarmerie* was established in 1812.[10] Under the impact of the *Gendarmerie*, though more, one suspects, as a reflection of the ending of the wars and the return of peace to the countryside, the great robber bands disappeared. The maintenance of order after 1815 depended, as we know from the work of Alf Lüdtke on Prussia, on the establishment of elaborate networks of surveillance and control by the new police forces of the 1820s and 1830s (1982).[11] Open public punishments such as the pillory and the scaffold had already begun to give way to the prison as the principal means of controlling criminality in the second half of the eighteenth century; by the 1840s the process was largely complete, and was backed up by a growing policy of co-operation between police forces in different parts of Germany, who increasingly circulated information about crimes and criminals in the form of *Polizei-Anzeiger* and *Steckbriefe*.[12] According to Lüdtke, the new police regime of the first half of the nineteenth century created such a comprehensive form of state coercion that it successfully dampened the chances of popular revolutionary resistance to the emerging exploitative social relations of capitalism and cowed the masses into a deep spirit of submission long-lasting enough to precondition even their failure to rise up against the coming of National Socialism in 1933.[13]

Here again, however, we need to remember that crime did not decline in Germany in the first half of the nineteenth century despite the introduction of new, more intrusive methods of policing. In particular, property crime rates increased strongly under the impact of the massive population growth and social immiseration of the *Vormärz* period; but crimes of violence also rose in incidence from the mid-1830s onwards, while rioting and civil disorder reached unprecedented heights in this, the classic period of 'social protest' in Germany.[14] In the mid-1830s, King Friedrich Wilhelm IV of Prussia was sufficiently concerned about rising crime rates to order a large-scale investigation of criminality across his realm, though with very limited practical consequences. Penal authorities were conscious that imprisonment did little to reform offenders.[15] Individual case-histories suggest that the ways and means by which criminals or '*Gauner*', increasingly regarded by mid-century as a separate social group constituting a shadowy obverse to respectable bourgeois society, could evade detection and control by the police, were virtually inexhaustible.[16] Despite the gathering pace of urbanization and industrialization, little was done to institute a professional police force in major towns and cities, which characteristically relied on a mixture of nightwatchmen, citizens' militias and military force, the latter for serious disturbances only.[17] The quality of the manpower used for policing the cities was frequently very poor. Moreover, like so many of the creations of the Prussian reform era, the *Gendarmerie* was seriously weakened and scaled-down after the victory over Napoleon, in particular by cuts imposed in 1820. These were not made good for many decades, mainly because of the resistance of aristocratic landowners to state policing, which left the rural police in Prussia weaker than in any other German state by the 1840s.[18] It was not least because of the lack of an adequate police force that state power crumbled so rapidly in Germany in March 1848.

Part of the reason for this was the fact that state authorities had been concentrating on dealing with a threat which may have been more obvious than crowd power, but which arguably turned out in 1848 to be no more dangerous: liberal, nationalist and radical political opposition. The development of institutional structures and practices in this area is the subject of Wolfram Siemann's book (1985), which offers a comprehensive history of the political police in Germany from 1806 to 1866. This is a thorough, detailed, and well-researched account which is likely to remain a standard work for many years to come. The notion of a political police was particularly strongly associated with the reactionary Austrian Chancellor Metternich, whose influence in persuading the states of the German Confederation to adopt repressive measures against liberals and revolutionaries has long been proverbial.[19] Unlike too many recent studies of Germany in the first half of the nineteenth century, therefore, Siemann devotes a properly large share of his scholarly attention to what was going on in Vienna.

Not surprisingly, Siemann finds that the Austrians made most of the running in the formation and expansion of political policing during this period. They constructed an elaborate system of surveillance, checked and opened the correspondence of revolutionaries, employed a substantial number of paid and unpaid spies and informers, and encouraged attempts to formalize co-operation with other political police forces in institutions such as the Frankfurt Central Investigation Authority and the Mainz Information Office, whose activities even extended to the pursuit of revolutionaries in neighbouring states outside the German Confederation as well. Other states, including Prussia, were more hesitant and less consistent in their activities, but gradually followed suit. Siemann presents a wealth of fascinating detail on the activities of Metternich's political policing of the German Confederation, including lists of agents with official descriptions ('precise, industrious, well-thought-of, unconditional loyalty'[20]), and accounts of specialist departments such as the Austrian Secret Code Office, whose sole task was to break the secret codes used by politicians who knew their correspondence to be under surveillance. All this denoted an increasing degree of professionalization which justifies Siemann's characterization of this period as crucial in the formation of the practice of political policing in general.

II

For all its elaboration and professionalization, neither Metternich's political police force nor any of its counterparts in the other German states was particularly large. By twentieth-century standards their numbers were pitiful and their methods primitive. Whatever their influence in the 1820s and 1830s, they were in the end unable to stem the tide of liberalism, nationalism and revolution ('declining zeal, did not fulfil expectations in Berlin in Spring of 1848, therefore Feb.–Apr. 1848 no pay'[21]). Indeed, knowledge of their underhand methods and activities had probably done a good deal to strengthen liberals and democrats in their resolve to overthrow the old political system. What now became crucial was the fact that the political police was unaccountable to anyone but the monarch and those who wielded power on his behalf, and operated in the strictest secrecy, doing its best to stay as far as possible out of the public eye. During the reaction period of the 1850s, as German states re-established their authority and looked for effective means of preventing a recrudescence of the revolutionary threat, political policing in the German Confederation was put on a new footing with the formation of the *Polizeiverein*, which achieved a new level of sophistication and organization in the co-ordination of political policing across the various German states.[22] In Berlin this was the era of Carl Ludwig von Hinckeldey, the Berlin police chief who became Prussian General Director of Police in 1853 and was given wide-ranging powers by King Friedrich Wilhelm IV, against the bitter opposition of the Interior Ministry. Under Hinckeldey, items of political policing business dealt with by the Central Office of the Berlin police increased from 2,927 in 1850 to 7,156 in 1851 and 9,423 in 1852. They came in at over 5,000 a year for the next three years, before declining to under 1,000 by 1862.[23]

At the same time, Hinckeldey reformed the criminal police in Berlin, which now became a virtually separate branch of the police, and co-operated closely with the political branch. His collaborator in this enterprise was the notorious figure of Wilhelm Stieber, who despite a very chequered past was put in charge of the criminal police in 1850. A moving force behind the Cologne Communists' trial made famous by Karl Marx and Friedrich Engels, Stieber developed many of the techniques which were to give the Prussian police so much notoriety in subsequent decades: deliberate provocations, bribery, deception, theft of documents, forgery and perjury were all his stock-in-trade.[24] His 'memoirs', first published in 1978, an unintentionally hilarious book which culminates in the amazing claim that Stieber ran a network of no fewer than 30,000 spies in France in the late 1860s, are dismissed by Siemann as a forgery, although the question of their authenticity remains finally to be resolved.[25] With Stieber, indeed, we enter a new underworld of deception, where nothing was quite what it seemed to be. A characteristic figure in this baleful new tradition of political policing was the head of the Berlin political police in the 1870s, Baron von Meerscheidt-Hüllessem, who besides being the founder of the photographic *Album of Criminals*, an early example of new technology being used in the service of crimefighting, also functioned from time to time as an *agent provocateur*. During the *Kulturkampf*, he was sent to the Saarland village of Marpingen to gather evidence against the informal cult which had sprung up after the supposed visions of the Virgin Mary seen by some young girls in the village in 1876. Like Stieber before him, he manufactured evidence and lied on a colossal scale in order to get the convictions he wanted. When he was forced to take the stand in the witness box, however, his entire story was exposed as a tissue of fabrications and the case collapsed.[26] The situation was no better in the 1880s and 1890s, when, as it emerged in 1897, the Berlin Police Commissar Eugen von Tausch had been selling confidential information from the files of the political police to the press in order to finance his extravagant lifestyle. During his trial for perjury, the court discovered that he had also been selling obscene letters. Despite all this, he was acquitted, only to be dismissed from office after the state prosecutor had entered an appeal against the judgement.[27] Not long afterwards, the Berlin Criminal Inspector, Thiel, was obliged to confess to having accepted a bribe from a private detective hired by the defendant in the Sternberg trial, in which a millionaire businessman was accused of rape, while another, more junior policeman, Constable Stierstädter, was transferred to other duties when he showed too much zeal in pursuing the case. 'As a result of this trial,' commented a newspaper, 'calls for a thoroughgoing reform of the Berlin police, which this time has sustained far more serious damage than four years ago in the Tausch–Leckert–Lützow trial, are becoming ever louder and more urgent.'[28]

The manifest corruption and dishonesty of Berlin's criminal and political police at the highest level was above all a legacy of the Stieber–Hinckeldey era, but its ultimate cause was the secrecy and unaccountability with which the police operated. Internal investigations seldom bore fruit, and even the few convictions obtained were usually effectively nullified by the liberal use of the royal pardon.[29] The many cases detailed in the proceedings of the Association Against Bribery revealed a world far removed from the traditional reputation of Prussian state servants for honesty and reliability.[30] All this exacerbated the notorious interference of the police on the ground with the human rights of the ordinary German. The Revolution of 1848 made a valiant attempt to establish a set of Basic Rights of the German People, and some states translated a version of some of these into legislation in a number of areas, for example through a law on the protection of personal freedom passed in Prussia on 24 September 1848 and revised on 12 February 1850.[31] The Prussian Criminal Code of 1851 also brought many improvements in these respects, including trial in open court and a diminished reliance on the confession as the 'queen of proofs' in criminal trials. But the police considered the law on personal freedom, which among other things limited their ability to conduct house searches, as a 'licence for thieves', and soon the courts were complaining 'about numerous violations of the law of 12 February 1850 on the part of the police authorities'. By 1860 the Prussian Minister of Interior, Simons, was forced to recognize the existence of serious 'abuses' in this area at the same time.[32]

However, not a lot was done about either police corruption or the fact that the police frequently exceeded their already quite considerable powers in the second half of the nineteenth century. Moreover, there was considerable bourgeois sympathy for the police's attitude. 'In recent times,' remarked one Association for the Protection of Property in January 1849, 'and in particular since the promulgation of the Habeas-Corpus-Act, common theft has increased to such an alarming extent', that it was already time for the police to be given more powers again.[33] It would be wrong, therefore, to regard the idea of a police force such as it developed in Prussia after 1848 as simply 'neo-Absolutist' or 'premodern', a vehicle of the neo-feudal authoritarian state opposed by the mass of the liberal middle classes. The growth of police power and its relationship with the concept of the state working through legal norms, the *Rechtsstaat,* is the subject of Albrecht Funk's study of the police in Prussia from 1848 to 1914 (1986), a product of the Berlin political science school. Funk too deals in some detail with the impact of the 1848 Revolution and the following reaction on the history of policing in Germany. Although this is primarily an institutional study, Funk has a sharp eye for telling detail. It was said by wits, for example, that the most lasting achievement of the 1848 Revolution in Berlin was the ending of the police ban on smoking in public places. To demonstrate the limitations of this achievement, however, and to indicate the wide-ranging nature of police powers over public assemblies after 1848, Funk cites the example of a policeman who in 1853 was overseeing a meeting in Berlin at which those present decided there should be a ban on smoking in the hall. Taking his cigar out of his mouth, the policeman dissolved the meeting with the words: 'I dissolve this assembly! Smoking is legal in Prussia!'[34]

Funk's interest is focused primarily on the political functions of the police, and to this extent he sticks to well-worn tracks as he covers the policing of meetings, the control of the press, the persecution of socialists under the Anti-Socialist Law of 1878–90, and the development of the law of emergency powers. Where his work is most valuable is in its insistence that the place of the police in Prussian society in these decades was founded on a compromise between the middle classes and the state. In the 1870s and 1880s, even the most liberal of bourgeois citizens demanded better protection against the looming presence of drunks, vagrants, prostitutes, pimps, thieves and loafers on the streets of Berlin. The idea of the constable on the beat, protecting the security and property of the honest citizen, was highly appealing to the middle classes. As far as they were concerned, there should be no doubt about whom the policeman was protecting: it was above all themselves. They had no objections when the police used their own uncontrolled powers of arrest and imprisonment (*Polizeihaft*) in increasing measure to carry out these functions. And they were keen for the police to become more professional and more efficient in the fight against crime and disorder. There was far less concern about the arbitrariness and frequent illegality with which the police treated other sectors of the population.

The most obvious victims of police discrimination were Catholics during the *Kulturkampf* and socialists under the Anti-Socialist Law, but seen in social as well as political terms, the subjects of police arbitrariness in Imperial Germany included the working classes and the vagrant and impoverished underclass;[35] ethnic minorities such as the Poles and gypsies;[36] and women: not just the prostitutes under the control of the Morals Police, but all women, for whom walking alone in any major town or city, especially in the evening, meant running the risk of being stopped, questioned and as often as not verbally abused by policemen ostensibly searching for 'ladies of the night'.[37] Moreover, the control functions of the police were emphasized by their essentially military organization and style. Most policemen in Prussia, and increasingly in other German states too, were *Militäranwärter*, NCOs from the Prussian Army who had a legal right on retiring from their job to obtain a position in one of the state services, such as the post office or the police. Funk argues that the gradual intrusion of the police into everyday life during the second half of the nineteenth century thus amounted to an important step towards the militarization of everyday life. It was a price that the middle classes were well prepared to pay.

Funk analyses the development of the police in Prussia in terms of the Weberian concepts of rationalization and bureaucratization. This approach helps him give coherence to his story, but it also leads him to neglect the dysfunctional aspects of the Prussian style of policing: the alienation of large sectors of the population, the corruption and arbitrariness born of a lack of proper democratic accountability, and the inefficiency which the American observer Raymond Fosdick for one saw as a consequence of cumbersome and over-bureaucratized working methods and administrative structures. A military style of policing could do more to provoke riotous assemblies than to calm them.[38] The staffing of the police with former long-service soldiers also, in Fosdick's view, tended to make them rather elderly and thus slow-moving and slow-witted in comparison to their British counterparts. He also criticized what he saw as the obsession of police staff regulations with questions of military discipline rather than techniques of crime prevention and solution. Indeed, the growth of the Prussian police failed to keep pace with the growth of population in many major centres, and crimes of violence began to rise again in the Wilhelmine period, much to the dismay of contemporaries of all social classes.[39]

III

Both Funk and Nitschke see the history of the police, among other things, in Weberian terms as a history of the state monopolization of violence. The patrimonial jurisdictions of aristocratic East-Elbian landowners and urban associations such as citizens' militias were gradually forced to surrender their powers of policing and law enforcement to the state. But this process, like most historical processes, was both uneven and incomplete. As Ralph Jessen shows in his well-researched study of the police in the Westphalian Ruhr (1991), employers in the area set up *Zechenschutzwehren*, protection squads composed of 'reliable' workers, whose number increased dramatically after the great miners' strike of 1905. Although they were not encouraged to do so by the authorities, employers retained control over these auxiliary police forces.[40] In view of his thesis that the state monopolization of policing was an aspect of 'modernization', Jessen is anxious to sugggest that the employers' search for state legitimation of the *Zechenschutzwehren* was 'traditionalistic'; but from the point of view of the late twentieth century, when private security firms carry out many duties formerly within the competence of the police, or indeed from the point of view of employers in the late nineteenth- and early twentieth-century USA, who regularly sought to defend their interests against strikers through the use of small armies of Pinkerton agents, it was the use of private police forces by large capitalist enterprises that was 'modern'. It had its parallel in other parts of Germany besides the Ruhr, too, as strikebreakers brought with them their own armed security apparatus, as during the Bremen tramdrivers' strike of October 1910, when work volunteers fired on a hostile crowd.[41]

The demilitarization of policing was another aspect of 'modernization' which proceeded unevenly and partially in the Ruhr. Jessen shows that the proportion of *Militäranwärter* among police forces was declining under the impact of massive expansion in the 1890s and 1900s, and was only a minority in most towns and cities in the Ruhr by the eve of the First World War. The police force was recruited increasingly from the working class. Training and professionalization began to replace the former reliance on military experience. But these processes had their limits. The minority of ex-soldiers remained influential. Military patterns of behaviour continued to be encouraged. Training, as Jessen shows, emphasized virtues such as 'an upright gait', and 'a spotless uniform worn according to the regulations' and took place 'in a strictly military manner'. Contemporary criticisms of the military elements in police behaviour may have encouraged police training schools to soften the soldierly arrogance of the ex-NCO, but the professional ideals which they held up to all who passed through them were still to a large extent military ideals. And the police proved in 1912 unable to do without the military in the combating of strikes. Thus Jessen, in the end, modifies rather than overthrows the conventional picture painted by critical contemporaries such as Fosdick.[42]

Jessen's view from the provinces is a valuable corrective to the customary concentration of historians of the Prussian police on Berlin.[43] He takes a broad view of the police's activities, not confining himself to the obvious area of the policing of industrial relations, but also examining the police's role in dealing with – and defining – criminality. His local statistics, and his discussion of how they were arrived at, are closely linked to a discussion of the ever-increasing control exercised by the police over everyday life and should be required reading for historians who rely on crime statistics on a national level.[44] Of course, as he points out, the police's powers to regulate, arrest, fine and imprison were not confined to the working class; moreover, with the emergence of the social welfare system came a plethora of other forms of control and regulation as well.[45] However successful such disciplining processes may have been – for example, in persuading the Social Democrats to operate in an orderly, law-abiding fashion[46] – they never managed to persuade the mass of the working class to accept or even tolerate the police as a social institution of real value to themselves. The increasing proportion of policemen drawn directly from the ranks of the working class did nothing to soften the hostility with which they were widely regarded in the proletarian milieu. Nevertheless, such evidence as we have of working-class attitudes towards the police does suggest that workers not only accepted the principle of policing as such but had an ideal picture of how a police force should operate when it was freed from the constraints of the system of 'class justice' to which they believed it was shackled under the Empire. What happened, then, when the Social Democrats gained power, or at least a strong influence, after 1918?

Unlike the history of German policing in the nineteenth century, which until recently – indeed, virtually until the publication of the books reviewed above – remained in a serious state of scholarly neglect, the police in the Weimar Republic have been studied by a number of historians over the years, and for an obvious reason: the problem of public order was, both at the beginning and the end of the Republic, far more serious than it had been at any time since the 1840s, and played a major part in the Republic's eventual downfall. Most of this work, however, has been very specialized;[47] Peter Lessmann's Bochum dissertation casts its net a good deal wider than most, covering not only the whole of Prussia but also dealing with questions such as police training and recruitment (1991). The disorder of the early Weimar Republic saw the collapse of the state monopoly of violence which had been gradually established in the nineteenth century, as workers' and soldiers' councils, neighbourhood protection squads, Free Corps, and republican or revolutionary armed groups such as the Red Army in the Ruhr all sought to impose their own particular concept of internal order on German society, while the most effective armed force, the German army, refused to accept the legitimacy of the new state and did nothing to support it either during the Kapp *putsch* of 1920 or the final débâcle of 1932–3. The Prussian *Schutzpolizei* was the nearest thing there was to a republican guard, created above all by the Social Democratic Prussian Interior Minister Carl Severing, who wanted to build an organization free from the military character of the Wilhelmine police. The reality turned out, as Lessmann shows, to be very different.

To start with, the *Schutzpolizei* were recruited almost entirely from ex-soldiers – not surprisingly, since such a high proportion of the able-bodied men of the eligible age-groups had served in the war. Then the influx of former Free Corps members and professional soldiers into the middle and higher ranks of the organization meant that a military tone was set from above. The experience of using the *Schutzpolizei* against organized Communist uprisings in 1919 and 1921 in the province of Saxony confirmed the Social Democratic leadership in its belief that a heavily armed, quasi-military police force was necessary for the maintenance of order. In fact, as we have seen, the militarization of the police was more a continuation of old behavioural patterns than anything else. And the lumbering apparatus of the *Schutzpolizei* was no match for the rapid manoeuvrings adopted by National Socalist and Communist street-fighters in the second half of the decade. By the early 1930s the sheer scale of street conflict was beginning to overwhelm the force, whose members were often continuously in action for days on end. With the advent of Franz von Papen as Reich Chancellor in 1932 and his tendency to tolerate National Socialist violence, the *Schutzpolizei* found itself at a political disadvantage just as serious as the legal disadvantage it had long suffered before conservative judges trying cases of alleged police brutality brought by paramilitaries of the far right. Meanwhile, discontent was spreading through the upper ranks of the force, as the sergeants (*Wachtmeister*) saw their post-retirement rights whittled away under the impact of cuts in the state budget, and the officers were successfully targeted by National Socialist recruiting drives. It was hardly surprising that the *Schutzpolizei* proved itself unreliable as a pillar of the Republic during the final Nazi assault, and almost predictable that, apart from a small number of mostly top-level administrators, the force stayed on post after Hitler took over power as Chancellor in January 1933 and willingly helped establish the National Socialist dictatorship during the following months.

None of this is, to be sure, particularly surprising. It fits in with what we know of the other branch of the Weimar Republic's police force that has been extensively studied – namely, the political police.[48] What we still need for the period is a study not of the political aspects of policing but of the everyday history of the force; Liang's study, though pioneering for its time, must in most respects now count as badly in need of replacement, and in any case, as usual, only deals with Berlin. As Richard Bessel points out in his brief but wide-ranging survey, the police under Weimar also had to contend with huge waves of petty crime, especially during periods of economic difficulty such as the inflation and the depression,[49] as well as with organized crime along the lines of the notorious Berlin *Ringvereine*, the German equivalent of the Chicago gangster mobs. Professional policemen were keen to develop new, efficient and scientific methods to deal with all this. Already laid out in handbooks such as Gustav Roscher's impressive *Grossstadtpolizei* ('Big-City Policing') of 1912,[50] modern methods of policing were further refined through the work of men like Ernst Gennat, the celebrated head of the Berlin homicide squad during the 1920s, and gained wide currency through popular media such as film, most obviously in Fritz

76

Lang's portrayal of the fictional equivalent of Gennat in *M*. Yet, as Bessel points out, the police felt frustrated in their drive to professionalize the fight against crime through having to devote so much time and energy to combating and controlling political unrest. Here is yet another reason why they, like so many other groups in German society, welcomed the coming of the 'Third Reich' in the belief that it represented a return to normality.

The failure of the police in the Weimar Republic was not merely political, therefore. It was exemplified in the scandals caused by many of the most notorious murder cases of the era, from Fritz Haarmann, the serial killer in Hanover whose status as an unofficial police agent was the main factor in allowing him to continue committing his crimes undisturbed long after sufficient evidence was available for his arrest, to Peter Kürten, the 'Düsseldorf vampire', who led the police by the nose for many months, even writing them sarcastic letters ridiculing their incompetence, while he went on with his career of sexual murder. For those on the left, the case of Josef Jakuboski, a Polish-Russian labourer executed for murder in 1926, they believed unjustly, provided another example not only of police incompetence, as a series of fresh investigations failed to clear the matter up to their satisfaction, but also of the police and judicial system's allergic reactions to public criticisms and stonewalling of attempts to overturn decisions once arrived at.[51] For those on the right, law enforcement appeared as weak and indecisive under the Weimar Republic, with do-gooders, sentimentalists and interfering lawyers and politicians preventing the police from working properly and stopping criminals getting their just deserts. It was hardly surprising that the police themselves tired of being caught in the crossfire and opted for a regime in which not even the slightest word of criticism was allowed.

IV

The studies reviewed above show that the historiography of the German police has been transformed since the middle of the 1980s. No longer can it be said to be, as it was little over a decade ago, neglected by historical research.[52] A number of factors are responsible for this change. In the first place, the role of the police in modern society has come under serious critical scrutiny (as distinct from being subjected to crude Marxist-Leninist or revolutionary polemics) in recent years, and wide public discussion as to the proper limits and exercise of police power in the Federal Republic has clearly had its influence on research: Albrecht Funk's book, reviewed above, for instance, is part of a broader project whose main focus is on the police after 1945.[53] In this connection, it is perhaps surprising that so few of the works under review venture any explicit statement of what they think a proper police force should be and how it should behave; the use of Weberian concepts of rationalization and modernization, common to a number of these studies, seems to be more a way of avoiding such normative questions than anything else.

Secondly, the past decade or so has seen a number of central institutions of modern German history at last come under critical scrutiny, after many years in which their leading representatives have somehow managed to fend it off. The medical profession, the legal profession, and the army are only three institutions whose part in the 'Third Reich' has only very recently become the subject of critical investigation. The same could be said of the police, where official and semi-official histories dominated until the 1980s. Even the role of the Gestapo and the SS in the construction, maintenance and operation of the terror system under the National Socialists was relatively neglected until recently.[54] Research on the police in the Third Reich is bound to open up the question of continuity and lead to research on earlier periods, though once again, none of the authors whose work is considered here explicitly addresses the question apart from Lessmann.

Thirdly, the coming of social history to Germany, above all in the 1980s, has directed attention to previously neglected areas such as crime and law enforcement and opened up new areas of research. It is scarcely possible to write the history of the everyday life of ordinary people, for instance, without either dealing with their clashes with the police and the law, or using the sources generated by the agencies of surveillance and control.[55] This approach is most noticeable here in the work of Nitschke and Jessen. Yet what is still striking is the continuing neglect by historians of what one might call the everyday functions of the police, and the continuing concentration, exemplified here by the work of Siemann, Funk and Lessmann – all of them excellent in their different ways – on the political aspects of policing. Rather than look at police and criminality in their symbiotic relationship to one another, as Jessen suggests, historians still tend to treat them in isolation, or become interested in criminality only if they (implicitly) think it consists of political activities that really should not have been criminalized at all.

This is not to plead, of course, for a rejection of politics in the study of police history. Rather, we need to think of politics and power in a different way. One of the most striking things about the books under review is their continued allegiance to Weberian theory and their continuing use of concepts like rationalization, bureaucratization and modernization as organizing principles. This is all well and good, but it prevents them from asking equally pertinent questions about other things – police corruption, for instance, or the abuse of police power. In England, France and the USA historians since the 1980s have turned instead to Foucault for new questions to ask about power, authority, law and control in the past. Foucault is conspicuous in the books under review mainly by his absence. That is not to say that a Foucauldian approach should be applied uncritically, of course; but the work of Robert Gellately in particular shows how it can be used imaginatively to generate a new and fruitful perspective on even such an obvious topic as the nature of Nazi rule (1990). Rather than conceiving of power as something that operates directly, from the top down, Gellately uses a more diffuse and complex model of power, derived from Foucault, in analysing the role of the Gestapo, Himmler's feared Secret State Police, in the Third Reich. This enables him to come up with some startling yet convincing new perspectives on how it operated.[56]

According to Eugen Kogon, author of perhaps the first major study of the SS and its system of concentration camps, published shortly after the war,[57] the Gestapo was maintaining an 'army' of agents numbering as many as a quarter of a million by the early 1940s. This view has been widely shared. Yet Gellately shows it to be startlingly inaccurate. The actual number of full-time, paid Gestapo officials was in fact very small: 126 in Düsseldorf, for example, in 1937; forty-three in Essen, twenty-eight in Duisburg – all cities with more than 400,000 inhabitants each. Moreover, a fair number of these officials pursued administrative rather than policing duties. For an organization charged with the hunting-down of all kinds of dissidence and non-conformity, from membership in banned organizations to unconventional leisure activities and listening to foreign radio programmes, such numbers seemed far too small to be effective. How then did the Gestapo succeed in gaining its fearsome reputation as the all-seeing, all-knowing agency of political control in the Third Reich? The answer is, through the receipt of denunciations sent in, unsolicited, by ordinary German citizens. These, as Gellately shows, were supplemented by information supplied by paid informers, by the Security Service of the SS, by party officials, and by the regular police force. But they remained the most important source of information by far. Using the Gestapo files for the city of Würzburg, which along with those for Düsseldorf constitute the only major surviving Gestapo archive at this level, Gellately shows that, for example, out of 175 cases of 'friendship to Jews' investigated by the local Gestapo between 1933 and 1945, the majority – 57 per cent – were initiated by denunciations from the population. By contrast, only 9 per cent originated in information provided by National Socialist Party organizations, and only 5 per cent were based on reports by other institutions of political control and surveillance. The rest mostly emerged from incriminating statements given to the Gestapo itself during interrogations (15 per cent), from 'political evaluations' (3 per cent) or from unknown sources (11 per cent).

Gellately, it should be said, is not the first historian to have noted the importance of this phenomenon. Characteristically, it was the late Martin Broszat who first drew attention to it; but the brief article in which he did so, published in the *Archivalische Zeitschrift*, went largely unnoticed when it appeared in 1977. Some use was made of the Düsseldorf Gestapo files by the American historian Sarah Gordon in her book *Hitler, Germans and the*

'Jewish Question' (Princeton, 1984), but it was rendered somewhat problematical by Gordon's assumption that all the people denounced for protecting Jews had in fact been doing so. As Gellately shows, numerous malicious denunciations were sent in, and the Gestapo, who investigated all of them, irrespective of the sometimes rather personal motives from which they were made, frequently came to the conclusion that they were baseless. Two young historians, both sadly no longer with us, Detlev Peukert and Reinhard Mann, also made use of the Düsseldorf files, and the late Peter Hüttenberger's study of malicious gossip cases brought before the Nazi 'Special Court' in Munich uncovered a further hoard of denunciatory material. But Mann's work, as Gellately shows, though very valuable, is vitiated by his decision to exclude from his sample all cases involving Jews and foreigners, even though many of these covered offences of the same kind which he did include in his sample. As a result, Gellately suggests, Mann seriously underestimated the role of denunciations from ordinary citizens in initiating Gestapo action (in Mann's sample, indeed, only 33 per cent of cases originate in a denunciation, as compared to 57 per cent in Gellately's sample). The other three historians mentioned did not have the work of the Gestapo and its relationship to denunciation as their central focus, as Gellately does.

Even Hitler complained in May 1933 that 'we are living at present in a sea of denunciations and human meanness'. The motives for denouncing someone to the Gestapo were varied in the extreme. Husbands denounced wives whom they wished to be rid of; neighbours denounced each other as a new way of pursuing long-standing quarrels; ambitious business people denounced rivals whose property they coveted. To dismiss these actions as irrelevant to the question of whether or not the National Socialists' ideology on matters such as political conformity and racial purity had met with general acceptance is, Gellately argues, beside the point. The point is, he says, that

> denunciations from the population were the key link in the three-way interaction between the police, people and policy in Nazi Germany. Popular participation by provision of information was one of the most important factors in making the terror system work. That conclusion suggests rethinking the notion of the Gestapo as an 'instrument of domination'; if it was an instrument, it was one which was constructed within German society and whose functioning was structurally dependent on the continuing co-operation of German citizens.

This argument, Gellately notes, is a good exemplifier of Foucault's thesis that 'the exercise of power is not violence, nor is it consent . . . It is a total structure of actions brought to bear upon possible actions.' Gellately's sober and chilling analysis in no way diminishes the Gestapo's well-merited reputation for ruthlessness, brutality and violence. One of the most telling sections of his book, indeed, details the methods of intimidation, blackmail, extortion and entrapment deployed by the Gestapo to convict people or force them to confess. But his approach does place the Gestapo's activities in their proper social context and makes their effectiveness easier to comprehend. As he notes, in a discussion of the success of the Gestapo in enforcing the laws forbidding contact between Jews and non-Jews in Nazi Germany,

> In attempting to understand the routine operations of the Nazi system, the question of the popularity of the regime is to a very large extent beside the point . . . Successful enforcement of Nazi racial policies depended on the actions of enough citizens, operating out of an endless variety of motives, who contributed to the isolation of the Jews by offering information to the Gestapo or other authorities of Party or state.

This sophisticated understanding of power and how it operated could be employed fruitfully in the study of the German police under other regimes and at other times as well.[58]

Foucault is not the only modern social theorist neglected by historians of modern Germany. In the Netherlands in particular, the history of crime and law enforcement has been dominated above all by the civilization theory of Norbert Elias. While there is some evidence that it is seen as relevant to their research by German historians working on the early modern period, it has scarcely been used at all by historians concerned with more recent times. As the historiography of modern Germany continues to circulate around the now rather threadbare concepts generated by the work of the late 1960s and early 1970s and deriving ultimately from the American neo-Weberian sociology of the 1950s, it is difficult not to feel – even after a reading of the books under review, all of them important, carefully researched, thorough and original contributions to scholarship – that it is time for something new. This is particularly the case because of the new problems of research and interpretation confronting historians as a result of the collapse of the German Democratic Republic. Since 1989, with the opening of government and party files and the establishment of the 'Gauck Office', which gives access to individuals and researchers seeking information from the vast archive of the State Security Service, the ill-famed Stasi, it has become clear that the scale and intrusiveness of political policing in Communist East Germany was unprecedented, even in the Third Reich. Over 200,000 paid and unpaid, formal and informal agents were working for the Stasi by the last decade or so of the regime's existence, in a population of little over 16 million. Numerous publications have appeared detailing the Stasi's operations in many areas and at many levels of society.[59] Here was a true Foucauldian dystopia, where surveillance was almost universal. The thoroughness of the police system's operations in the German Democratic

Republic inevitably put policing in earlier periods of German history into a different perspective. It makes the approach taken, and the theories applied, by the majority of German historians of the police, whatever period they are dealing with, seem obsolete and beside the point. No doubt the Stasi was 'rational' and 'bureaucratic' like any other police force, at least in the way it operated and the methods it employed, but is this really the most important thing there is to be said about it?

NOTES

1 Peter Nitschke, *Verbrechensbekämpfung und Verwaltung. Die Entstehung der Polizei in der Grafschaft Lippe 1700–1814* (Münster/New York, 1990); Alf Lüdtke (ed.), *'Sicherheit' und 'Wohlfahrt'. Polizei, Gesellschaft und Herrschaft im 19. und 20. Jahrhundert*, Suhrkamp Taschenbuch Wissenschaft 991 (Frankfurt am Main, 1992); Wolfram Siemann, *'Deutschlands Ruhe, Sicherheit und Ordnung.' Die Anfänge der politischen Polizei 1806–1866*, Studien und Texte zur Sozialgeschichte der Literatur, Vol. 14 (Tübingen, 1985); Albrecht Funk, *Polizei und Rechtsstaat. Die Entwicklung des staatlichen Gewaltmonopols in Preussen 1848–1918* (Frankfurt/New York, 1986); Ralph Jessen, *Polizei im Industrierevier. Modernisierung und Herrschaftspraxis im westfälischen Ruhrgebiet 1848–1914*, Kritische Studien zur Geschichtswissenschaft, Vol. 91 (Göttingen, Vandenhoeck and Ruprecht, 1991); Peter Lessmann, *Die preussische Schutzpolizei in der Weimarer Republik. Streifendienst und Strassenkampf* (Düsseldorf, 1991); Robert Gellately, *The Gestapo and German Society. Enforcing Racial Policy 1933–1945* (Oxford, 1990).
2 Jerome K. Jerome, *Three Men on the Bummel* (London, 1900), pp. 129–31.
3 Ray Stannard Baker, *Seen in Germany* (New York, 1901), p. 8.
4 Raymond B. Fosdick, *European Police Systems* (New York, 1915), pp. 9, 27–8.
5 Franz-Ludwig Knemeyer, 'Polizei', in Otto Brunner *et al.* (eds.), *Geschichtliche Grundbegriffe. Historisches Lexikon zur politisch-sozialen Sprache in Deutschland*, Vol. 4 (Stuttgart, 1978), pp. 875–97; Alf Lüdtke, 'Von der "tätigen Verfassung" zur Abwehr von "Störern". Zur Theoriegeschichte von "Polizei" und staatlicher Zwangsgewalt im 19. und frühen 20. Jahrhundert', *Der Staat*, Vol. 20 (1981), pp. 210–28; idem, 'Einleitung: "Sicherheit" und "Wohlfahrt". Aspekte der Polizeigeschichte', in idem (ed.), *'Sicherheit' und 'Wohlfahrt'*, pp. 7–33; R. Schulze, *Policey und Gesetzgebungslehre im 18. Jahrhundert* (Berlin, 1982); P. Preu, *Polizeibegriff und Staatszwecklehre. Die Entwicklung des Polizeibegriffs durch die Rechts- und Staatswissenschaften des 18. Jahrhunderts* (Berlin, 1983); Hans Maier, *Die ältere deutsche Staats- und Verwaltungslehre (Polizeiwissenschaft). Ein Beitrag zur Geschichte der politischen Wissenschaft in Deutschland* (Neuwied, 1966). The books under review by Nitschke and Siemann provide many further references to the substantial literature on this topic.
6 Clive Emsley, *Policing and its Context 1750–1870*, Themes in Comparative History, (London, 1983), is a useful comparative survey. See also William R. Miller, *Cops and Bobbies. Police Authority in New York and London, 1830–1870* (Chicago, 1977); Douglas Hay and F. Snyder (eds), *Policing and Prosecution in Britain 1750–1850* (Oxford, 1989).
7 Marc Raeff, 'Der wohlgeordnete Polizeistaat und die Entwicklung der Moderne im Europa des 17. und 18. Jahrhunderts. Versuch eines vergleichenden Ansatzes', in Ernst Hinrichs (ed.), *Absolutismus* (Frankfurt am Main, 1986).

8 Carsten Küther, *Räuber und Gauner in Deutschland. Das organisierte Bandenwesen im 18. und frühen 19. Jahrhundert*, Kritische Studien zur Geschichtswissenschaft, Vol. 20 (Göttingen, 1976).

9 B. Becker, *Actenmässige Geschichte der Räuberbanden an den beyden Ufern des Rheins*, 2 vols (Cologne, 1804); Manfred Franke, *Schinderhannes. Das kurze, wilde Leben des Johannes Bückler. Nach alten Dokumenten neu erzählt* (Düsseldorf, 1984); Paul Anselm Ritter von Feuerbach, *Aktenmässige Darstellung merkwürdiger Verbrechen*, 2 vols (Giessen, 1828–9); and, dealing with an earlier period and emphasizing the effectiveness of state controls in normal times, Uwe Danker, *Räuberbanden im Alten Reich um 1700*, Suhrkamp Taschenbuch Wissenschaft 707, 2 vols (Frankfurt am Main, 1988).

10 Geheimes Staatsarchiv Preussischer Kulturbesitz (GStA) Berlin, Rep. 84a/10734 (Die Errichtung einer Gensdarmerie für den Preussischen Staat), S. 9–26: Promemoria über die Errichtung einer Gensdarmerie für den Preussischen Staat, 4 April 1810.

11 Alf Lüdtke, *'Gemeinwohl', Polzei und 'Festungspraxis'. Staatliche Gewaltsamkeit und innere Verwaltung in Preussen, 1815–1850*, Veröffentlichungen des Max-Planck-Instituts für Geschichte, Vol. 73 (Göttingen, 1982). For examples of the formation of new police forces in this period see Bernd Wirsing, ' "Gleichsam mit Soldatenstrenge": Neue Polizei in süddeutschen Städten. Zu Polizeiverhalten und Bürger-Widersetzlichkeit im Vormärz', in Alf Lüdtke (ed.), *'Sicherheit' und 'Wohlfahrt'*, pp. 65–94.

12 Peter Becker, 'Vom "Haltlosen" zur "Bestie". Das polizeiliche Bild des "Verbrechers" im 19. Jahrhundert', in Lüdtke, *'Sicherheit' und 'Wohlfahrt'*, pp. 97–131.

13 For a concise statement of this thesis, see Alf Lüdtke, 'The Role of State Violence in the Period of Transition to Industrial Capitalism: the Example of Prussia from 1815 to 1848', *Social History*, Vol. 4 (1979); and idem, 'Praxis und Funktion staatlicher Repression: Preussen 1815–50', *Geschichte und Gesellschaft*, Vol. 3 (1977), pp. 190–211.

14 Dirk Blasius, *Kriminalität und Alltag. Zur Konfliktgeschichte des Alltagslebens im 19. Jahrhundert*, Kleine Vandenhoeck–Reihe 1448 (Göttingen, 1978); Arno Herzig, *Unterschichtenprotest in Deutschland 1790–1870*, Kleine Vandenhoeck–Reihe 1534 (Göttingen, 1988), summarizing a large and mostly recent scholarly literature.

15 Dirk Blasius, *Bürgerliche Gesellschaft und Kriminalität. Zur Sozialgeschichte Preussens im Vormärz*, Kritische Studien zur Geschichtswissenschaft, Vol. 22 (Göttingen, 1975).

16 See Richard J. Evans, *Szenen aus der deutschen Unterwelt. Verbrechen und Strafe im 19. Jahrhundert* (Reinbek bei Hamburg, 1997).

17 For Berlin, see Frank Thomason, 'The Prussian Police State in Berlin 1848–1871' (Ph.D., Johns Hopkins University, 1978); idem, 'The Criminal Division of the Berlin Police Organization, 1877–1910', *Journal of Police Science and Administration*, Vol. 2 (1974), pp. 429–43; idem, 'Uniformed Police in the City of Berlin under the Empire', in E.C. Viano and J.H. Reiman (eds), *The Police in Society* (Toronto, 1975), pp. 105–19; for Hamburg, Richard J. Evans, *Death in Hamburg: Society and Politics in the Cholera Years 1830–1910* (Oxford, 1987), pp. 87–9. See also Albrecht Funk and Norbert Pütter, 'Polizei und Miliz als "Bürgerorgane" ', in Lüdtke (ed.), *'Sicherheit' und 'Wohlfahrt'*, pp. 37–64.

18 Hermann-Josef Rupieper, 'Die Polizei und die Fahndungen anlässlich der deutschen Revolution von 1848/49', *Vierteljahrschrift zur Sozial- und Wirtschaftsgeschichte*, Vol. 64 (1977), pp. 311–25.

19 See H. Adler (ed.), *Literarische Geheimberichte. Protokolle der Metternich-Agenten* 2 vols (Cologne, 1977/81).
20 Siemann, *'Deutschlands Ruhe'*, p. 167.
21 Ibid.
22 See Wolfram Siemann (ed.), *Der 'Polizeiverein' deutscher Staaten. Eine Dokumentation zur überwachung der öffentlichkeit nach der Revolution von 1848/49*, Studien und Texte zur Sozialgeschichte der Literatur, Vol. 9 (Tübingen, 1983).
23 Siemann, *'Deutschlands Ruhe'*, p. 357.
24 Karl Marx, 'Enthüllungen über den Kommunistenprozess zu Köln' (Basel, 1853), also in *Marx-Engels Werke*, Vol. 8 (East Berlin, 1960), pp. 405–70.
25 Wilhelm J.C.E. Stieber, *Spion des Kanzlers. Die Enthüllungen von Bismarcks Geheimdienstchef* (Stuttgart, 1978); Siemann, *'Deutschlands Ruhe'*, p. 23, n. 100. Since Stieber was an accomplished, indeed professional liar, the obvious falsehoods in his book do nothing in themselves to suggest that he did not write it himself.
26 For the full story, see David Blackbourn, *Marpingen. Apparitions of the Virgin Mary in Bismarckian Germany* (Oxford, 1994).
27 Dieter Fricke, *Bismarcks Prätorianer. Die Berliner politische Polizei im Kampf gegen die deutsche Arbeiterbewegung (1871–1898)* (East Berlin, 1962), pp. 288–303.
28 GStA Berlin, Rep. 84a/9260 (Äusserungen der Presse über das Polizeiwesen in Berlin): *Rheinischer Kurier*, 10 Dec. 1900.
29 GStA Berlin, Rep. 84a/8265: Zusammenstellungen und Nachweisungen über Verurteilungen, Freisprechungen bzw. Begnadigungen von Polizeibeamten wegen übertretung ihrer Amtsbefugnisse 1896–1906.
30 GStA Berlin, Rep. 84a/8260, 8261, 8262, 8263, 8264, 8265: Die Untersuchung und Bestrafung der von Beamten begangenen Verbrechen 1803–1934.
31 GStA Berlin, Rep. 84a/3712: Schutz der persönlichen Freiheit, Bl. 35–36; *Gesetz-Sammlung für die Königlichen Preussischen Staaten*, Nr. 42 (Nr. 3035).
32 GStA Berlin, Rep. 84a/3712: Schutz der persönlichen Freiheit, Bl. 41, 61, 118; GstA Berlin, Rep. 84a/3714: Schutz der persönlichen Freiheit, Bl. 31, 38–42.
33 GStA Berlin, Rep. 84a/3712: Schutz der persönlichen Freiheit, Bl. 61.
34 Funk, *Polizei und Rechtsstaat*, p. 77.
35 Klaus Saul, 'Der Staat und die "Mächte des Umsturzes". Ein Beitrag zu den Methoden antisozialistischer Repression und Agitation vom Scheitern des Sozialistengesetzes bis zur Jahrhundertwende', *Archiv für Sozialgeschichte*, Vol. 12 (1972), pp. 293–350.
36 Michael Zimmermann, 'Ausgrenzung, Ermordung, Ausgrenzung. Normalität und Exzess in der polizeilichen Zigeunerverfolgung in Deutschland (1870–1980), in Lüdtke (ed.), *'Sicherheit' und 'Wohlfahrt'*, pp. 344–70.
37 For an elaboration of this argument, see Evans, *Szenen*, Chapter 5.
38 Ibid., Chapter 6.
39 See Eric A. Johnson, *Urbanization and Crime. Germany 1871–1918* (New York, 1995).
40 See also Ralph Jessen, 'Unternehmerschaft und staatliches Gewaltmonopol. Hüttenpolizisten und Zechenwehren im Ruhrgebiet (1870–1914)', in Lüdtke (ed.), *'Sicherheit' und 'Wohlfahrt'*, pp. 262–86.
41 Staatsarchiv Bremen 4,14/1.V.G.4.1–7a: Streik der Strassenbahner 1910/11 und dadurch hervorgerufene Unruhen.
42 See also Elaine Glovka Spencer, 'Police–Military Relations in Prussia, 1848–1914', *Journal of Social History*, Vol. 19 (1985), pp. 305–17, and idem, *Police and the*

Social Order in German Cities: The Düsseldorf District 1848–1914 (DeKalb, Ill., 1992).

43 See also Elaine Glovka Spencer, 'State Power and Local Interests in Prussian Cities: Police in the Düsseldorf District, 1848–1914', *Central European History*, Vol. 19 (1986), pp. 293–313.

44 Johnson, *Urbanization and Crime.*

45 Christoph Sachsse (ed.), *Soziale Sicherheit und soziale Disziplinierung. Beträge zu einer historischen Theorie der Sozialpolitik* (Frankfurt am Main, Suhrkamp, 1986).

46 Cf. Heinz-Gerhard Haupt, 'Staatliche Bürokratie und Arbeiterbewegung: Zum Einfluss der Polizei auf die Konstituierung der Arbeiterbewegung und Arbeiterklasse in Deutschland und Frankreich zwischen 1848 und 1880', in Jürgen Kocka (ed.), *Arbeiter und Bürger im 19. Jahrhundert* (Munich, 1986), pp. 219–54; and Klaus Tenfelde, 'Polizei und Klasseverhältnisse. Deutschfranzösiche Unterschiede', in Kocka (ed.), *Arbeiter und Bürger*, pp. 255–60.

47 Hsi-Huey Liang, *Die Berliner Polizei in der Weimarer Republik* (Berlin, 1977); Eric D. Kohler, 'The Crisis in the Prussian Schutzpolizei 1930–32', in George L. Mosse (ed.), *Police Forces in History* (London, 1975), pp. 131–51; Siegfried Zalka, *Polizeigeschichte. Die Exekutive im Lichte der historischen Konfliktforschung. Untersuchungen über die Theorie und Praxis der preussischen Schutzpolizei in der Weimarer Republik zur Verhinderung und Bekämpfung innerer Unruhen* (Lübeck, 1979); Jürgen Siggemann, *Die kasernierte Polizei und das Problem der inneren Sicherheit in der Weimarer Republik. Eine Studie zum Auf- und Ausbau des innerstaatlichen Sicherheitssystems in Deutschland 1918/19–1933* (Frankfurt am Main, 1980); Johannes Buder, *Die Reorganisation der preussischen Polizei 1918–1923* (Frankfurt am Main, 1986).

48 C. Graf, *Politische Polizei zwischen Demokratie und Diktatur. Die Entwicklung der preussischen Politischen Polizei von Staatsschutzorgan der Weimarer Republik zum Geheimen Staatspolizeiamt des Dritten Reiches* (Berlin, 1983).

49 Richard Bessel, 'Militarisierung und Modernisierung: Polizeiliches Handeln in der Weimarer Republik', in Lüdtke (ed.), *'Sicherheit' und 'Wohlfahrt'*, pp. 323–43.

50 Gustav Roscher, *Grossstadtpolizei. Ein prakisches Handbuch der deutschen Polizei* (Hamburg, 1912).

51 See Richard J. Evans, *Rituals of Retribution: Capital Punishment in Germany 1600–1987* (Oxford, 1996), Chapters 11–13. Cf. Haupt, 'Staatliche Bürokratie' and Tenfelde, 'Polizei'. ,

52 See for example the surveys by Heinz-Gerhard Haupt and Wolf-Dieter Narr, 'Vom Polizey-Staat zum Polizeistaat? Ein Forschungsbericht anhand neuerer Literatur', *Neue Politische Literatur*, Vol. 23 (1978), pp. 185–218, and Wolfgang Kopitzsch, 'Neue Beiträge zur Polizeigeschichte', *Jahrbuch des Instituts für Deutsche Geschichte (Tel-Aviv)*, Vol. 10 (1981), pp. 445–50.

53 H. Busch *et al.*, *Die Polizei in der Bundesrepublik* (Frankfurt am Main, 1985); F. Werkentin, *Die Restauration der deutschen Polizei. Innere Rüstung von 1945 bis zur Notstandsgesetzgebung* (Frankfurt am Main, 1984).

54 Robert Gellately, 'Gestapo und Terror. Perspektiven auf die Sozialgeschichte des nationalsozialistischen Herrschaftssystems', in Lüdtke (ed.), *'Sicherheit' und 'Wohlfahrt'*, pp. 371–92; Karl-Leo Terhorst, *Polizeiliche planmässige überwachung und polizeiliche Vorbeugungshaft im Dritten Reich* (Heidelberg, 1985) (mainly legal); Reinhard Mann, *Protest und Kontrolle im Dritten Reich. Nationalsozialistische Herrschaft im Alltag einer Grossstadt* (Frankfurt am Main, 1987); W.O. Weyrauch, *Gestapo V-Leute* (Frankfurt am Main, 1989).

55 See Richard J. Evans (ed.), *Kneipengespräche im Kaiserreich. Die Stimmungs-berichte der Hamburger Politischen Polizei 1892 bis 1914* (Reinbek bei Hamburg, 1989).
56 Gellately, *The Gestapo and German Society*.
57 Eugen Kogon, *Der SS-Staat. Das System der deutschen Konzentrationslager* (Frankfurt am Main, 1946).
58 For a recent German study of the Gestapo largely supporting Gellately's conclusions, see Klaus-Michael Mallmann and Gerhard Paul, 'Omniscient, Omnipotent, Omnipresent? Gestapo, Society and Resistance', in David F. Crew (ed.), *Nazism and German Society 1933–1945* (London, 1994), pp. 166–96.
59 See for example Karl Wilhelm Fricke, *MfS intern. Macht, Strukturen, Auflösung der DDR-Staatsscherheit* (Cologne, 1991), and Johannes Beleites *et al.*, *Stasi intern. Macht und Banalität* (2nd edn, Leipzig, 1991).

7

THE CATHOLIC COMMUNITY AND THE PRUSSIAN STATE[1]

On Monday 3 July 1876, Margarethe Kunz and two other young girls in the village of Marpingen, in the Saarland, returned home in a state of considerable agitation. Obviously frightened, they described having seen a woman in white in the meadows on their way back from gathering bilberries in the woods. On the following days, they described further encounters. The woman told them: 'I am the Immaculately Conceived.' Adults in the village confidently identified her as the Virgin Mary. News of the encounter spread rapidly. Soon there were hundreds of pilgrims at the scene, and miraculous cures were being reported at a nearby spring which the children said the Virgin had indicated as a source of healing. Within a week there were said to be 20,000 pilgrims in the village, and people were speaking of Marpingen as 'the German Lourdes'.

In his new book (1993), David Blackbourn takes this incident as the starting-point for a detailed examination of Catholic culture, both popular and ecclesiastical, and its relations with politics and the state in Bismarckian Germany. Blackbourn's previous work presented the Catholic Centre Party as a normal part of the political scene in the *Kaiserreich*, and in so doing gave us political Catholicism with the religion left out. Here he makes amends with a sensitive and elegantly written exploration of the religious world in which political Catholicism was rooted. Once more, however, it is the political and social dimensions of the subject which interest him most. This is not a study of Catholic spirituality, or an anthropology of popular belief. Politics still occupy centre-stage.

Given the furore which the incident aroused, this is perhaps unsurprising. For the visions at Marpingen were reported at the height of the Bismarckian *Kulturkampf*. Blackbourn reminds us in graphic detail of the extent and ferocity of the persecution to which Catholics were subjected at this period. In the diocese of Trier, in which Marpingen was situated in 1876, the bishop had just died (shortly after his release from nine months in gaol), 250 priests had been brought before the courts, nearly a third of the parishes were without an incumbent, and 150,000 Catholics lacked a priest. The Prussian authorities were hounding and harassing the Catholic community, and tensions with local Protestants and the local authorities had risen sharply. 'Prussia in the 1870s', as Blackbourn notes in an illuminating parallel, 'became a less bloody version of France in the 1790s.' All this took place at a time of deep economic crisis following the crash of 1873. In the Saarland, overpopulation, agricultural depression and the rapid growth of the coal-mining industry had turned villages like Marpingen into dormitories, with the men forced to live away in pithead barracks during the week. Here too the economic depression created serious tensions and strains. Marpingen had become a *Weiberdorf*, a village of women and children. Economic crisis, social change, political repression and religious persecution combined to engender a strong collective desire for redemption and deliverance among the villagers.

Such circumstances, as Blackbourn points out in a chapter comparing Marpingen with other, similar incidents in nineteenth-century Europe, often provided the backdrop to 'clusters' of apparitions across a wide area within a short space of time. And those who claimed to have seen the Virgin at other times and in other places also bore remarkable similarities to Margarethe Kunz: intelligent, enterprising, but from impoverished and broken families, recently bereaved, and socially marginal or at least under threat of becoming so. Bernadette Soubirous herself was one such; and the widely publicized example of her visions at Lourdes, where 100,000 Catholics, including thirty-five bishops, were celebrating the crowning of a statue of the Virgin on the very day on which the first apparitions were reported in Marpingen, undoubtedly had an influence on the German Catholic community, which had sent its first organized pilgrimage to the French grotto the previous year. Patriotism prompted the thought that it would not be long before the Virgin graced German soil with her presence as well, and no doubt helped account for the readiness with which many German Catholics, in Marpingen and beyond, accepted Margarethe Kunz's tale.

The advantages for them in doing so were not merely psychological. The thousands of pilgrims who flocked to the village had to be fed and watered, they needed accommodation, and they were eager to buy holy water from the well, water which was soon being posted in tin containers to recipients all over Germany. Medallions were struck, booths were set up to sell religious *kitsch*, and hawkers moved in to exploit the visitors' piety. A future more lucrative still beckoned to the villagers, if the example of Lourdes, with its grand hotels and aristocratic patronage, was anything to go by. But none of this came to pass. For this, two main factors were responsible. First, the Catholic Church in Germany, unlike its counterpart in France, failed to back the authenticity of the visions. While the local priest, the decent Father Neureuter, overcame his initial scepticism and endorsed the visions with genuine enthusiasm, what was left of the Catholic hierarchy in Germany demurred. When a parallel set of apparitions in Mettenbuch, Bavaria, was reported in December 1876, the local bishop moved swiftly into action, interrogated the visionaries, and forced them to confess that they had made the whole thing up. In the absence of an episcopal incumbent in Trier, however, no formal canonical investigation was ever held in Marpingen, an omission which was probably one of the factors that allowed the cult to develop. Such was the political sensitivity of the issue that either an open endorsement or a public denial of the visions by the Church would have played with equal ease into the hands of the Prussian authorities. Margarethe Kunz and her companions were eventually interrogated, in a nunnery to which they were removed in 1878, but while a confidential ecclesiastical report described their visions as inauthentic, even diabolical in origin, it was never published, and in the absence of a formal refutation by the Church, the cult lingered on in an attenuated form for many years afterwards. For most Catholics, however, the failure of the Church to give the Marpingen apparitions its official blessing was enough.

Essentially, therefore, the Catholic hierarchy in Germany was cowed into submission by the Prussian government. The hostility of the secular authorities was the second major reason for the evanescence of the religious enthusiasm which the apparitions generated. On hearing of the mass gatherings at Marpingen, the local authorities ordered the troops out, and on 13 July 1876, the men of the 8th Company of the 4th Rhenish Infantry Regiment arrived at the scene, fixed bayonets, cleared away several thousand singing and praying pilgrims with considerable violence, and proceeded to billet themselves upon the appalled villagers for the next two weeks. In this atmosphere, the judicial authorities launched a full-scale criminal investigation. But after several weeks of interrogating the villagers, they failed to garner any concrete evidence of illegality. This alarmed their masters in Berlin, who decided to bring matters to a head by sending in a plain-clothes detective to act as an *agent provocateur*.

The Berlin detective, Baron von Meerscheidt-Hüllessem, arrived in Marpingen on 1 October 1876 and immediately tried to ingratiate himself with the villagers by buying them no fewer than 60 litres of beer in the village inn the same evening. He proceeded to collect, and manufacture, a great deal of allegedly incriminating evidence on the basis of which a number of the villagers – though not the visionaries themselves – were brought to trial for fraud and other offences. Meerscheidt-Hüllessem cut a sorry figure in the witness box, however, and the accused were all acquitted. Blackbourn draws the conclusion that the affair illustrated 'the weaknesses of the Prussian state'. But while it is true to say that it demonstrated that Prussian citizens lived under the rule of law (after a fashion), it is also evident that politically at least, the military occupation of the village, the ensuing heavy police presence, the criminal investigation, and the highly publicized trial, all achieved their purpose. Not only the Church hierarchy, but also the mass of Catholic laity, were browbeaten into distancing themselves from the apparitions.

During his sojourn in the village, the Berlin detective posed, somewhat improbably, as an Irish journalist and, wonderfully, took the alias of 'Marlow'. The name gains its true retrospective appropriateness not so much through its resemblance to that of the detective hero of Raymond Chandler's novels, as through its coincidence with that of the narrator of Joseph Conrad's novella *Heart of Darkness*. For in the eyes of German liberals in particular, Marpingen was indeed the heart of darkness, symbolizing in the most graphic possible way the dangers of what they saw as the intransigence, low cunning, gullibility and superstition of the 'ultramontanes' and their constituency. It was a liberal, Rudolf Virchow, after all, who had coined the term *Kulturkampf*, dignifying the brutal repression of Catholicism in the 1870s as a struggle between progress and obscurantism. The liberals' attitude to the affair revealed some of their most fateful weaknesses. The eagerness with which they wrote off the cult's supporters as 'hysterical women' and gullible peasants demonstrated all too clearly the gender- and class-based elitism which proved such an obstacle to their winning mass support. And the way in which they applauded the repressive measures taken in Marpingen by the Prussian state suggested strongly the extent to which they were prepared to sacrifice their liberal principles on the altar of what they saw as progress, whether it was embodied in German unity, in anticlerical rationality, in the defence of society against left-wing violence, or – eventually – in the promise of national regeneration.

Blackbourn tells this complex and sometimes unsavoury story with immense subtlety and sophistication, pouring into it all the knowledge he has gained in more than twenty years of working on Imperial Germany, and basing it on a mass of meticulous research into what must often have been quite difficult manuscript material in the archives. It is a measure of his skill as a story-teller that he reveals almost at the very outset that Margarethe Kunz admitted some years later that she had invented the visions, and that – as other evidence also showed – many of the details, such as the confused phrase about the Immaculate Conception said to have been uttered by the Virgin, had first been suggested to her by leading questions put by adult inhabitants of the village. If only people had not believed her so readily, said the adult Kunz, instead of calming her down, she and her friends would not have been tempted to have gone on embroidering their stories and making up new ones until the costs of turning back became too great. The apparitions, she confessed, were 'one big lie'. As Blackbourn demonstrates in a careful assessment of the evidence, there is no reason to believe that she was doing anything but freely telling the truth when she made this dramatic admission.

The visions, therefore, were not authentic. Their prosaic, everyday quality, indeed, contrasted strongly with the more exalted, other-worldly nature of the apparitions reported by the classic visionaries of the nineteenth century such as Bernadette Soubirous. By opening his narrative of the Marpingen apparitions with this revelation, Blackbourn turns his book into an explicit study in irrationality, an attempt to explain why so many people believed something that was palpably false. In this way, it rather resembles Georges Lefebvre's *The Great Fear of 1789*, and it is a measure of the quality of Blackbourn's work that it can easily stand comparison with the great French historian's classic study. But *Marpingen* also belongs to a much more contemporary historical genre, the micro-history of a single, often strange or bizarre incident, in which a small, seemingly trivial case is used as a point of departure for reflections on much larger and wider historical issues, often seen through this process in an unfamiliar light, or from a novel and original angle: Le Roy Ladurie's *Montaillou* and Natalie Zemon Davis's *The Return of Martin Guerre* are examples mentioned by Blackbourn himself in the Introduction to his book; Robert Darnton's *The Great Cat Massacre* would be another.

Yet parallels of this sort are in the end rather less convincing. Blackbourn is an historian's historian: his scholarship is too scrupulous, his craftsmanship too skilled, for him to be drawn into the kind of vertiginous speculation and imaginative reinterpretation of the evidence which not only made those other works so exciting, but also invited so much hostile, and often devastating criticism from other historians. As a result, while *Marpingen* has many delights to offer the reader who already has some knowledge of Imperial Germany, it is probably too exacting a work of scholarship to enjoy a wider appeal. And rather than modish postmodern uncertainty, it is probably good old-fashioned scholarly caution that prevents Blackbourn from drawing any particularly novel or exciting lessons from the story he has to tell. His three main conclusions – that religion was a power in nineteenth-century Europe, that the Prussian state was not simply or uniformly authoritarian, and that Marpingen was not merely a revolt against modernity but also showed the dark, repressive and dehumanizing side of liberalism, rationalism and progress – are hardly going to surprise anybody. When he says, in the final sentence of the book, that 'any larger conclusions we wish to draw from these events must surely be ambiguous', the reader is entitled to sniff a cop-out. Lefebvre's work was important precisely because it dealt with a decisive event which had major implications for the course of the French Revolution. Marpingen, on the other hand, had no wider significance or impact on German politics and society. Given the essentialy political approach which this book takes, it seems that the drawback of 'micro-history' may perhaps lie in the fact that the seemingly trivial incidents on which it is based often turn out on closer inspection to be really trivial in the end.

Blackbourn may thus be justified in refusing to venture any firm generalizations on the basis of what he has discovered; and it is a measure of his scrupulousness as a historian that he resists the temptation to do so. This is not, therefore, a book that overturns accepted views of the

Kulturkampf or makes us rethink our views on Bismarckian Germany. Yet such criticism, in a way, is beside the point. The real achievement of *Marpingen* lies in the details, in its wonderfully rich and nuanced re-creation of the world of Catholic society and secular politics in the 1870s, and in its beautifully crafted, sympathetic and stylishly written exploration of the thoughts, words and deeds of people who have languished in the dustbin of history for too long.

NOTES

1 David Blackbourn, *Marpingen. Apparitions of the Virgin Mary in Bismarckian Germany* (Oxford, Clarendon Press, 1993).

8

WORKERS' CO-OPERATIVES IN THE NINETEENTH CENTURY[1]

Big has been beautiful in the German economy for a very long time, but never more so than in recent years. Mammoth enterprises and conglomerates stretch their tentacles across every branch of industry, while the high streets and pedestrian precincts of West German towns are lined with those temples of consumerism, the local branches of the great department-store chains, identical in every respect, so that as you walk past the serried ranks of Hertie and Kaufhof, Karstadt and Kaufhalle, you scarcely know any longer whether you are in Göttingen or Marburg, Bielefeld or Bonn. Yet there are signs of a consumer revolt. Away from the 'city', as the Germans now like to call what used to be known as the *Stadtmitte*, you can find here and there an alternative commercial scene, above all if you go to the older parts of town, where the grey and shabby tenements, the run-down public facilities and the absence of neon and gloss speak of an area soon to fall under the developer's axe. In makeshift shops, run by enthusiasts with a minimum of advertising hype, you can buy organic fruit and vegetables, homespun garments, non-pollutant cleaning materials, alternative books and newspapers, you can sit in a sparsely furnished café and read a copy of *Die Tageszeitung* over a cup of camomile tea, you can hire a bicycle or take your own to be repaired, or you can inspect, and perhaps purchase, the pottery, art, ceramics and other goods made by producer co-operatives in the neighbourhood.

It is not only the outward appearance of such enterprises that assigns them to the 'alternative economy'; it is also their inner structure and organization. As Walter Hesselbach points out, they are owned by those who work in them, are democratically run, orient themselves to what they believe to be the customer's needs, and lay almost as much stress on the self-expression of those who operate them as they do on sales and profits. The alternative economy can be seen, too, as a form of co-operative self-help at a time of mass unemployment, a way not just of creating jobs, but of doing so with minimum damage to the environment and maximum help to the self-respect of those involved – a self-respect too often assaulted in the past by the brutal compulsion inherent in so many of the massive job creation and public works schemes into which the young unemployed have been drafted by the state. Not surprisingly, therefore, such new forms of co-operative self-help have aroused increasing interest in the Federal Republic, and not only among the Greens. One result of this has been a growing volume of literature on the subject, quite a lot of it historical, for such ideas, however contemporary their expression, are not entirely new.

Christiane Eisenberg's study of the co-operative movement in the 1860s and 1870s (1985) was clearly inspired by this new interest, but despite this it relates mainly to a series of very detailed scholarly debates about continuities in the early German labour movement and the reasons for labour's break with the liberals, and these debates are not made any more accessible to the reader by the author's turgid style and pedantic excess (over thirty pages of closely printed footnotes for less than seventy pages of text). Her strange decision to banish discussion of the co-operatives themselves to a numbered list of 304 of them, whose fates are individually recounted in an appendix that is longer than the book's main text, also prevents her from enlivening the very tedious argument with many real examples. Anyone who wants a readable introduction to the history of German co-operatives had better go elsewhere.[2] Nevertheless, it is possible, painfully, to extract some points of wider interest, and these are particularly worth discussing in view of the recent general revival of interest in the subject.

The early socialist theorists imagined the future society as based on a network of producer co-operatives, and this vision was shared at least to some extent by the labour movement in Germany after the 1848 Revolution. Even Marx, in his Inaugural Address of 1864, agreed that 'co-operative factories' showed that industry could exist without exploitation and wage labour (p. 17). The appeal of such an idea depended heavily on the presence in the labour movement of artisan producers who saw co-operative production as a means of regaining some of the status they had lost with the decline of the guilds. As the Productive Association of Berlin Printers declared in 1872, 'The transition from wage to co-operative production is an act in the social sphere comparable to that of a transition from monarchy to republic in the political: liberation from tutelage over and instrumentalization of the individual's destiny' (p. 29). As with other ideas of the early German labour movement, this was fundamentally forward looking and future oriented, whatever the motives from which it was developed, the more so since both the ADAV and the SDAP, the two branches of the socialist party that eventually united at Gotha in 1875, envisaged that co-operatives would obtain state support after the democratic revolution. Thus the co-operative idea was an integral part of socialism: it was not, as has often been assumed, an invention of liberal reformers like Schulze-Delitzsch, whose interpretation of the co-operative idea entirely lacked this radical political thrust. Concern for the petty-bourgeois interests present in the liberal movement would not allow Schulze-Delitzsch to envisage ploughing back profits into productive co-operatives, but led him to plan for them to be distributed to members, so co-operatives would have limited powers of growth and expansion, thus allowing petty-bourgeois artisanal production to continue. Nor would they bring wage labour to an end, though Schulze-Delitzsch thought that their success in competing with capitalist industry would force employers to strike back by raising wages, so a general reduction in social conflict would be the result.

It was not the co-operative idea in itself, therefore, so much as the specifics of Schulze-Delitzsch's version of it, that deterred the labour movement from going along with the liberals in the 1860s. In this period, and even more, perhaps, in the 1870s, a large number of producer co-operatives were founded in the belief that a democratic alternative to wage-labour exploitation could be provided. They ranged from groups of four or five members engaged in skilled woodwork and carpentry, or the Solingen Steel and Ironware Co-operative – founded in 1867 with twenty-seven members (including former members of the League of Communists) in explicit opposition to Schulze-Delitzsch's principles – to the 300-member General German Co-operative Printing Society (1875), which printed socialist party newspapers. Co-operatives were organized on a variety of principles. But they all faced a number of similar problems which, in the end, they were unable to overcome.

The co-operatives could only make a profit if they freed themselves from the very considerable debts with which most of them began. This meant exploiting market opportunities. In a period of rapid fluctuations in demand, whether upwards, as in the unification boom of 1870–3, or downwards, after the crash of 1873, this necessitated increasing or reducing the workforce as required. This policy in turn could only be done by engaging wage labour and so departing from the principles on which the co-operatives were founded. The alternative of sticking to their principles and keeping a static workforce meant that members exploited themselves by working excessive hours when demand was high or getting poor rewards when demand was low. Moreover, they were further hampered by the Co-operative Law of 1867, designed by Schulze-Delitzsch to protect petty-bourgeois co-operatives by requiring collective liability and so deterring workers from joining for fear of bankruptcy if the enterprise failed. German capitalism was expanding so fast in the 1860s and – despite the crash – the 1870s, particularly in the area of heavy industry, that it was illusory to suppose that the co-operative movement could ever keep pace, let alone swallow up the rest of the economy. As for the political affiliations of the co-operatives, most of them soon found that joining the Social Democrats was bad for business, while economic success distanced them once more from the party, because it could only be achieved by compromising their principles. The co-operative tradition was overtaken by the rise of trade unions, who accepted the fact of wage labour and based their strategy on the strike, rejecting alternatives such as co-operative production as unrealistic and, in any case, too expensive for their meagre funds to support. By the end of the 1870s, therefore, most of the co-operatives had folded. The dream was over.

In the meantime, however, a new version of the co-operative idea was emerging, based on the worker as consumer rather than producer. The consumer co-operatives in Hamburg and elsewhere soon became immensely successful and by the turn of the century had hundreds of thousands of members. At their height, around 1930, their membership numbered nearly four million. What were the reasons for their success? Workers found it advantageous to club together to reduce prices and ensure fair trading, and the fact that the annual profits were divided up equally between the members meant that everyone had an incentive to join and to purchase more goods. Thus consumer co-operatives avoided the contradictions that had undermined producer co-operatives. It is quite probable that the co-operatives were closely linked to the Social Democratic milieu, to the 'alternative culture' created by the SPD and the 'Free' Trade Unions, yet the movement and its leading figures (such as Adolph von Elm in Hamburg) do not seem to have played much of a role in the party. Perhaps they were too self-consciously reformist and oriented towards the practicalities of daily existence. Even further removed from the party were the co-operative building societies that emerged towards the end of the century: the capital that had to be raised initially was much greater, the cost for each member was much higher, and the organization involved in building was often very complex, requiring professional legal and financial expertise. Before 1914 building societies seem to have catered mainly to the petty bourgeoisie: the payments they required were beyond the pockets of most workers. More successful were the building societies set up by the construction workers' union after the 1918 Revolution. But here too, despite 82,000 small dwellings built by 1929, little impact was made on the state of the housing situation overall.[3]

The co-operative movement was prominent enough, however, to be one of the many factors that alienated small retailers and other sections of the petty bourgeoisie from the SPD: indeed some of the leading Social Democrats in Hamburg, who thought it necessary to woo the lower middle class in a city where it was particularly substantial, were critical of the co-operative movement for precisely this reason.[4] The co-ops also fell foul of the persistent German tendency to introduce protective legislation to safeguard the interests of the *Mittelstand*. This tendency reached its height in the Third Reich, when the co-ops were wound up altogether – one of the areas, it seems, where the Nazis really did keep their promises to their beleaguered petty-bourgeois supporters. Even in the 1950s the Adenauer government restricted co-op discounts by law to the same allowed normal retailers, and though there were two and a half million co-op members once more by 1961, they could no longer call on the loyalties engendered by the Social Democratic milieu, and now had to face the competition generated by the lowering of retail prices by the large supermarkets and department stores on the one hand, and the emergence of common bulk purchase arrangements by small retailers organized in chains such as the Spar group on the other. With the 'economic miracle' and the arrival of the affluent society, who cared about a few *pfennigs* saved here and there anyway? The remaining co-ops in West German today have opened their doors to all and become, of necessity, virtually indistinguishable from other retail stores.

Nevertheless, West German consumers are not satisfied. Not only in the alternative scene but even on the high streets, a change in retailing is taking place: shops are getting smaller again. As the standard of living of West Germans passes from the super-affluent to the ultra-affluent, the department store, even on the grandest scale, no longer satisfies their needs. What is in demand now is the small, specialized, high-price luxury goods shop, providing a feeling of intimacy and personal service lost in the anonymity of the big store. In Hamburg in recent years, a whole series of passages and courtyards with such shops have been built in the inner city, around the Gänsemarkt and the big stores on the main shopping street, the Mönckebergstrasse, have now lost so much trade to them that they too are busy converting to a 'small' image. None of this has much to do with co-operatives, of course, still less with the alternative scene. But it does show that the consumer revolt against bigness is very widespread, and this may well benefit the alternative co-operatives as well. The kind of products they deal in, if not the way they are organized, will probably spread beyond the alternative scene too. All these developments mean more choice for the consumer, and if they bring about a wider availability of safe and pollutant-free foodstuffs and natural products, that is another reason to welcome them as well. The advent of high technology could further the decentralization of retailing. Conditions for the small co-operative today, whether retail or productive, are probably in their way a good deal more promising than they were a century or so ago. There is every reason, therefore, for a revival and critical examination of Germany's co-operative tradition, and for this reason if no other, Eisenberg's book is a welcome addition to the literature.

NOTES

1 Christiane Eisenberg, *Frühe Arbeiterbewegung und Genossenschaften. Theorie und Praxis der Produktivgenossenschaften in der deutschen Sozialdemokratie und den Gewerkschaften der 1860er/1870er Jahre.* (Bonn-Bad Godesberg, 1985).

2 Older standard works include Erwin Hasselmann, *Geschichte der deutschen Komsumgenosenschaften* (Frankfurt, 1977), and Helmut Faust, *Geschichte der Genossenschaftsbewegung. Ursprung und Aufbruch der Genossenschaftsbewegung in England, Frankreich und Deutschland, sowie ihre weitere Entwicklung im deutschen Sprachraum* (3rd edn, Frankfurt, 1977). Newer work is often locally based: see for example Gerhard Huck, 'Arbeiterkonsumverein und Verbraucherorganisation. Die Entwicklung der Konsumgenossenschaften im Ruhrgebiet 1860–1914', in Jürgen Reulecke and Wolfhard Weber (eds), *Fabrik-Familie-Feierabend* (Wuppertal, 1978), pp. 215–45. This literature is overwhelmingly concerned with consumer co-operatives.

3 See Nicholas Bullock and James Read, *The Movement for Housing Reform in Germany and France 1840–1914* (Cambridge, 1985).

4 See Werner Ahrens, *Das sozialistische Genossenschaftswesen in Hamburg 1890–1914. Ein Beitrag zur Sozialgeschichte der Arbeiterbewegung* (Hamburg, 1970).

9

THE FAILURE OF GERMAN LABOUR IN THE WEIMAR REPUBLIC

I

In 1918 the abdication of the Kaiser and the fall of the German Empire created by Bismarck brought to power the one political and social organization that had remained outside the mainstream of Imperial German politics from the very beginning: the labour movement. Marxist in orientation, democratic in politics, the labour movement was still in 1918 formally committed to the overthrow of the capitalist social order and its replacement by a proletarian state. But in practice it had long since reconciled itself to using the methods of parliamentary democracy to achieve these ends. Fearful of the Bolshevik Revolution in Russia moving further westwards and engulfing them as it had done their moderate Menshevik counterparts in 1917, the German Social Democrats who took control in November 1918 put the restoration and maintenance of order above everything else. Determined to press forward to the election of a Constituent Assembly (which eventually met in Weimar in 1919), they did a deal with the army to ensure the peaceful demobilization of the troops from their battle stations in the East and West, and employed heavily armed gangs of ex-soldiers known as the *Freikorps* in order to put down revolutionary uprisings by Communists in Berlin, Munich and elsewhere early in 1919. A year later, in 1920, these same *Freikorps* were staging a *coup* in Berlin, with the partial backing of the army, aimed at restoring the monarchy and its authoritarian institutions to power. Right-wing thugs associated with them were responsible for a wave of assassinations, including those of the liberal Foreign Minister Walther Rathenau, the Catholic politician Matthias Erzberger and the left-wing socialist leader Hugo Haase, as well as the brutal murder of leading Communists Karl Liebknecht and Rosa Luxemburg in 1919. It was the overheated atmosphere of far-right plots and conspiracies which they fostered in the early 1920s, above all in Bavaria, that encouraged the emergence of Adolf Hitler as a serious political figure.

At the same time as compromising with the military forces of the right in this way, the Social Democrats exhibited a persistent reluctance to join with the political parties of the right in the creation of a stable political coalition that could steer the Republic's destinies through the troubles and turmoils of the 1920s. Unused to the experience of government, the Social Democrats found it difficult to make the necessary compromises with 'bourgeois' politicians. Partly as a result of this, Weimar cabinets were notoriously short-lived, and frequently foundered on the inability of their constituent parties to agree on policy. Thus on the one hand the Social Democrats were too willing to collaborate with the forces of the right, on the other hand they were not willing enough.

This paradox lies at the heart of Heinrich August Winkler's massive three-volume history of the labour movement and the working class in the Weimar Republic, published in the mid-1980s.[1] The moment for such a history was certainly right. Since the 1960s there had been an immense outpouring of detailed research in this area as historians began to exploit the vast riches of the German archives – above all, police surveillance reports – for the history of the labour movement. In the case of the Revolution of 1918–19 and the Weimar Republic there were also massive editions of source material. The ascendancy of the Social Democrats in the Brandt and Schmidt governments of the years 1969–82 was accompanied by a vast wave of scholarly publication on labour history and culminated in the project of an eight-volume history, published by the Social Democratic Dietz Verlag in Bonn, ending in the three volumes by Winkler on the Weimar Republic.

Winkler makes full use of all the detailed research done since the 1960s, producing as a result a vast work covering some 2,700 pages in all. The books are beautifully produced, clearly and accurately printed and stoutly bound, with footnotes at the bottom of the page, and for once a German publisher has actually gone to the trouble of providing a usable index. Despite its great length, Winkler's volumes, for the most part, read very easily, with plenty of well-turned phrases and memorable quotations. The author has a complete command over the literature, and his ability to structure his material in such a way as to sustain the reader's interest is very impressive. This is history on the grand scale, executed with consummate skill and learning.

Winkler defines his subject as 'that part of the German labour force whose political behaviour allows one to conclude that it felt itself to be the "working class" in the sense intended by Marx' (p. 9). He thus excludes consideration of liberal and Christian trade unionists and concentrates mainly on the socialist political parties, that is, the Social Democrats; the short-lived Independent Social Democrats, created by a split over the war issue in 1916/17 and effectively destroyed by the defection of most of their supporters to the Communists in 1922; and finally the Communists themselves. There is also some treatment of the 'free' trade unions, by this time loosely allied to the Social Democrats, and of smaller syndicalist organizations. This immediately presents some problems, as the fracturing of the labour movement's unity in the First World War obliges Winkler to construct the book not around a single narrative but around several parallel narratives dealing separately with the Social Democrats, the Independents, the Communists, and the trade unions. Inevitably, this introduces a certain amount of confusion, as the same events are discussed from different angles in different sections or alluded to in one section before they are fully recounted in another. More seriously, one is left wondering at the end whether the separate development of these different organizations allows one to speak of a general labour movement at all after 1918, especially since Winkler goes out of his way to emphasize the power of Moscow over the Communists, who thus appear primarily as a political force directed from outside. The rather 'top-down' approach of the book makes it difficult to constitute the labour movement as a single object of study.

Winkler approaches his subject from what one might call a moderate reformist point of view. His obvious efforts to be balanced and fair-minded, and the care with which he outlines and discusses rival interpretations of the very controversial events he is describing, are models of how this kind of synthesis should be done. Yet his overall thesis appears to rest on a contradiction. On the one hand, he argues that the central issue on which labour movement politics in this period have to be judged is the degree to which they helped keep the Republic going in the face of those who were determined to overthrow it, and whose efforts eventually met with success in 1933. Correspondingly, Winkler is consistently critical of the Social Democrats for their lack of willingness to compromise with other parties sufficiently to keep coalition governments in office. He takes them to task for not pushing through a more strongly parliamentary constitution in 1919, leaving the office of President with powers which were to be used to destroy the Republic little more than a decade later. He makes clear his strong disapproval of the Social Democrats' inability to distance themselves from the right-wing view that Germany bore little or no responsibility for the outbreak of the First World War in August 1914, and that therefore the Treaty of Versailles was an utterly unjust settlement imposed on an innocent but defeated nation by the grasping and unscrupulous victor powers. Finally, he repeats at a number of points his view that the party needed to rid itself of the 'ideological ballast' of Marxism and the doctrine of the class struggle at the earliest possible opportunity; in his view, its failure to do so was a major factor in inhibiting it from fully supporting the 'bourgeois' Weimar Republic and its institutions.

On the other hand, Winkler also criticizes the Social Democrats' failure to curb the power of the military, to push through a limited socialization programme (above all, the take-over of the mining industry by the state), and to find an alternative to the removal by Presidential decree and by force of the legally constituted ultra-left state government in Saxony in 1923, a step which provided a fatal precedent for the similar removal of the legally constituted Social Democratic government in Prussia by the far-right Reich Chancellor Franz von Papen nine years later. The failure to extend state ownership over significant parts of industry and the brusque and barely legal dismissal of the Saxon government alienated large sections of the working class from the Social Democrats and led to heavy electoral losses. A large part of the bitterness which so deeply divided Communists and Social Democrats in the Republic's final years, one may add, was also due to the latter's employment of the brutal 'Free Corps' in the suppression of revolutionary uprisings at the beginning of the Republic; many left-wing workers made the Social Democrats and leading figures among them, such as Gustav Noske, responsible for the deaths of Rosa Luxemburg and Karl Liebknecht and the slaughter of workers in the 'white terror' of 1919 in Munich.

Yet in the circumstances of the time, it was precisely the Social Democrats' shedding of so much of their 'ideological ballast' of the pre-war years that led to these latter problems in the first place. If they had remained more firmly Marxist, more clearly wedded to the doctrine of class struggle which Winkler so abhors, they would have been much more inclined to socialise industry and to tolerate the Saxon radicals. At one point Winkler argues that the only way to have avoided giving a free hand to the army and the Free Corps in the early years of the Republic, with all the disastrous consequences this implied for the viability and stability of Weimar democracy, was for the Social Democrats to have created an armed people's militia. But he then goes on later in the book to damn the creation of just such a militia – the 'Red Army' mobilized against the Kapp *putsch* in the Ruhr in 1920 – as leading to 'extortion, destruction, murder and anarchy'. Thus Winkler's judgements of the labour movement, and particularly the Social Democrats, in this period are riven with contradictions.

The reason for this is ultimately Winkler's excessively teleological model of German history: early twentieth-century Germany, he argues, was an industrialized society, and therefore it should have had a parliamentary, democratic political system with broadly based, undogmatic political parties collaborating in coalition governments, just as it did from the 1950s onwards: Weimar should have been Bonn, in other words. This kind of approach, unfortunately, does not get us very far towards understanding the reasons why the Social Democrats of the years 1918–24 made the choices they did. In the circumstances of the time, the chances of Weimar becoming Bonn were, in truth, negligible. Reformism and distrust of Marxist ideology on the one hand went inevitably together with fear of Bolshevism and social unrest and a tendency to trust the traditional forces of order to overcome it rather than to put arms in the hands of possibly radical and therefore unreliable workers on the other.

The most rational policy for the labour movement in this situation was surely to try to restore the political unity of the working class, shattered by the war, rather than to sacrifice everything in an attempt to shore up the shaky edifice of Weimar constitutionalism at the price of losing millions of the Social Democrats' traditional supporters. It is in the end neither analytically useful not historically realistic to base the argument of an entire book such as this on the demand that the German labour movement of the 1920s should have behaved like the West German Social Democrats of the 1970s.

II

In the first volume of his trilogy (1984), Heinrich August Winkler usefully reminds the reader constantly of the social and economic background to the turbulent political events of the years 1918–24. He includes, for example, an extensive discussion of the effects of the monetary inflation of these years on working-class living standards. And on a number of occasions he provides a useful analysis of the social basis of the electoral and organizational support of the political parties on whose fortunes he concentrates. However, the really detailed analysis of the inner structure, consciousness and culture of the German working class in the 1920s is saved for the opening section of the second volume, *Der Schein der Normalität* ('The Semblance of Normality') (1985).

Here Winkler combines a useful analysis of the official occupational census of 1925 with an effective synthesis of the relevant secondary literature. The census revealed the labour movement's demographic optimism of pre-war days to be illusory. Before 1914, the Social Democrats had believed that capitalism was inexorably dividing German society into two social classes, the bourgeoisie and the proletariat. The class that constituted the overwhelming majority of their own supporters, the proletariat, would continue to grow in numbers until it formed the majority of the German population, at which point it would be in a position to bring the Social Democratic Party to power because it would numerically outnumber all other parties put together at the polls. But the 1925 census showed that manual labour had in fact passed its numerical peak and was already declining relative to the emerging service sector. To be sure, as Marxism predicted, workers were being concentrated into larger units of production, and industrial cartels on the other hand were growing in size and power. Real wages, apart from the disastrous months of hyperinflation in 1923, were also rising, though (argues Winkler, taking issue here with the economic historian Knut Borchardt, who has made 'excessive' real wages partly responsible for the alienation of big industry from the Weimar Republic), compared both to other countries and to pre-war levels, they were still by no means particularly high. Moreover, hours and conditions of work did not deteriorate as severely in the mid-1920s as much of the literature on the industrial rationalization of these years has claimed. The worker's lot in the Weimar Republic, therefore was in Winkler's view a moderately happy one.

Yet all in all, the data he presents make the weakness of labour's position in the Weimar era painfully clear; rationalization in particular weakened labour's bargaining position, and the growing diversity of the social composition and material interests of the workforce made it more difficult for workers to act in concert. It is a pity, perhaps, that Winkler concentrates so much on describing the social structures of the wage-labour sector and that he does not spell out more explicitly the political implications of the evidence he synthesizes with such mastery. Still, he goes on to give a superb account of workers' culture and to show that it was undermined, or by-passed, by the growth of the mass communications media. Radio and cinema in particular brought entertainment with which male-voice choirs, circulation libraries, cycling clubs and pigeon-fancying associations simply could not compete. Winkler describes the common values and customs shared by the cultural organizations, and the membership, of both the Social Democrats and the Communists, but he portrays the split between the cultural and leisure organizations of the two parties as an artificial import from the political world. He thus neglects the opportunity to explore the internal origins of the fatal split in the sociocultural institutions of the left, in the gulf between the employed and the unemployed, in the growing generation gap between young workers and old, and in the cultural memories of the events of 1918–20. Moreover, in view of the role that violence and crime played in the final years of the Republic, Winkler's account of working-class deviance is disappointingly brief and weak, perhaps because this might be interpreted as revealing an 'ugly' side of proletarian culture and values that would run counter to the generally positive and upbeat picture painted in this book.

After this lengthy opening analysis of the social and cultural situation of the working class, Winkler launches into a detailed narrative of party-political developments, elections, and cabinet politics between 1924 and 1928. His major thesis, as in the first volume of his trilogy, is that the Weimar Republic would have stood a better chance of surviving had the Social Democratic Party been more willing to compromise with other political groups and take on more governmental responsibility than it did. This view informs virtually every aspect of his analysis of the ins-and-outs of party-political negotiations and manoeuvrings in these middle years of the Republic's history, years when the Social Democrats, in Winkler's view, left far too much of the business of governing the country and stabilizing Weimar democracy to others less well equipped and more reluctant to do it than themselves. In 1928, however, the party finally took the plunge and formed the Grand Coalition government under the Social Democratic Reich Chancellor Hermann Müller. The fortunes of his ministry form the subject of the third and final part of Winkler's second volume.

Winkler is surely right to regard the Grand Coalition as Weimar's last chance: after its fall in 1930, Germany, under the anti-democratic Chancellorships of Brüning, Schleicher and Papen, was ruled by emergency decree and democracy was effectively dead. Yet the lesson Winkler draws from this – that the Social Democrats should have kept the coalition going at any price – ignores the problem of whether the mass of the party's supporters, whose interests would have been to a large extent sacrificed had this course been taken, would have remained loyal. The party had minimal room for manoeuvre in a situation where businesses were collapsing in their hundreds and industrial workers being thrown out of their jobs in their millions under the impact of the Depression following the American stock-market crash of 1929. Winkler's claim that a supposedly flexible and mature attitude like that of the Labour Party in Britain would have overcome these problems was certainly not borne out by Labour's fate in 1931, when its leader Ramsay Macdonald's entry into a broad coalition government led to a major split in the party and the defection of the majority of its most active members, destroying its power for more than a decade.

Interwoven with this narrative of Social Democratic politicking in Winkler's second volume is a detailed account of the Bolshevization and then Stalinization of the Communist Party, ending in its adherence to the thesis that the Social Democrats were 'social fascists' who posed a greater threat even than the Nazis did because they were dedicated to winning over workers to the support of allegedly 'bourgeois' and therefore 'objectively' 'fascist' political projects, such as the maintenance of the Weimar Republic. Winkler's grasp of recent literature on this subject is impressive, but his unremitting hostility to the Communists leads to a complete failure of historical imagination when it comes to explaining why the Communists took this course, why so many millions of workers supported them, or, indeed, why they enjoyed such sympathy among Weimar's left-wing intellectuals. Winkler virtually ascribes the successful transition of the Communists from an insurrectionary elite group in the early 1920s to a disciplined mass formation by the end of the decade to the manipulative genius of Stalin, aided and abetted by the limited intelligence and abilities of the German Communist leader Ernst Thälmann. Yet attributing the size of the Communist electorate in the late Republic to a protest vote by the unemployed or to the radicalizing effects of the war on younger German workers does not really explain how such a disastrous policy as the 'social fascism' thesis could have had such a wide appeal.

The popularity of the Communist Party surely reflected the place of Russia in the mythology of the left in this period. As far as intellectuals were concerned, it was a centre of massive artistic creativity and experimentation. For the workers, it was the one example of a successful social revolution, the world's only proletarian state. But the Communists' appeal was due to negative factors as well as positive ones. Explaining the mass support of the

Communists inevitably involves exploring some of the weaknesses and inadequacies of the Social Democrats, an enterprise in which Winkler is all too reluctant to engage. At almost every point, *parti pris* for the Social Democrats infuses the analysis. Thus while he concedes that the Social Democratic police chief in Berlin, Karl Zörgiebel, made a foolish decision in banning Communist demonstrations in the capital on May Day 1929, when over thirty demonstrators were killed by the police, Winkler concentrates in his account of the incident on the ways in which the Communists exploited the disturbances for propaganda purposes, more or less ignoring in the process the inadequacies the affair revealed in the Social Democrats' attitude to the forces of law and order which were supposedly under their control. Many incidents of this sort, from 1919 onwards, turned left-inclined workers against the Social Democrats; had the latter's dealings with police, Free Corps and army been more robust, such alienation might not have occurred.

III

The third volume of Winkler's trilogy, *Der Weg in die Katastrophe* ('The Road to Catastrophe') (1987), opens with a 100-page survey of unemployment, the problem that did so much to shape working-class experience in the years 1930–3. Mass joblessness led to political apathy among workers. It deepened divisions between the employed, who tended to stick with the Social Democrats, and the unemployed, who gravitated towards the Communists. And it robbed the unions of the political instruments, such as the general strike, with which to defeat assaults on democracy, as they had done with the Kapp *putsch* in 1920, for even if millions could be persuaded to lay down their tools, millions more were waiting in the wings ready to pick them up again regardless of the political consequences. The impotence of the labour movement was compounded, as Winkler already noted in the second volume of his survey, by the spread of mass culture. This, Winkler argues, was an indicator not so much of *embourgeoisement*, as contemporary sociologists maintained, as of 'deproletarianization'. It undermined the class consciousness that bound workers to socialism and laid them open to the blandishments of populist demagogues like Hitler.

Against this backdrop of mass unemployment and the decay of labour movement institutions and traditions, Winkler then brings forward a political narrative which occupies the greater part of the book. The central problem of these final years of the ill-fated Republic was in his view the Social Democrats' toleration of the governments that succeeded the Grand Coalition of 1928–30. Had they been determined to vote against ratifying Chancellor Brüning's emergency decrees, on which the signature of the aged President Hindenburg had to be approved by the Reichstag if their legal effect was not to be nullified, they could have brought the business of government to a stop, with who knows what effect. But they did not do so, and swallowed in the process a series of increasingly undemocratic policies, along with economic measures that arguably worsened the situation of the workers through their strongly deflationary effects. Such a policy might have been justifiable as the price the party paid for keeping Brüning from interfering with its control over the powerful state government of Prussia. But it was hardly justifiable once Brüning left the Chancellorship in the Spring of 1932, to be succeeded by the arch-reactionary Franz von Papen, a man who quite obviously intended to get rid of the Prussian Social Democratic cabinet in order to pave the way for an authoritarian regime of his own.

Winkler describes in some detail the Social Democrats' pathetic decision to back Field Marshal von Hindenburg, a man who was not only a dyed-in-the-wool monarchist but also so senile that he was clearly open to manipulation from the far right, for President in the elections of 1932. Their choice was theoretically justifiable on the grounds that he was the only man who could prevent the election of Adolf Hitler to the job. But Hindenburg was endorsed with such enthusiasm by the Social Democratic Minister-President of Prussia, Otto Braun, in terms of such ringing enthusiasm, that one is left with no very favourable impression of the party's sense of political realism at this stage of the Republic's decay. When Braun's government was illegally removed at Papen's behest in what was in effect a military *coup d'état* in July 1932, the possibilities of successful resistance, whether by legal action, general strike, or armed struggle, were, Winkler argues, very limited. Legal action was indeed commenced, but it dragged on for many months, and in the circumstances in any case would have had little practical effect on the realities of power. A general strike was out of the question. And an armed uprising would have stood no chance against the well-armed and well-organized Reichswehr which was the main instrument of Papen's *coup*. The example of the Austrian socialists, who were far better equipped for an armed struggle than their German counterparts, was instructive: in February 1934, when they attempted to resist a right-wing *coup* by force, they were overwhelmed in a few days by the Austrian army, which was far less impressive as a military organization than the German *Reichswehr* was.

Even so, Winkler concedes, the Social Democrats did so little to prepare for the Papen *coup*, despite knowing about it weeks in advance, that their removal from office was 'more a farce than a tragedy' (p. 679). Still worse was to come in early 1933 when the trade unions detached themselves from the Social Democrats and vainly tried to save themselves by collaborating with Hitler after he came to power as Reich Chancellor. In the Reichstag, the Social Democratic deputies covered themselves in shame, however defensible their motives, by voting for the Hitler government's mendacious disarmament declaration on 17 May. Only Otto Wels's moving final speech in the chamber in March, reaffirming democratic values in the face of the Nazi onslaught, provided a glimmer of light in the enveloping gloom. As for the Communists, Winkler makes clear once more his view that their policy of outright hostility to the Social Democrats contributed significantly to the Republic's downfall. Their view was that the Republic was a 'bourgeois' state which was not worth saving; after its collapse, Nazi rule would be no more than a brief interlude, opening the way to a proletarian revolution which would usher in a new, Communist, state. Even had the Communists not fallen prey to these fantasies, even had they been prepared to compromise sufficiently with the Social Democrats to join forces with them instead of insisting on unity on such terms that would have amounted to a take-over, it is still difficult to see how an effective resistance to the Nazi seizure of power could have been organized. The disunity of the labour movement was politically disastrous indeed, but it would have taken much more than labour movement unity to stop Hitler in 1933.

Winkler tells this miserable story with the same stylistic clarity, intellectual openness and scholarly thoroughness which distinguished the first two volumes of his trilogy. Yet the work's faults weigh particularly heavy in the final volume. Once more, Winkler subordinates everything to the question of how the Social Democrats could have saved Weimar, so that he allots far too much space to a minutely detailed narrative of their increasingly pointless politicking in Berlin. As their actions became progressively more irrelevant to the real course of events, which was determined to an ever greater extent in the President's and Chancellor's offices, in the Nazi party headquarters, and on the streets of Germany's towns and cities, so Winkler devotes more and more space to analysing theoretical newspaper and magazine articles by Social Democratic intellectuals who were merely observing events from a distance without having any discernible impact on them at all. Quite why he considers them so important is therefore something of a mystery.

Moreover, the individual actors in the drama never acquire any real human identity in the book; they remain just names, with the single exception of Hermann Müller, the real hero of the trilogy, who is the subject of an uncharacteristically emotional obituary from Winkler's pen (pp. 295–7). New figures constantly appear in the party leadership without the reader learning who they were, how they got there, or what were their relations with one another. In what is for very long stretches a political narrative of the most traditional kind, the lack of a human dimension, so characteristic of the writings of the generation of structural historians to which Winkler belongs, becomes a real disadvantage and detracts seriously from the book's otherwise outstanding readability. In all these volumes, the author's great strengths are his ability to portray complex issues and events clearly, his skill in synthesizing a vast and diverse literature, and his calm, unpolemical handling of the difficult and often acrimonious scholarly disputes which surround almost every topic he deals with. On the other hand, the material is sometimes not very well integrated, and particularly in the second volume it is so disparate that the reader gets the impression of a collection of essays on subjects whose relation to one another is never made really clear.

Winkler's trilogy covers a vast range of subjects, from the role of women and young people in the labour movement to the policies of the employers and the tactics of strike leaders in industrial disputes. Yet, especially in the final volume, Winkler's concentration on the Reichstag and government means an unfortunate neglect of many other aspects of labour movement history, from the performance and policies of Social Democratic administrations at every level – from the Prussian government down to the municipalities – to the party's attitude to issues such as policing and judicial reform. Winkler is even less informative about Communist policies than he is about Social Democratic. He has little to say about the theoretical debates which raged among German Communists in the 1920s, and he neglects both Communist and Social Democratic party organization, the party press, and many other subjects. Ultimately, too, his concern to defend the Social Democrats' actions in the revolution of 1918–19 undermines his attempt to explain their failures and compromises in the crisis of 1930–3.

These volumes cannot be regarded as the definitive text on the social history of the working class, which occupies only about 15 per cent of the work as a whole. The final volume is particularly sketchy and unsatisfactory in this respect, with much of the space on the working class being taken up with an account of unemployment in Austria and a discussion of various theoretical writings by contemporary German sociologists. As far as the main focus of the volumes is concerned – the political history of the labour movement and its two main political parties, the Communists and the Social Democrats – it has to be questioned whether the perspective of modern Social Democracy in the era of Willy Brandt, Helmut Schmidt and their successors is really the most helpful one to adopt in assessing the actions of their predecessors in the totally different context of the 1920s. Historians are of course perfectly at liberty to speculate about what might have happened in the past had things been rather different from what they turned out to be. But their main task, surely, is to understand and explain what actually did happen. Wishful thinking led by present-day political beliefs does not, in the end, get us very far.

NOTES

1 Heinrich August Winkler, *Von der Revolution zur Stabilisierung: Arbeiter und Arbeiterbewegung in der Weimarer Republik, 1918 bis 1924* (Berlin, 1984); idem, *Der Schein der Normalität: Arbeiter und Arbeiterbewegung in der Weimarer Republik 1924 bis 1930,* (Berlin, 1985); idem, *Der Weg in die Katastrophe: Arbeiter und Arbeiterbewegung in der Weimarer Republik 1930 bis 1933* (Berlin, 1987).

Part III

IDEOLOGICAL ORIGINS OF NAZISM

In Part III, we turn to the vexed questions of where the Nazis got their ideas from and how far these ideas were generally acceptable in German society and among German elites. From the late 1960s to the late 1980s, it is fair to say, the intellectual history of Nazism was a rather neglected subject. A long tradition of tracing back a variety of National Socialist ideas to great thinkers of the German past, from Novalis to Nietzsche, had fallen into disrepute as a result of contextualized studies of these thinkers which had revealed the many different readings to which their work had been subjected. Nietzsche, for instance, as the late Richard Hinton Thomas showed, was widely regarded in Wilhelmine Germany as a liberal, even a left-wing thinker whose message was fundamentally one of human liberation and personal autonomy. Under the influence of Marxism and social history, research turned instead to detailed, often quantitative investigations of the class basis of Nazism and its antecedents in the discontents of the petty bourgeoisie, expressed in organizations such as the Anti-Semitic Parties, the Fatherland Party, and pressure-groups of the lower middle classes.

By the end of the 1980s, however, attention was turning back to ideas. This was partly because the social theory of Nazism had seemed to have reached the limits of its explanatory power, and partly because of the emergence, in however diluted a form, of postmodernist approaches to history, from psychoanalysis to discourse theory, which focused more on what people were saying than on what they were doing. But it also reflected a broader shift in the way that historians understood the whole phenomenon of the Third Reich. The rediscovery of the 'forgotten victims of Nazism', from gypsies and the 'antisocial' to the mentally and physically handicapped who were first sterilized and then exterminated in the so-called 'euthanasia' programme launched at the beginning of the Second World War, moved racism, eugenics and Social Darwinism into the centre of the picture, displacing class analysis, proletarian resistance and elite collaboration, all subjects which had dominated research during the

1970s, into the margins. The roots of Nazi violence towards disadvantaged minorities became a vital new topic of research.

One of the first serious works to explore this topic was Klaus Theweleit's *Male Fantasies*, discussed in Chapter 10. Theweleit's extraordinary book, published in the late 1970s and reissued in an English translation in the late 1980s, presaged the new wave of writing about the Third Reich in several important ways, from its use of gender analysis and theories of sexuality to its concentration on close readings of literary texts. The 'Free Corps' organizations formed at the end of the First World War to combat revolution within Germany and defend German claims on territory outside the shrunken borders of the Weimar Republic quickly became notorious for the insensate violence and brutality they showed towards their opponents. Theweleit's analysis owes much to the sexual-political theories of the Freudian revolutionary Wilhelm Reich, whose work became widely influential during the student movement of the late 1960s and early 1970s. It shows both the power and the limitations of the psychoanalytical approaches to history which have become such a significant part of the turn to postmodernism in the 1990s. More particularly, by placing gender, the relations between men and women, and the categorization of women in the 'male fantasies' of the book's title, at the centre of his analysis, Theweleit presaged much of the feminist work which has had such an influence on our understanding of the Third Reich in recent years.

If the violence of the Free Corps was largely uncontrolled and often 'spontaneous', then that of the Third Reich, at least after the initial 'seizure of power' during the first six months of 1933, was increasingly regulated and planned. At its heart was the doctrine of Social Darwinism. Ever since the 1960s, historians have sought to delineate the contours of this theory and trace the links between the Darwinian ideas of the nineteenth century and the murderous racialism and aggression of the Nazi regime in the twentieth. But this task has proved extraordinarily difficult to achieve. At the heart of the problem is the issue of teleology. Chapter 13 began as a commentary on a paper attacking a supposed dominance of teleological approaches to this subject, presented at a conference on medical science in modern Germany, held in Washington in 1993. But on surveying the development of controversy and interpretation in the history of German Social Darwinism over the last three decades, it soon became apparent that attacks of this kind were largely misplaced. Chapter 11 argues that much of the disagreement which has existed between historians rests on a confusion between the search for origins and the postulate of inevitability. Just because we can identify some ideas current at the turn of the century which were subsequently to be taken up by the Nazis does not mean that those ideas were necessarily 'Nazi' in themselves, or that they would inevitably lead to the kind of murderous eugenic selectionism practised by the Third Reich.

That selectionism was carried out in particular with the advice and collaboration of medical scientists, and Chapter 12, originally written for a special science number of the book review section of *The Times Higher Education Supplement*, takes a close look at the scientific theories which underlay the sterilization and 'euthanasia' campaigns. Here too, tracing the ideological origins of Nazi policy is a difficult task, and early scientific eugenicists have more of a claim to be regarded as left-wing democrats than as proto-Nazis. Nevertheless, lines of continuity can be drawn, and they became stronger as the discipline of 'racial hygiene' grew more influential. The rediscovery of racist traditions in German science has a particular resonance in the late 1980s and 1990s, too, for, as we shall see in Part V, racism has become one of the central issues in the post-reunification era.

In the final chapter in Part III, the focus is on the history of German antisemitism. In 1996 the publication of a best-selling book by the young American political scientist Daniel Jonah Goldhagen, called *Hitler's Willing Executioners*, roused a considerable storm on both sides of the Atlantic by arguing that the men who carried out the extermination of the Jews in the Third Reich did not do so because they were locked into a German tradition of obedience or because they were Nazi fanatics but because they were, like all other Germans, fanatical antisemites who not only enjoyed killing Jews but had been keen to do so for a long time. Goldhagen's indictment of German political culture in the nineteenth century for harbouring a deep-seated and pervasive eliminationist antisemitism was based on an explicit assertion that a similar factor was not present in any other country. At a time when some German commentators, in newspapers such as the *Frankfurter Allgemeine Zeitung*, were arguing for a post-reunification reassertion of national self-confidence, and suggesting that the traumas of the past could now be largely forgotten, this seemed to suggest that the rest of the world was determined to perpetuate the idea of German guilt for centuries to come.

Chapter 13 subjects Goldhagen's arguments and evidence to close scrutiny and argues that they are sweeping and unconvincing, especially when confronted with a mass of evidence for the virtual absence of antisemitism within the German labour movement, which Goldhagen's book totally ignores. It also discusses the reasons why the book has attracted such widespread attention – reasons which have as much to do with the current political situation in the countries where it has sold well (namely America, Germany, Britain and Israel), as with its general qualities of stark simplicity, black-and-white argument, emotional commitment, and powerful empirical detail. The horrors of the Nazi past, it argues, will not go away because they have now become a general, symbolic part of Western culture as well as of German political discourse.

10

THE DYNAMICS OF VIOLENCE

Since its appearance in Germany in 1977, Klaus Theweleit's psycho-analytical study of fascist literature[1] has graduated from the status of a cult work to that of a classic. Rereading it in English, a decade after my first, rather sceptical perusal, it is easy to see why. Much of what made Theweleit's book so startlingly original in the mid-1970s has since become relatively conventional in literary and historical studies, from the Foucauldian analysis of literary discourse, and the exploration of the political history of the human body, to a feminist perspective on sex and power. Yet in the intervening period, the book has not lost its capacity to shock and disturb. Much of its power comes from its author's unerring eye for the startling quotation. Consider this passage from a novel by Franz Schauwecker which was published in 1929.

> They lie next to each other. She lifts her arms and her dress slips off. Underneath it she is naked. Her nakedness assaults him with a sudden glowing shudder, a gust of wind across a placid lake. He says nothing, but with a jolt his breath rushes into his blood, filling it with pearls of pure, quivering bubbles, a gushing froth, just as the blood of men shot in the lungs leaves them lying yellow and silent like corpses, while the blood spurts endlessly, gurgling and seething at every breath – breath which they heave up, groaning, as if by a block and tackle, the air is so heavy and laden.

Sex and death are never very far apart in the literature that is the subject of Theweleit's analysis.

Theweleit is concerned not with the literature of the Nazi movement but with that of its much smaller military precursor, the *Freikorps* movement of the years between 1918 and 1923. The *Freikorps* were heavily armed bands of right-wing thugs, including many ex-soldiers, who were used by the Social Democratic-dominated governments of the early Weimar Republic to put down revolutionary uprisings such as those of the Spartacists in January 1919, the Communists in Munich later the same year, or the 'Red Army' in the Ruhr in the spring of 1920. Recently the *Freikorps* have had their defenders: some historians have suggested that they helped stabilize Weimar democracy in its formative phase, or that they were a basically legitimate means by which the German middle classes defended themselves against the Bolshevik threat. No one who reads this book, however, can come away without feeling that these men were pathological murderers who despised the values Weimar represented and hated the 'bourgeoisie' as decadent and corrupt.

For some of the authors of the two hundred-odd novels and memoirs discussed in this book, a continued state of warfare, lasting beyond 1918 and well into the 1920s, was the only way to exist. For others who had not fought in 1914–18, violence was also a psychological necessity. 'Blood, blood, blood must flow,' they sang, 'thick as a rain of blows.' An attack, wrote Ernst von Salomon, 'represented the ultimate, liberating intensification of energy; we longed for the confirmation it would bring of our sense that we were made for every possible destiny. In the attack, we expected to experience the true values of the world within us.' The world within them, according to Theweleit, was full of terrible tensions that sought a violent outlet. As children from traditionally strict bourgeois households, as graduates of brutally disciplinarian military academies, as soldiers in the rigidly hierarchical German army, they had been drilled to repress desire, and they could find release only in annihilating the symbols of desire they found in the world around them.

Hence the 'passionate rage' of the *Freikorps* soldiers as they murdered the women they found amongst their opponents. Erich Balla, for example, writing in 1932 about his adventures as part of a *Freikorps* operating in the Baltic area just after the end of the First World War, described how the troop found two Latvian women suspected of helping the Red Army murder some German soldiers: 'The dull thudding of clubs is heard. Both women lie dead on the floor of the room, their blood exactly the same colour as the roses blooming in extravagant profusion outside the window.' 'With their screams and filthy giggling,' wrote Kurt Eggers in his novel *Rebel Mountain* (1937), 'vulgar women excite men's urges. Let our revulsion flow into a single river of destruction. A destruction which will be incomplete if it does not also trample their hearts and souls.'

Such passages – and there are many more of them in *Male Fantasies* – show clearly enough the dialectic of repression and release that powered the *Freikorps* men's 'pleasure in destruction', as one writer called it, or, in another writer's rather different assessment, their 'cold and merciless will to destruction'. It was not fear that lay behind the brutal killing of Rosa Luxemburg and Karl Liebknecht or the assassination of leading republican politicians like Erzberger and Rathenau. It is Theweleit's achievement, which appears even more striking now than it did a decade or so ago, to have uncovered the more complex psychological roots of this blood-lust and aggression.

It is good news, therefore, that Theweleit's book has at last appeared in English. The translation reads fluently. But there are signs of carelessness. 'Lickspittles' appears as 'split-lickers', while *zärtlich* ('tender') is mistranslated as 'light', thus missing the sexual undertone. The legend on the phallic Zeppelin doesn't just say, 'Your health, brothers': it also, in a rare example of a German pun, says, 'Shove away, brothers!', as the observer whose eyes lighted upon the jolly waitress straddling the airship would immediately realize. Careless proofreading has caused ten lines of the text to be repeated in the Introduction to Volume II. A number of pictures included in the German edition have been omitted from the Anglo-American. Some of the pictures that actually are included are just as offensive as the ones omitted, so I can only think that, at least in some instances, legal reasons must have been involved.

The doubts and questions which were raised about Theweleit's analysis on its first publication have also been strengthened by the intervening period. In the first place, the question of what, or whom, he is actually writing about seems more vexed than ever. Theweleit's project began when the historian Erhard Lucas, then completing the third volume of his study of the 'Red Army' and the 'March revolution' in the Ruhr – in its own way a classic of committed historiography – asked him to analyse the large body of literature he had found relating to the revolution's suppression by those who put it down. But if Theweleit's subject is the writings of the *Freikorps*, why does he devote so much space to a novel like Goebbels's *Michael*, whose author was never in the *Freikorps*? On the other hand, if he is writing about the literature of fascism, why does he spend so much time on a writer like Ernst Jünger, who never was a Nazi? Come to think of it, why is he so obsessed by Martin Niemöller, who was not only not in the *Freikorps* but was also a leading figure in the German resistance – a fact to which Theweleit alludes at the beginning, but never satisfactorily explains?

The extent to which one can assume the *Freikorps* to have been 'fascist' remains in the end uncertain, especially in view of the fact that antisemitism plays a virtually negligible role in Theweleit's book. It may simply be the case that what Theweleit is describing is not a political phenomenon in the conventional sense at all: that his analysis may be equally applicable to soldiers, secret policemen and torturers of left-wing as well as right-wing views. Where Theweleit actually wants to extend his analysis is not to soldiers and policemen involved in the violent suppression of freedom, but to the bourgeois male. 'I don't', he writes, 'want to make any categorical distinction between the types of men who are the subject of this book and all other men. Our subjects are equivalent to the tip of the patriarchal iceberg.' Thus the violent contrast which his authors draw between their conventional, bourgeois wives, asexual, pure, anonymous, 'white', and the raging, shrieking, demonic, castrating 'red' whores whom they see on the side of their opponents, seems to Theweleit but a colourful exaggeration of the paler dichotomies common in the conventional perceptions of women by men in general. Elsewhere, Theweleit says that 'fascism is a current reality whenever we try to establish what kinds of reality present-day male–female relations produce'. All this makes it very difficult to isolate what exactly it was that turned a small minority of bourgeois men into *Freikorps* thugs, or even what made a rather larger number of them fascists.

Theweleit's tendency to expand the application of his analysis further and further, his broad, at times seemingly limitless concept of fascism, his claim that 'the pathway to a non-fascist life is marked out a little further by every act of love-making in which the participants touch neither as images nor as bearers of *names* defined by the social', his vision of desire as a politically liberating force – all these features of the book stamp it indelibly as a product of the student movement of the 1960s, in which indeed Theweleit himself was a moderately prominent activist. Viewed from the perspective of the 1990s, his argument appears politically utopian, and – given the work that has been done by Peter Gay and others on exposing the gulf that lay between the prim nostrums of Victorian moralists and the pulsating realities of the sexual culture they were trying to define – historically inadequate.

Moreover, the book's structure is as rambling and disorganized as ever. One can appreciate the fact that Theweleit is caught by his own argument that regimentation, order and discipline are fascist and repressive, so that instead of lining up those ideas and arguments in nice, neat rows and marching them out before the reader in an orderly fashion, he prefers to let them sprawl all over the place, come back again in a different guise, or wander off at a tangent. It doesn't make the book particularly easy to follow. Then there are those pictures – a couple of hundred of them at least, drawn from sources as varied as American adult comics, inter-war cinema, Modernist art, First World War posters and postcards, Nazi murals, nineteenth-century caricatures, and, of course, that wonderful source for the eroticization of political symbolism, the early twentieth-century illustrator 'Fidus'. Intended as a commentary, sometimes direct, sometimes oblique, on the text, these illustrations are as often as not a distraction from it. Yet they share with the text a propensity which one ought, perhaps, to see, in the end, as positive: both words and pictures, rather than compelling the reader to reach conclusions, are open-ended; they raise questions, suggest ideas, which go well beyond the subject of the book itself.

NOTES

1 Klaus Thewelheit, *Male Fantasies*. Vol. I: *Women, Floods, Bodies, History*, Vol. II: *Male Bodies: Psychoanalysing the White Terror*, translated by Chris Turner, Erica Carter and Stephen Conway (Cambridge, Polity, 1987/9).

11

IN SEARCH OF GERMAN SOCIAL DARWINISM

I

At a lunchtime meeting held on 20 August 1942 to mark the occasion of the appointment of Otto-Georg Thierack as Reich Justice Minister and Roland Freisler as President of the 'People's Court', Hitler launched into one of his characteristic monologues. The judicial system, he said, was soft. Criminals were being allowed to get away with far too much on the home front. Looting and petty crime were being punished with mere prison sentences instead of the death penalty. The result of this in the longer term would be disastrous:

> Every war leads to a negative selection. The positive elements die in masses. The choice of the most dangerous military service is already a selection: the really brave ones become airmen, or join the U-boats. And even in these services there is always the call: who wants to volunteer? And it's always the best men who then get killed. All this time, the absolute ne'er-do-well is cared for lovingly in body and spirit. Anyone who ever enters a prison knows with absolute certainty that nothing more is going to happen to him. If you can imagine this going on for another three or four years, then you can see a gradual shift in the balance of the nation taking place: an over-exploitation on the one side; absolute conservation on the other!

In order to re-establish the balance, Hitler declared, the 'negative' elements in the German population had to be killed in much larger numbers.[1] In the following months, Thierack and his officials redefined the role of penal policy. Punishment, he told German judges on 1 June 1943, 'in our time has to carry out the popular-hygienic task of continually cleansing the body of the race by the ruthless elimination of criminals unworthy of life'.[2] The judges did not demur. By the end of the war, more than 16,000 offenders, many of them guilty of extremely trivial misdemeanours, had been sentenced to death by Hitler's courts; untold thousands more had been handed over to the Gestapo for 'elimination', or transferred from Germany's prisons to the concentration camps of the SS for 'extermination through labour'.[3] By 1944, such a fate was reserved for all 'community aliens' who showed themselves unworthy of belonging to the German race by their immorality, laziness, or even 'frivolity', 'disorderliness while drunk', and 'irritability'.[4] After all, as Hitler had remarked on another occasion, 'apes trample outsiders to death as community aliens. And what holds good for apes, must hold good for humans to an even greater extent.'[5]

Hitler's espousal of a ruthless policy of negative eugenic selection – even more, perhaps, the analogy he drew between the natural world and human society, between apes and people – reflected deeply held views, and found an expression in other areas beside the judicial – most notoriously, perhaps, in his extermination of the mentally and physically handicapped and the chronically ill in Germany under the code-name of 'Action T4'.[6] Hitler, as is well known, believed that world history consisted of a struggle for survival between races. The Jewish race was plotting to undermine the German; 'inferior' groups such as the Slavs were also threatening the future of the Aryan 'master-race'; and degenerative tendencies within the German race itself had to be countered if disaster was not to ensue. His views on these subjects have often been called Social Darwinist. Yet historians have signally failed to agree on what Social Darwinism was, or on how it developed from its scientific beginnings in the nineteenth century into a central component of an ideology of mass murder and racial warfare in the twentieth. The debate about Social Darwinism and its relation to Nazism involves wider questions about the relationship of science and society, medicine and politics, about historical continuity, and about the problems and possibilities of tracing back Nazi ideology to its (real or imagined) nineteenth-century roots.

II

Ever since the early 1960s, Social Darwinism has played a central role in arguments among historians about the ideological origins of Nazism. Hans-Günter Zmarzlik was the first serious German historian to tackle a subject which had hitherto been dominated by propagandists, polemicists and philosophers.[7] Zmarzlik began his seminal article, published in 1963, by pointing out:

> Darwinism has been claimed as an authority for very different interpretations of social processes. Proponents of altruistic ethics have rested their case on it, but so too have the spokesmen of a brutally elitist morality; liberal-progressive thought has called on it for legitimation, but so too has crass historical fatalism. Pioneers of the theory of socialist egalitarianism have employed it, but so too have the authors of manifestos of racial inequality.[8]

Subsequent historians who have made Zmarzlik responsible for a teleological approach which reads back the whole of Nazi ideology into the configurations of Social Darwinism before the First World War are therefore wide of the mark.[9] From the very beginning, the modern historiography of Social Darwinism made its links with non-racist and progressive ideologies absolutely clear. Of course, Zmarzlik did not stop at establishing Social Darwinism's political diversity. He went on to argue that, subject to these reservations, the varieties of Social Darwinism could be roughly subsumed under two headings. First, there was evolutionary Social Darwinism, in which ideas of mutual aid were often as prominent as ideas of competition. Popular among liberals and on the left in the 1860s and 1870s, this variant began to be superseded in the 1890s by a second, stressing the struggle for the survival of the fittest. From about the turn of the century, racist and imperialist ideas entered the mixture as well, and some Social Darwinists began to think of racial and social engineering in the interests of the nation. This chronology, of course, was only approximate, and Zmarzlik was careful to point out that older, evolutionary forms of the ideology continued to be held, for example among the Social Democrats, well after the turn of the century. He also differentiated carefully between the Social Darwinism of racial anthropologists, racial hygienists and other scientific groups, many of whom, he said, made 'valuable contributions' to social and scientific theory and practice, and the vulgarization, popularization and political exploitation of Social Darwinism by imperialists and pan-Germans, who took up 'more or less isolated slogans, without applying the Darwinist explanation of nature to the interpretation of political–social processes in a consistent way'.[10] Hitler and others like him, he argued, only adopted vulgarized elements of 'certain Darwinisms', not the whole ideology, and the Nazis only purveyed a 'primitive version' of Social Darwinism.[11] And Zmarzlik warned against either making Social Darwinism responsible for the Nazi 'descent into barbarism' or confusing the Social Darwinist slogans adopted by Hitler with the social and political programmes of more thoroughgoing Social Darwinists, many of whom wanted their aims to be realized humanely and without violence or coercion.[12]

Zmarzlik's central points – the existence of different varieties of Social Darwinism, the supersession of liberal-leftist, evolutionary variants by rightist, selectionist variants from the 1890s, the vulgarized, sloganizing oversimplifications of the Nazis, and the dangers of drawing a straight line from Social Darwinism *per se* to Nazism – have been echoed by many subsequent writers on the subject. In 1974, for instance, Hans-Ulrich Wehler insisted in almost identical terms to those employed by Zmarzlik on 'the enormous, many-sided variety of Social Darwinism as a kind of kaleidoscope, which could be shaken into place according to purpose'.[13] In the 1860s and 1870s it helped form the ideology of the Social Democrats, and justified the competitive capitalism of early German industrialization. Later on, a 'vulgarized Social Darwinism' brought the concept of the 'struggle for existence' to the fore in political discourse, reducing it to warfare and violence in the process.[14] While Zmarzlik saw the shift in Social Darwinist ideology that occurred in the 1890s as a reflection of the wider political shift to the era of Wilhelmine *Weltpolitik*, however, Wehler added his own inimitable twist to the argument by suggesting that the adoption of a vulgarized, inegalitarian and selectionist version of the ideology reflected instead 'the so-called feudalization of the bourgeoisie, the influence of neo-aristocratic modes of behaviour, norms, values and aims in life' which made the German middle classes more receptive to such an interpretation than were their counterparts in the USA.[15] The influence of selectionist Social Darwinism in Germany could thus be seen as an aspect of Germany's 'special path' (*Sonderweg*) to modernity, reflecting the historic weakness of the German bourgeoisie. This was not a particularly plausible argument; it lacked any credible evidence to back it up, and it rested on a series of assumptions about the dominance of aristocratic values and the 'bourgeois' nature of egalitarianism in the late nineteenth century that have not been confirmed by subsequent research.[16] Nevertheless, Wehler was persuasive when, like Zmarzlik, he stressed the many-faceted nature of Social Darwinism, and emphasized the shift in the dominant Darwinian discourse from evolutionism to selectionism in the 1890s. Another member of the 'Bielefeld school', Hans-Walter Schmuhl, has also followed Zmarzlik in pointing out that

> Social Darwinism allowed its name to be lent to very diverse interpretations of social processes, according to which aspect of the Darwinist theory of evolution and selection was placed at the centre of Social Darwinist doctrine. Both Social Democrats and 'social aristocrats' claimed the authority of Darwinism, as did both adherents of *laissez-faire* liberalism and champions of the modern interventionist state, protagonists of altruistic ethics on the basis of 'social instincts' and apologists for a 'morality of the master race' which emphasized the right of the stronger, as did both militarists and pacifists.[17]

Schmuhl supported the consensus view, and concurred with other historians that Social Darwinism had undergone a rightward shift in the 1890s.[18] However, Schmuhl's view, typical for the Bielefeld school, that Social Darwinism on the whole served the interests of 'system-stabilization' after the turn of the century, is not only unsupported by evidence, but demonstrably wrong.[19] In so far as Social Darwinist views were held by radical groups of right and left in Wilhelmine Germany, it seems clear enough that they operated against the stability of the political system rather than in its favour.[20]

Writing not about Social Darwinism in general but rather about the ideological origins of Nazism, Michael Burleigh and Wolfgang Wippermann also insisted that 'Social Darwinism was not an exclusively right-wing concern . . . Social Darwinians . . . could be conservative, liberal, socialist, or fascist'[21] (1991). In their delineation of the prehistory of Nazi racism, they were careful to distinguish between the 'collectivist and state interventionist variety' of Social Darwinism which eventually triumphed in Germany, and other varieties, and to delimit all of the variants of Social Darwinism from 'racial anti-semitic theories'.[22] Similarly, although the medical historian Gerhard Baader's rather simple-minded Marxism made him want to deny the label 'Social Darwinist' to what he admitted was the labour movement's espousal of a Darwinian 'theory of descent', he too devoted some space to outlining the liberal, *laissez-faire* and especially anticlerical affiliations of Social Darwinism in the 1860s and also in the 1870s, the time of the *Kulturkampf*. He followed existing orthodoxy in pointing to a change of direction by Social Darwinism in the 1890s, although the new, selectionist Social Darwinists, he cautioned, were, initially at least, 'nationalistic writers, who used Darwinist concepts like the struggle for existence to embellish their arguments'.[23] Baader's article (1980), though rather brief and in some ways not very satisfactory, does not present a monolithic view of Social Darwinism as leading to Nazism, but on the contrary, points up its varieties – laissez-faire and nationalist, moderate and extreme, scientific and vulgar – in what had by the time he wrote it become a thoroughly orthodox manner.

Not only did historians after Zmarzlik customarily emphasize the diversity of Social Darwinism, they were also well aware of its role, and the wider role of biological ideas, in informing movements of sexual liberation on the left. Writing about the feminist movement in Wilhelmine Germany in 1976, I commented for example that Helene Stöcker's League for the Protection of Motherhood

> attempted to ally liberalism, Social Darwinism and Nietzscheanism into a new social ideology that would preserve the most libertarian and individualist elements in all three creeds and translate them into the practical demand that the individual woman should be allowed to dispose over her own body without interference from the state.[24]

Correspondingly the League rejected the more authoritarian variants of Social Darwinism, despite their growing influence in public discourse, in the first years of its existence. While, as I wrote, 'all the *Mutterschutz* enthusiasts believed to some extent in some form of racial hygiene',[25] the pacifist views of the majority made them reject the argument that racial hygiene should be administered by the state using a form of legal compulsion. The feminist Maria Lischnewska, for example, 'whose strong nationalism distinguished her from the bulk of the leading radical feminists and gave her Social Darwinist views a strongly authoritarian tint',[26] had little influence at this time. The League's failure to persuade the mainstream feminist movement to adopt its radical policies in 1908 led to a serious crisis in its affairs, and many of its leading members resigned. This opened the way to the triumph in both the League and the feminist movement as a whole of a more right-wing variant of Social Darwinism, in which racial hygiene was administered by the state against 'degenerate' elements in the population, in order to 'improve' the German race in the struggle for survival against the Latins and the Slavs.[27] Such views, I was careful to emphasize, were only one variant of Social Darwinism among many. 'Social Darwinism', I wrote, 'had of course its progressive aspects. In the early years of the *Mutterschutz* movement, it clearly provided support for the movement's radical ideas about marriage, contraception and abortion.' But 'the variety of Social Darwinism that took root in the German women's movement in the years 1908-1914 contained a strong element of authoritarianism'. I mention this not because I would wish to claim any particular originality for these views, but rather in order to illustrate that in the 1970s it was so conventional to emphasize the diversity of Social Darwinism and its appeal to both left and right in Wilhelmine Germany that there was no question of using its presence in the ideology of radical feminism to 'revise' a supposed view that Social Darwinism was a purely conservative or 'proto-fascist' set of doctrines; such a view never existed in the first place.[28]

The orthodox line was usefully summed up in 1982 by Ted Benton, who concluded: 'Feminists and anti-feminists, revolutionaries and revisionists, socialists, liberals and conservatives, imperialists and internationalists: all, or almost all, seemed to find something in Darwinism and the idea of evolution which benefited their cases.'[29] Rolf-Dieter Sieferle's emphasis on Social Darwinism's complex and contradictory nature underlines this generally accepted point (1994).[30] And it has been repeated most recently by Paul Crook, who has emphasized the 'cultural malleability' of German Social Darwinism, which precludes any 'correct' reading of the implications of Darwin's ideas, or of those associated with him, for human society. Crook too concludes that in the early years German Social Darwinism was 'mainly influential on the left half of the political spectrum', but that 'as liberalism weakened, there came to the fore an organicist and authoritarian' version of 'Social Darwinism marked by eugenic proposals to save the nation or race', fusing eventually with Gobineau's race theories to create a dangerous new mix.[31] This line has also been followed by the British medical historian Paul Weindling, who, like Zmarzlik, has emphasized that 'Social Darwinism gave legitimacy to a variety of interests in an expanding industrial society, and cannot be identified as an exclusively right-wing racist ideology.'[32] Like Zmarzlik, Weindling has posited a 'transition in Darwinism from being a liberal and secular ideology of social reform during the 1860s' to meshing with 'the social imperialism of the 1890s' so that 'from the turn of the century, the doctrine of the "survival of the fittest" became increasingly

124

useful to doctrines of racial superiority.'[33] In his book on the cell biologist Oskar Hertwig (1991), Weindling showed how Hertwig attacked militarists such as Bernhardi as being 'Social Darwinists' using Darwin's theories to justify war, accused Social Darwinism of contributing to the overheated, militaristic political atmosphere before 1914, and criticized Social Darwinists for advocating selective breeding. Hertwig's tract against Social Darwinism, published in 1918,[34] 'stands', in Weindling's view,

> as an important commentary on the strength of Social Darwinism and the racial hygiene movement. By 1918 it was possible to see these as fundamental threats to German liberal ideals and the international community . . . Hertwig's achievement was to demonstrate that there was already a concerted body of opinion which could be described as 'Social Darwinism'.[35]

There is not much mention here of the varied and diverse nature of Social Darwinism, nor of its differential political implications. Yet elsewhere Weindling claims that 'the positive side to Darwinism' has been 'overlooked by historians',[36] who have tended to provide 'schematic accounts of Social Darwinism as a proto-fascist ideology'.[37] Not only does he fail to provide convincing evidence to show that such accounts really have been widespread in the literature, however, but, as we have seen from his own account of Oscar Hertwig, the assumption that Social Darwinism by the First World War was a uniform doctrine that was mainly or even exclusively racist, nationalist and militarist seems to be present not least in the work of Hertwig and indeed in the writings of Weindling himself.

In fact, of course, as we have seen, the positive side to Darwinism has not been overlooked by historians. The only historian of whom this could plausibly be claimed is Daniel Gasman, who argued in 1971 that all forms of Social Darwinism were part of the 'scientific origins of National Socialism', to borrow the title of his book on Ernst Haeckel. Haeckel, a leading German popularizer of Darwin's views, had long been regarded as a liberal, but Gasman went to the other extreme and portrayed him instead as a fascist *avant la lettre*. Haeckel for example supported capital punishment because, as he said, 'it has a directly beneficial effect as a selection process' by 'rendering incorrigible criminals harmless', and for good measure he added that modern methods such as chemical injections and electrocution should be used, and should also be applied to the mentally ill, because psychological disturbances were the expression of a physical degeneracy of the brain which could hold up human progress unless it was eliminated from the chain of heredity.[38] These views undoubtedly bore a close resemblance to those taken up later by the Nazis. Yet Haeckel also believed that war was wrong because it meant the slaughter of the best and bravest of the nation's youth, which would be a eugenic disaster. The 'Monist League', which he founded, was therefore a pacifist organization, as far removed from Nazism in this respect as it was possible to be. Here is a classic example of how some aspects of an ideologue's thought can legitimately be regarded as precursors of aspects of Nazi thought, while others cannot. It was quite wrong of Gasman, therefore, to reduce Haeckel *in toto* to the originator of 'the scientific origins of National Socialism'.[39] This was recognized by other historians right away, however. In 1976, I reflected a widespread view when I wrote that 'Gasman's account, though a valuable corrective to earlier works, is in general disappointingly one-sided.'[40] Three years later, Robert Bannister added that 'Gasman's definition of "Social Darwinism" compounds every confusion in the literature of the subject.'[41] In 1981, Alfred Kelly added to the chorus of disapproval of Gasman's work. 'If Haeckel and the Monist League can be forerunners of Nazism', he commented, 'then so can most any other thinker or organization.'[42] Further opprobrium came from Piet de Rooy in 1990, who pointed out that Haeckel's works were removed from German public libraries by the Nazis in 1935.[43]

Gasman's interpretation in fact ultimately derives from Allied wartime propaganda, which cannot really be considered serious in scholarly terms. Books such as William McGovern's *From Luther to Hitler*, published in 1941 and containing a chapter on 'Social Darwinists and their Allies', or Rohan Butler's *The Roots of National Socialism*, published the previous year, trawled German writings in the past, from Novalis to Nietzsche, not only in the search for antecedents of Nazism but also in the attempt to prove that all German 'ideology' had always been Nazi in one way or another, and that Nazism, in essence, was not new. Such arguments were related to the anti-German racism which was prominent in Allied propaganda during the Second World War, and which early postwar German historians such as Gerhard Ritter attempted to counter by arguing that the Nazis got most of their ideas from other countries – racism from France (through Gobineau), antisemitism from Austria, and so on. Ritter in particular saw the origins of National Socialism not in a long-term continuity of German values, but in their collapse after the First World War. He did not have anything to say in detail about Social Darwinism, and made no specific reference at all to any putative links with Nazi exterminism. Where he did draw a link, rather oddly, was between Hitler's geopolitical doctrine of *Lebensraum*, the claim for more territorial 'living space' for the Germans, and 'Darwinian theories which had been influencing the political literature of Europe for many years, and which caused disturbing symptoms in the writings of other countries too.' Here Ritter was trying both to attribute the idea of *Lebensraum* to a non-German source, detaching it from the specificities of Germany's historical development in the process, and to suggest that other countries were as prone to territorial aggrandisement (above all, in the First World War) as Germany was.[44] The Christian-conservative Ritter went on to argue that Social Darwinism was an aspect of the materialist world-view of the

Weimar Republic, which encompassed Marxism and atheism as well, and displaced the religious values which he thought had dominated in the Imperial period and which alone, he thought, could guarantee political stability in the age of the masses. Historians on both sides of this dispute thus paid scant attention to the nuances of ideology, or the historical context of ideas, in their desire to heap collective historical blame upon the Germans for Nazism, or to absolve them from responsibility for it. It was precisely this kind of unhistorical approach from which the more differentiated search for the origins of Nazi ideology undertaken from the 1960s onwards was trying to escape.[45] In this respect, Gasman's work represented a throwback to an earlier style of writing about ideas in German history, not the historiographical orthodoxy of the last thirty years. It is not surprising that it has had little or no influence among historians.

III

The prevailing orthodoxy on the history of Social Darwinist ideology in Germany has not gone unchallenged. A number of historians have been dissatisfied with it for a whole variety of different reasons. The feminist historian Gisela Bock, for example, rejected the term 'Social Darwinism' in the context of her work on compulsory sterilization in the Third Reich (1986), as 'partly unjustified, partly unsatisfactory, partly unnecessary.'[46] This was because, according to Bock, Social Darwinism was essentially a liberal ideology. 'If liberalism and the competitiveness of modern industrial society were the godparents of Darwin's interpretation of "nature",' she claimed, 'this certainly did not hold good for the racial hygiene movement.'[47] Racial hygiene and biology, Bock pointed out, were unknown to Darwin. The idea that natural selection had to be replaced by deliberate policy was alien to Darwin's thought. Racial hygiene, in fact, according to Bock, was

> less a movement in the history of ideas, than above all a sociopolitical movement with practical aims. Its theories did not address themselves, as Darwin's does, to the past, but to the present. Its interest was directed not towards the socioeconomic 'struggle for existence', but to the socio-sexual 'struggle' for reproduction. In this sphere it demanded not the 'right of the stronger' in free competition, but its regulation by the state; practical racial hygiene . . . For these reasons it seemed advisable not to define racial hygiene or eugenics as Social Darwinism, as thought and action that could be more or less reduced to Darwin, but instead to treat them as independent innovations.[48]

Feminist historians in general seem rather uncomfortable with the concept of Social Darwinism, perhaps because it does not of itself imply sufficient sharpness of focus on the issues that concern them, above all the 'politics of the body' and women's reproductive role. Cornelie Usborne made no use of the term in her book on reproductive politics in the Weimar Republic (1992), mentioning it only once, in passing, at the very beginning of her book. Nor did Ann Taylor Allen use the concept in her work in this area, except in a purely marginal way.[49] But this austere disdain for the concept of Social Darwinism, its restriction to what Darwin himself thought, does not convince. Darwin himself, as has long been recognized, took common social ideas of his time – above all, the competitiveness of early industrial capitalism – and applied them to nature.[50] Other ideas described as Darwinian even in his own day, including the 'survival of the fittest', may have derived originally not from Darwin himself, but from others (in this case, Herbert Spencer),[51] and after his death, different people interpreted Darwin, as historians have noted, in their own way, and in the process produced combinations of ideas which Darwin himself might not have recognized. But none of this made these ideas any less 'Darwinian'. Karl Marx, after all, is said to have complained, on reading the work of some of his disciples, that 'All I know is, I am not a Marxist'; and it is well known that Lenin, Kautsky, Plekhanov and even Engels introduced new ideas or variant readings which radically changed the nature of Marx's original thought.[52] Nevertheless, it would be foolish and pedantic to deny them the label 'Marxist' because of this. In a similar way, if Social Darwinism means the application to human society, however crudely or loosely, of concepts ultimately derived from Darwin, or approved by him as conforming to his theories, or appealing to his authority (principally evolution, the struggle for existence and the survival of the fittest), then the policy of the compulsory sterilization of the 'unfit', the subject of Bock's work, was certainly Social Darwinist.

More recently, Richard Weikart has also criticised Zmarzlik's two-stage model of the transition of Social Darwinism from liberal competitiveness to radical-reactionary selectionism because, he says,

> From the earliest expressions of Social Darwinism in the 1860s until the turn of the century, numerous German scholars used the Darwinian theory to defend individualist economic competition and laissez faire, others emphasized a collectivist struggle for existence between societies, while *most upheld both simultaneously*. A synthesis of individualism and collectivism had great appeal to German liberals in the 1860s and 1870s, since the long-standing twin ideals of German liberalism were individual liberty and German national unity. While the idea of individualist struggle may have faded after 1890 as classical liberalism declined in Germany, it would be incorrect to speak of a shift from stress on individualist to collectivist struggle, since collective competition received emphasis from the start.[53]

In practice, therefore, on a close reading of this passage ('may have faded after 1890'), it *does* appear that Weikart conceded that there was a shift in emphasis. Moreover, an inspection of his footnotes reveals that most of his references to 'collectivist' Social Darwinism, insofar as it applied to German society, date from 1890 onwards, further undermining his basic point. He also shows that many early Social Darwinists were National Liberals. They applied their advocacy of a society as based on free competition between individuals to Germany, while transposing it onto the global scale by making analogies with the competition between races. In an age of imperialism, a cause to which National Liberals became strongly attached, this was not surprising. It has long been recognized that the emergence of Wilhelmine *Weltpolitik* provided the context for such views to be turned back on German society itself; and if we accept the connections between National Liberalism and Social Darwinism, then the context also included the precipitate decline of the National Liberals from the mid-1880s and their turn towards more aggressive forms of nationalism and a more authoritarian view of society.[54] Weikart points out that even if laissez-faire Social Darwinism was not important in the USA before the last years of the nineteenth century,[55] the same cannot be said of Germany, for 'Darwinism had its greatest impact in Germany'.[56] While he pays insufficient attention to the Social Democratic version of Social Darwinism, on the whole, therefore, Weikart confirms rather than overthrows the existing orthodoxy on the subject, despite his rhetorical sallies against it.[57]

Perhaps the most radical attempt to restrict the concept of Social Darwinism was undertaken some years ago by Alfred Kelly. According to Kelly,

> the common historical treatment of German Social Darwinism as a theoretical rehearsal for Nazism is a mistake . . . Cast in the role of proto-Nazism, Social Darwinism almost inevitably takes on not only a malevolence, but also a prominence, coherence, and direction that it lacked in reality.

Kelly argued that the 'rhetoric of struggle', which (in his view) was usually equated with Social Darwinism, antedated Darwin. Militarists did not need Darwinian language to tell themselves and the world that war was a good thing. The occasional appropriation of 'a Darwinian phrase or two' did not make someone a Social Darwinist. The real Social Darwinists, according to Kelly – that is, 'those who undertook a sustained and detailed application of Darwin to human society' – were few in number and relatively without influence. Historians in his view had failed to distinguish between the earlier, moderate phase of Social Darwinism, and the later, radical phase from the 1890s, when 'ominous changes' in the ideology took place, mainly because 'many Darwinists had come under the influence of August Weismann's germ plasm theory', which implied a need to preserve the 'best' germ plasm in the race and ensure it was passed on to the next generation.

Social Darwinism thus became mixed up with racism and eugenics in the writings of people such as Schallmeyer, Ploetz and Ammon. 'The full dehumanizing brutality of radical Social Darwinism', Kelly noted, 'becomes evident in the work of Alexander Tille', who advocated the killing of the mentally and physically disabled. But these radical Social Darwinists were few in number. They were 'largely unread figures'. Many racists and antisemites were not Social Darwinists, and many eugenicists, such as Fritz Lenz, rejected antisemitism. Of the alleged ideological precursors of Nazism, Houston Stewart Chamberlain only 'flirted with Darwinism', while the leader of the Pan-German League, Heinrich Class, did not use Darwinian language at all. Social Darwinism was not popular among the German middle classes, and Social Darwinism in no sense 'caused' Nazism.[58] In a similar vein, Britta Rupp-Eisenreich has recently attacked Zmarzlik, Wehler, and other historians for allegedly reading Nazism back into Social Darwinism by expanding the concept and making it so imprecise that it has become a kind of 'negative myth'. She too has argued that the term can only legitimately be applied to a small group of individual scientists such as Ploetz, Schallmeyer, and Gumplowicz.[59]

But there are a number of problems with these arguments. In the first place, although Kelly conceded at the beginning of his treatment of the subject that Darwinism was applied to human society in terms of evolution as well as selection, he ignored this 'progressive' aspect in the rest of his analysis.[60] Secondly, Kelly confused the search for the ideological origins of Nazism with the equation of earlier thinkers with Hitler. The point is simple but fundamental. Zmarzlik argued over a third of a century ago that the Nazis only took certain ideas from Social Darwinists, vulgarizing them and combining them with other crude political doctrines in the process. No sensible historian has argued that the total package of Nazism was present in earlier social or political movements or ideologies. What historians have tried to do is to find out where the different parts of Nazi ideology came from. Crucial distinctions are being blurred here, not only between the part and the whole, but also the embryonic and the fully grown. Similarly, nobody is really claiming that Social Darwinism 'caused' Nazism. Kelly presented no evidence in support of this odd assertion, nor could he; virtually everyone who has written on Nazism knows that its causes did not lie exclusively in the realm of ideas, let alone medical or biological ideas. Finally, Kelly's criterion for the popularity of Social Darwinism, Darwinism, and indeed by extension any idea in history, was extremely simplistic: he measured popularity exclusively in terms of book sales. A writer such as Haeckel, whose books sold widely, Kelly described as popular; a writer such as Ploetz, whose books did not, he described as unpopular. Then, crucially, Kelly transferred these assessments to the ideas which the books purveyed. But all this is deeply implausible. Ideas, rhetoric, concepts were and are spread by many other means than books. Magazines, newspapers, speeches, parliamentary debates, court cases, conversations, political manifestos, voluntary associations, pressure groups – all these were means of forming 'public opinion' in Imperial Germany and the Weimar Republic, and all of them were ignored in Kelly's account. One can see why Kelly did not investigate these mechanisms of popularization, which would have involved a very substantial amount of additional research. But the result is that the question of popularization is left largely unanswered by his book, despite the promise contained in its subtitle.

The major point at issue here is whether or not the kind of Social Darwinist ideas that were developed by the theorists Kelly mentioned were taken up in wider public debate. Zmarzlik, and the orthodox view which he did so much to shape, argued that they were, even if in a crude, vulgarized and unsystematic manner. Kelly said that they were not. But no one should suppose that elaborate scientific or even pseudo-scientific theories were or are ever adopted wholesale in public debate. Kelly's criteria for popularization were too strict. When scientific ideas enter the realm of public political discourse they inevitably do so in an imprecise, crude and highly selective manner. This is then the form in which they equally inevitably get discussed by general historians seeking to explain the broad contours of Germany's social and political development. This may be annoying to the specialist historian of science or the author of a detailed study in intellectual history, but it is none the less a reasonable enough procedure. In the political world, concepts of race and ethnicity were – still are, indeed – defined not by anthropological societies, university professors or research scientists, but by politicians, demagogues and the average citizen. This, therefore, is where most historians have located them.

The late Tim Mason, for example, called for a materialist account of Social Darwinism in a broad historical context, as part of his long and ultimately unsuccessful search for a Marxist reading of the Third Reich that overcame the greatest weakness of Marxism in this area – its inability to incorporate racism and exterminism into an integrated historical explanation of National Socialism.[61] Mason called for a study of Nazism and capitalism linked through the concept of Social Darwinism as the ideology of struggle. In summing up the debates of the 1970s between 'intentionalists' and 'functionalists' – not his terms, but epithets already bandied about by participants – Mason's intention was to transcend them and move research onto 'a Marxist approach, which attaches pre-eminent weight to the processes of capital accumulation and class conflict'.[62] It was not his fault that this plea went largely unheeded. Intellectual and political developments since Mason wrote have placed racism increasingly at the core of historians' appreciation of the Nazi phenomenon, pushing the idea of class struggle increasingly onto the periphery. Marxist approaches have become less rather than more influential. In the 1980s and 1990s, with the coming of postmodernism and the growing influence of thinkers such as Foucault, intellectual history has enjoyed something of a renaissance, forcing 'materialist history' into the background. Moreover, in making his plea for a materialist history of Social Darwinism, Mason narrowed the concept down to the idea of struggle, which, following Engels's original critique of Darwinism, he saw as an expression of the competitive ethos of capitalist society. Yet few historians have accepted this extremely narrow definition. As we have seen, the application of Darwin's ideas, or what were taken to be his ideas, to human society could equally involve a stress on evolution and mutuality, ideas which exercised a strong fascination over the German Social Democrats at the turn of the century. Social Darwinism cannot simply be equated with the principle and practice of struggle in capitalist society, as Mason tried to do. Nor, for that matter, can racism. Historians nowadays would be far more prepared than Mason ever was to recognize that ideas have a force of their own. Yet in one respect at least, Mason's comments are worth heeding. Social Darwinism, he thought, was involved in competition between states, national and ethnic conflict, and many other areas of society. It was a protean and many-sided phenomenon. It was not simply part of medical and scientific discourses, but reached far beyond them.

IV

In Germany before 1914, Social Darwinist concepts can be found in three major areas of public debate.[63] First, there was the Social Democratic labour movement, where evolutionary concepts were being applied to historical change in a manner that strengthened the movement's already existing tendency to political immobilism. Darwinism had an appeal, not only as a means of allegedly refuting the ideological premisses of Christianity but also as a way of bolstering the Social Democrats' conviction that the future was theirs. In substituting an evolutionary for a dialectical view of human history, the majority of Social Democrats convinced themselves that there was a scientifically proven 'law of evolution' of society towards socialism, so that the end of capitalism would come, as it were, of its own accord, without the party having to do very much about it. Industrialization would simply continue until the working class formed the majority of the population, and the Social Democrats would then win a majority of seats in the Reichstag and come to power. By giving the labour movement the assurance that revolution would come peacefully, the Darwinian, evolutionary element in German Marxism played an integrating role in the Social Democratic Party and helped bind it together as the world's largest and most cohesive socialist organization before 1914. Beyond this, too, it also informed the party's views on class struggle and welfare. It is possible to argue that faith in Social Darwinism, and the habit of using Darwinian language, laid some Social Democrats at least open to the lure of selectionist eugenics, especially in the

1920s. But on the whole, there is no doubting the fact that the concept of evolution played the more prominent role. [64]

Secondly, a very different set of Social Darwinist ideas and concepts found their way into the ideology of Pan-Germanism by 1914. This indeed is how they first came to the attention of general historians. Social Darwinism's place in the ideological synthesis that underpinned the policies of the Pan-German League has been precisely delineated by, among others, Roger Chickering. Pan-Germanism, Chickering has remarked, was not a scientific ideology. Some of the men who created it around the turn of the century possessed scientific credentials, 'most did not':

> The feat they as a group accomplished required, in any event, the ingenuity of dilettantes. They managed to fuse Gobineau's historical panorama, Wagner's theory of regeneration, antisemitism, and theories of natural selection drawn from Darwin. The infusion of Darwinism, for which most of the credit belongs to the anthropologist Ludwig Woltmann, was the leavening in the synthesis, for it provided these thinkers with a biological metaphor in which to discuss regeneration. Regeneration would take place in the context of interracial struggle, in which the purest race would survive. Darwinism also made it possible to discard Gobineau's fatalism and, with the *imprimatur* of Schemann himself, to identify racial breeding as the key to arrest race-mixing and the cultural and physical degeneration still associated with it.[65]

Thus the Pan-Germanists' ideology was not simply 'Social Darwinism', but rather a synthesis which incorporated particular elements of it interpreted in a particular way.[66] Chickering cautions that no complete or systematic statement of this rather eclectic theory appeared before the First World War. Yet of the centrality of this version of Darwinian ideas to Pan-Germanism, Chickering is in no doubt. This ideology was tirelessly propagated in the Pan-German League's magazine, in meetings of its local chapters, and in a variety of other racist organizations which the League came to influence. Scientific racists such as Ludwig Woltmann and Otto Schmidt-Gibichenfels lectured to the League's meetings, and the League's publisher, J.F. Lehmann, was also a leading publisher of books on racial hygiene. 'Fusing Gobineau and Darwin', as Chickering remarks, 'led to the view that the inherent tendency in history was toward cultural degeneration, but that decisive intervention could still reverse, or at least arrest it.' From this fusion came not only a campaign to increase the German birth rate (among other things, by providing homes for illegitimate children to improve their survival chances), unite the ethnic Germans across Europe, and find *Lebensraum* for them to live in, but also a vision of international politics as the struggle for the survival of the fittest between Latins, Teutons and Slavs that could only be resolved by war.[67] Not everyone who supported any of these causes was necessarily a pan-German, and many people espoused one or other of them without accepting the whole package. But that there was such an ideological synthesis, and that it was held by a significant number of people on the Pan-German far right, cannot seriously be doubted.

The Pan-German League was a minority movement in Imperial Germany, but in the approach to the First World War it put increasing pressure on the government to adopt a more aggressive foreign policy, and its influence on public opinion was growing. Startling evidence for this influence can be found in the writings of the Reich leadership just before the war. The most notorious of these, General Friedrich von Bernhardi's book *Germany and the Next War*, published in 1912, while stemming from the pen of a man who had only been head of the historical section of the General Staff, and had retired in 1909, was widely debated and undoubtedly expressed the views of many within the military leadership. Bernhardi described war, famously, as a 'biological necessity': 'Without war, inferior or decaying races would easily choke the growth of healthy budding elements, and a universal decadence would follow.'[68] Georg Alexander von Müller, Chief of the Imperial Naval Cabinet, saw a prime target of German foreign policy as consisting in 'the preservation of the Germanic race against Slavs and Romans'.[69] Kurt Riezler, an important adviser of Reich Chancellor Bethmann Hollweg, took the view on the eve of war in 1914 that the major nations of the world were engaged in a ceaseless struggle with one another for the survival of the fittest.[70] The Kaiser himself, and even more the Crown Prince, shared such views of international relations. Erich von Falkenhayn, appointed War Minister in 1913 and Chief of the General Staff in September 1914, also believed strongly that science had proved nations and races to be engaged in a 'struggle for existence' of which military aggression was a necessary part. Recent research, based on Falkenhayn's newly discovered diaries and letters, shows that he despised the Kaiser for failing to bring about war, conspired in July 1914 to create circumstances in which war could be presented to Bethmann Hollweg as a military necessity, looked forward from the start to a war of attrition lasting three or four years rather than the short war so naively expected by many of the troops, and was quite prepared from the beginning to accept that Germany might well lose if that is what the Darwinist logic of world history and racial struggle dictated.[71] The point here is not that all these men were 'Social Darwinists'; nor that they all agreed with everything the Pan-German League said – Bethmann Hollweg and Riezler, for example, rejected many of the League's more far-reaching demands and while prepared to risk war in 1914, do not seem on currently available evidence to have deliberately brought it about. Rather, the point is that the Darwinian language of racial struggle had come to infuse many people's thinking abut the relations between states by 1914, above all in Germany. These were not marginal figures on the fringes of academia, nor were they unrepresentative or unimportant. These were the men who led the destinies of Imperial Germany. The view of international relations as interracial struggle for the survival of the fittest according to laws supposedly discovered by Charles Darwin was one of what James Joll described as the 'unconscious assumptions' on which statesmen based their conduct of foreign policy at this time. 'The linkage of Darwinism with militarism and imperialism', Paul Crook has concluded, 'was probably closest in Germany.'[72] It was more than merely a confirmation of the existing professional bellicosity of military men. On balance, it made war more rather than less likely to break out.[73]

Linked to these assumptions to a greater or lesser extent was a third major area of public debate in which Social Darwinist ideas featured prominently. This was the advocacy of policies of 'racial hygiene', which became steadily more influential in the emerging welfare sector before the First World War. I have suggested elsewhere how elements of the pan-German ideological mixture entered the feminist movement before the war, in the defeat of arguments for legalized abortion advanced by many influential women in the movement on the grounds that the international survival of the German race in a future war required a high birth rate.[74] Another illustration of the permeation of welfarist discourse by the language of racial hygiene can be found in the field of criminology and forensic psychiatry. One of the leading criminologists of the day, Gustav Aschaffenburg, thought that at least half of all penitentiary inmates were incorrigible, probably on hereditary grounds. The vast majority of criminals, he said, came from 'inferior human material'. Almost inevitably, they had 'physically and spiritually inferior children' who would simply repeat the cycle of crime. It was time, he declared, to prevent them breeding. Criminals must recognize 'that society defends itself with all the means at its disposal'.[75] Aschaffenburg considered that the challenges of modern life were too great for the weak human material from which criminals were made:

> Life takes its course and crushes the man who cannot cope. Just as the struggle for existence is played out today and will surely be played out through eternity, just as popular morality forces everyone under the yoke of this struggle, so we must all reach an unprejudiced perception and judgement of the dangers to which we are all exposed. And these are far greater than the ability of all these inferior elements in society to withstand them.[76]

Hence the high degree of recidivism observable in the German prison population. Another standard textbook, on forensic psychiatry, published in 1901, accepted the argument that criminality could be recognized by physical signs such as malformations of the ear or the size and shape of the forehead. 'In general', wrote its editor, Alfred Hoche, later to become notorious as the advocate of the extermination of what he called 'life unworthy of life', 'the morbid reduction of a person's capacity to resist his criminal tendencies can be estimated to be the higher, the more he displays physical and mental signs of degeneration under investigation.'[77] Even for less dangerous criminals, German criminologists before the First World War came increasingly to believe that compulsory sterilization was the remedy. 'Individuals of an antisocial disposition' and 'moral idiots' had to be stopped from reproducing. They should be removed from society for an indefinite period, irrespective of the nature of their crime, in the interests of an 'improvement of social hygiene'.[78] Monstrous, inhuman specimens like Jack the Ripper should not be kept alive, with the possibility that they might reproduce: they should be eliminated from the chain of heredity.[79] Even if criminologists shied away from advocating capital punishment on a large enough scale to be eugenically effective, some at least were prepared to support it for the most extreme of human 'monsters'.[80] The particular branch of criminology which was most vociferous in advocating such policies – criminal anthropology – was dominated by Germans and Austrians.[81] But by 1914 such biologistic ways of thinking about crime had become widespread among forensic psychiatrists as well. The increasingly professional nature of policing and detective work in the late nineteenth century also helped spread these ideas and techniques. Policemen saw them as lending added legitimacy and status to their profession, and soon textbooks of policing too were filled with pages of photographs detailing the physiognomical features of various types of criminal, while prison authorities in cities such as Hamburg began to collect the death masks of executed capital offenders in the hope of applying anthropological techniques to them when they had eventually collected a sufficient number.[82]

Yet in order to underline the precise significance of these views, it is necessary to recall that criminologists such as Aschaffenburg actually opposed the death penalty, because they were unwilling to take the crucial step from arguing that there was a hereditary element in criminality to proposing that incorrigible criminals should therefore be killed. Another prominent criminologist of the early twentieth century, Hans von Hentig, declared: 'A large proportion of criminals belong to elements in the race which are dying out of themselves.' Investigation showed that they came from families with few children, and had few of their own. From this argument, von Hentig drew the conclusion that it was not necessary to remove them from the chain of heredity; they would do it themselves; eventually, indeed, he was to be dismissed by the Nazis from his university post because of his protests against their eugenic penal policies in 1933.[83] Clearly, the argument that serious criminality was inherited and therefore serious criminals were incorrigible could be used to justify their biological extermination.[84] Equally clearly, however, such extrapolations were fairly uncommon before the First World War. It took a whole series of historical changes, including mass slaughter in a world war, military defeat, the overthrow of the *Kaiserreich* and the Revolution of 1918, before criminologists and psychiatrists could seriously start arguing along these lines. It took a further, massive social and political crisis at the beginning of the 1930s before they could become part of official government ideology. And it took another world war to provide the circumstances in which they could be put into effect.[85]

V

Selectionist Social Darwinism – the idea that human society was governed by the struggle, whether between races or between individuals or families, for the survival of the fittest – and the language and concepts which it inserted into welfarist and criminological discourse before the First World War, had a widespread and growing influence in the discussion of social problems at this time. This was, of course, a language in which a variety of different and often conflicting policies could be articulated. Yet without the emergence of this language, Nazi ideology would not have been able to develop as it did. And its spread during the Weimar Republic helped reconcile those who used it, and for whom it had become an almost automatic way of thinking about society, to accept the policies which the Nazis advocated and in many cases to collaborate willingly in putting them into effect. It may be helpful to conceptualize Social Darwinism in these broader historical contexts, indeed, as a language, a collection of words which constituted a discursive framework for debate in these various areas, rather than a coherent set of ideas or a fully worked-out ideology. It certainly does not help to conflate it with organicist biology or eugenics; the reach of Social Darwinist discourses was far wider than that, as we have seen.[86] The history of Social Darwinism in Germany goes far beyond the narrow history of science and medicine.

In a similar way, the willing collaboration of the medical profession with Nazi policies in the Third Reich can be explained exclusively neither in terms of its professional interests nor in terms of its scientific ambitions.[87] Doctors were part of the educated middle class, and their social and political attitudes were shaped as much by this fact as by their own specialist training and concerns. They were educated at German universities, and were therefore exposed to the conservative, radical-nationalist and (after 1918) far-right politics which dominated both academic staff and student representation in these institutions.[88] More generally, as Jeremy Noakes has pointed out (1984), the *Bildungsbürgertum*, to which doctors belonged,

> was a group which, by the first decade of the twentieth century, was beginning to feel itself threatened by a number of social developments, notably the creation of a 'mass' urban society combined with the emergence of a powerful new rival moneyed elite, neither of which shared their values. They both despised and feared the

democratizing, levelling aspects of a mass society and what they saw as the crude materialism of the new elite.[89]

The underlying social processes in all this cannot be reduced to the professionalization of biology or the emergence of institutional power-bases in the medical field. As Günther Hecht, from the Racial-Political Office of the Nazi Party, once said: 'As a political movement, National Socialism rejects any equation with any scholars or researchers or with any branches of research within the life sciences . . . National Socialism is a political movement, not a scientific one.'[90] Yet Social Darwinist language conferred scientific legitimacy on its exponents, whatever line they took. The rhetoric of science was an important legitimating factor in Nazi imperialism.[91] Hitler took up this rhetoric, and used his own version of the language of Social Darwinism as a central element in the discursive practice of extermination. By the middle of the war, this discursive practice had been almost entirely cut loose from whatever moorings it might once have had in medicine, science and social policy. Hitler and the Nazi judicial and police apparatus defined as racially degenerate 'anyone whose personality and way of life make it clear that their natural tendency is to commit serious crimes', whether or not the offences in question had actually been committed.[92] The language of Social Darwinism in its Nazi variant had come to be a means of legitimizing terror and extermination against deviants, opponents of the regime, and indeed anyone who did not appear to be wholeheartedly devoted to the war effort. At the same time, however, it was not merely a cover for state terrorism, it also provided a discursive practice which allowed that terrorism to be exercised, and helped remove all restraint from those who directed it, carried it out and drove it on, by persuading them that what they were doing was justified by history, science and nature.

NOTES

1 Bundesarchiv Koblenz R22/4720: Abschrift, 20 August 1942; Werner Jochmann (ed.), *Adolf Hitler: Monologe im Führer-Hauptquartier 1941–1944. Die Aufzeichnungen Heinrich Heims* (Hamburg, 1980), pp. 347–54; Lothar Gruchmann (ed.), 'Hitler über die Justiz. Das Tischgespräch von 20. August 1942', *Vierteljahreshefte für Zeitgeschichte*, Vol. 12 (1964), pp. 86–101.
2 Heinz Boberach (ed.), *Richterbriefe. Dokumente zur Beeinflussung der deutschen Rechtsprechung 1942–1944* (Boppard, 1975), p. 132.
3 Richard J. Evans, *Rituals of Retribution. Capital Punishment in Germany 1600–1987* (Oxford, 1996), Chapter 16.
4 Detlev J.K. Peukert, 'Arbeitslager und Jugend-KZ: die Behandlung "Gemeinschaftsfremder" im Dritten Reich', in Detlev J.K. Peukert and Jürgen Reulecke (eds.), *Die Reihen fast geschlossen. Beiträge zur Geschichte des Alltags unterm Nationalsozialismus* (Wuppertal, 1981), pp. 413–34, here p. 416; see also Norbert Frei, *Der Führerstaat. Nationalsozialistische Herrschaft 1933 bis 1945* (Munich, 1987), pp. 202–8; and P. Wagner, 'Das Gesetz über die Behandlung

Gemeinschaftsfremder: die Kriminalpolizei und die "Vernichtung des Verbre-
chertums"', in Götz Aly *et al.* (eds.), *Feinderklärung und Prävention.
Kriminalbiologie, Zigeunerforschung und Asozialenpolitik* (Berlin, 1988),
pp. 75–100.

5 Henry Pickler (ed.), *Hitlers Tischgespräche im Führerhauptquartier* (Stuttgart,
1976), p. 302 (15 April 1942).

6 Michael Burleigh, *Death and Deliverance. 'Euthanasia' in Germany c. 1900–
1945* (Cambridge, 1994), is now the best study of these events.

7 For the attempt of one of Germany's most senior philosophers of the immediate
postwar years to come to terms with Social Darwinism, see Hedwig Conrad-
Martius, *Utopien der Menschenzüchtung. Der Sozialdarwinismus und seine
Folgen* (Munich, 1955). This work stands apart from the more strictly historical
literature on the subject. For a phenomenological approach to the subject, see
Gunter Mann, 'Biologie und der "Neue Mensch". Denkstufen und Pläne zur
Menschenzucht im Zweiten Kaiserreich', in Gunter Mann and Rolf Winau (eds),
*Medizin, Naturwissenschaft, Technik und das Zweite Kaiserreich. Vorträge eines
Kongresses vom 6. bis 11. September 1973 in Bad Nauheim* (Göttingen, 1977),
182–880.

8 Hans-Günter Zmarzlik, 'Der Sozialdarwinismus in Deutschland als geschicht-
liches Problem', *Vierteljahreshefte für Zeitgeschichte*, 11 (1963), pp. 246–73, here
p. 247. For an English version, see Hans-Günter Zmarzlik, 'Social Darwinism in
Germany. Seen as a Historical Problem', in Hajo Holborn (ed.), *From Republic to
Reich: The Making of the Nazi Revolution* (New York, 1972), 435–74. The
translation above, however, is mine, as are all in the present chapter. See also
Hans-Günter Zmarzlik, 'Social Darwinism in Germany: An Example of the
Sociopolitical Abuse of Scientific Knowledge', in Günter Altner (ed.), *The Human
Creature* (Garden City, 1974).

9 Dieter Groh, 'Marx, Engels und Darwin: Naturgesetzliche Entwicklung oder
Revolution', in G. Altner (ed.), *Der Darwinismus* (Darmstadt, 1981), pp. 217–41.
For Richard Weikart's criticisms of Zmarzlik, see this chapter, pp. 128–9.

10 Zmarlik, 'Der Sozialdarwinismus', p. 262.

11 Ibid., pp. 262, 246–7.

12 Ibid., pp. 266–9.

13 Hans-Ulrich Wehler, 'Sozialdarwinismus im expandierenden Industriestaat', in
Imanuel Geiss and Bernd-Jürgen Wendt (eds), *Deutschland in der Weltpolitik des
19. und 20. Jahrhunderts* (2nd edn., Düsseldorf, 1974), pp. 133–42, here p. 139.

14 Ibid., pp. 138–9.

15 Ibid., p. 142. More recently, Wehler has described Social Darwinism in the form it
took in Wilhelmine Germany as a justificatory ideology of the upper classes (Hans-
Ulrich Wehler, *Deutsche Gesellschaftsgeschichte*, Vol. 3: *Von der 'Deutschen
Doppelrevolution' bis zum Beginn des Ersten Weltkrieges 1848–1914* (Munich,
1995), pp. 1,081–5). But of course the idea of the 'survival of the fittest' in no way
committed its proponents to the view that the aristocracy were the fittest to survive;
on the contrary, Social Darwinists of the radical right could just as easily claim that
the aristocracy were by and large degenerate, effete and lacking in eugenic vigour.

16 See especially David Blackbourn, 'The Discreet Charm of the Bourgeoisie:
Reappraising German History in the Nineteenth Century', in David Blackbourn
and Geoff Eley (eds), *The Peculiarities of German History. Bourgeois Society and
Politics in Nineteenth-Century Germany* (Oxford, 1984), pp. 159–292; and David
Blackbourn and Richard J. Evans (eds), *The German Bourgeoisie. Essays on the
Social History of the German Middle Classes from the Late Eighteenth to the Early
Twentieth Century* (London, 1990).

17 Hans-Walter Schmuhl, *Rassenhygiene, Nationalsozialismus, Euthanasie* (Göttingen, 1987), p. 72.
18 Ibid., p. 53.
19 Ibid., pp. 74–5.
20 For the general context, see Geoff Eley, *Reshaping the German Right. Radical Nationalism and Political Change after Bismarck* (New Haven, 1980).
21 Michael Burleigh and Wolfgang Wippermann, *The Racial State. Germany 1933–1945* (Cambridge, 1991), p. 28.
22 Ibid., pp. 132–3.
23 Gerhard Baader, 'Zur Ideologie des Sozialdarwinismus', in Gerhard Baader and Ulrich Schultz (eds), *Medizin und Nationalsozialismus: Tabuisierte Vergangenheit – Ungebrochene Tradition?* Sonderband 15, *Forum für Medizin und Gesundheitspolitik* (Berlin, 1980), pp. 39–51, esp. pp. 42, 50.
24 Richard J. Evans, *The Feminist Movement in Germany 1894–1933* (London, 1976), p. 138.
25 Ibid., p. 138.
26 Ibid., p. 160.
27 Ibid., pp. 133–4, 136–7, 159.
28 Ibid., pp. 158–69. Pointing out in the orthodox fashion that 'speakers of all political persuasions drew on the stock vocabulary of Social Darwinism', Ann Taylor Allen has argued, however, that Stöcker and her movement used eugenics only in a radical, progressive way. This constituted an attempt to argue for greater control by women over their own bodies. Unfortunately, she fails to distinguish between the rapidly changing phases of the movement's development, dismissing other historians' attempts to do so as mere 'narrative history'. She accuses my own writing on Stöcker of arguing that 'the use of eugenic theory by the women's movement was in itself a symptom of a more general "conservative revolution"', and claims that this 'fails to take into account the popularity of these social-radical theories among left-wing and progressive circles in Germany and elsewhere'. Yet this accusation confuses the two periods in the movement's history, and ignores everything that I and others have written about the different varieties and shadings of Social Darwinism and eugenics. The examples of progressive and emancipatory eugenic ideas which Allen presents from the feminist movement's literature almost all date from the period before 1908, a period for which no historian has disputed their hegemony. But she altogether fails to demonstrate their continuity significantly beyond this point. Her confusion is underlined by her description of such ideas as 'responses' to a series of authoritarian, male-dominated initiatives in reproductive policy which her footnotes indicate mostly dated from a later period! See Ann Taylor Allen 'Mothers of the New Generation: Adele Schreiber, Helene Stöcker, and the Evolution of a German Idea of Motherhood, 1900–1914', *Signs*, 10 (1985), pp. 418–438, here pp. 438, 435. See also her articles, 'German Radical Feminism and Eugenics, 1900–1908', *German Studies Review*, 11 (1988), pp. 31–56, and 'Maternalism in German Feminist Movements', *Journal of Women's History*, 5 (1993), pp. 99–103, and her book, *Feminism and Motherhood in Germany 1800–1914* (New Brunswick, 1991). For the location of the origins and early development of authoritarian discourses on sexuality and birth control in the direction taken by Social Darwinism and eugenics before 1914, see Anna Bergmann, *Die verhütete Sexualität* (Hamburg, 1992).
29 Ted Benton, 'Social Darwinism and Socialist Darwinism in Germany: 1860 to 1900', *Rivista di Filosofia*, Vol. 23 (1982), pp. 79–121, esp. pp. 93–7.
30 Rolf-Dieter Sieferle, 'Sozialdarwinismus', in Bodo-Michael Baumunk and J. Riess (eds), *Darwin und Darwinismus* (Berlin, 1994), pp. 134–42.

31 Paul Crook, *Darwinism, War and History. The Debate Over the Biology of War from the 'Origin of Species' to the First World War* (Cambridge, 1994), p. 31. The consensus is usefully summarized in the standard work by Peter Weingart, Jürgen Kroll and Kurt Bayertz, *Rasse, Blut und Gene. Geschichte der Eugenik und Rassenhygiene in Deutschland* (Frankfurt am Main, 1992), esp. pp. 114–21.
32 Paul Weindling, *Health, Race and German politics between National Unification and Nazism 1870–1945* (Cambridge, 1989), p. 28.
33 Ibid., p. 25; Paul Julian Weindling, *Darwinism and Social Darwinism in Imperial Germany: The Contribution of the Cell Biologist Oscar Hertwig (1849–1922)*, Forschungen zur heueren Medizin- und Biologiegeschichte, Vol. 3 (Stuttgart/New York, 1991), p. 302.
34 Oskar Hertwig, *Zur Abwehr des ethischen, des socialen, des politischen Darwinismus* (1918).
35 Weindling, *Darwinism*, pp. 270–87, 302; quotation on p. 287.
36 Ibid., p. 11.
37 Paul Weindling, 'Theories of the Cell State in Imperial Germany', in Charles Webster (ed.), *Biology, Medicine and Society 1840–1940* (Cambridge, 1981), p. 101.
38 Alfred Fried, 'Die Todesstrafe im Urteil der Zeitgenossen', *Die Zeitgeist: Beiheft zum Berliner Tageblatt*, 2 December 1901 (copy in Geheimes Staatsarchiv Preussischer Kulturbesitz, Berlin-Dahlem, Rep. 84a/7784, Bl. 203–5); and the *Deutsche Juristen-Zeitung*, 16/1 (1 November, 1911) (copy in Bundesarchiv Abteilungen Potsdam, Auswärtiges Amt IIIa Nr. 51, Vol. 10, 135–6).
39 Daniel Gasman, *The Scientific Origins of Nazism. Social Darwinism in Ernst Haeckel and the Monist League* (New York, 1971). Moreover, Gasman went on to identify even the mutualist and evolutionist forms of Social Darwinism espoused by Engels and the ideologues of the German Social Democratic Party as part of the intellectual heritage of Nazism as well! All this was achieved only by suppressing many aspects of Social Darwinism, misrepresenting Haeckel's thought, and distorting the historical record. Haeckel was portrayed in positive terms by officially sponsored historians in the former German Democratic Republic. See Erika Krause, *Ernst Haeckel* (Leipzig, 1983) and Georg Uschmann, *Ernst Haeckel. Eine Biographie in Briefen* (Leipzig, 1983). For a recent, more negative assessment, see Jürgen Sandmann, *Der Bruch mit der humanitären Tradition. Die Biologisierung der Ethik bei Ernst Haeckel und anderen Darwinisten seiner Zeit* (Stuttgart, 1990).
40 Evans, *The Feminist Movement*, p. 173, n. 47.
41 Robert C. Bannister, *Social Darwinism. Science and Myth in Anglo-American Social Thought* (Philadelphia, 1979), p. 133.
42 Alfred Kelly, *The Descent of Darwin. The Popularization of Darwinism in Germany, 1860–1914* (Chapel Hill, 1981), p. 11.
43 Piet de Rooy, 'Of Monkeys, Blacks and Proles: Ernst Haeckel's Theory of Recapitulation', in Jan Breman (ed.), *Imperial Monkey Business: Racial Supremacy in Social Darwinist Theory and Colonial Practice* (Amsterdam, 1990), pp. 7–34.
44 See Gerhard Ritter, 'The Historical Foundations of the Rise of National-Socialism', in *The Third Reich* (London, International Council for Philosophy and Humanistic Studies, 1955), pp. 381–416, esp. pp. 392–3, 415–16. The writings of Hans Koch on Social Darwinism, published in the course of the 'Fischer controversy' over the origins of the First World War, fall into the same context; their main argument is that Social Darwinism was a general European ideology, rather than a specifically German mode of thought: Hans Koch, 'Social

Darwinism as a Factor in the New Imperialism', in H.W. Koch (ed.), *The Origins of the First World War: Great Power Rivalry and German War Aims* (London, 1972), pp. 329–54, paradoxically manages to deal with the subject without mentioning a single German Social Darwinist. See also Hansjoachim W. Koch, *Der Sozialdarwinismus: Seine Genese und sein Einfluss auf das imperialistische Denken* (Munich, 1973).

45 See the critique in Richard J. Evans (ed.), *Society and Politics in Wilhelmine Germany* (London, 1978), Chapter 1, and in idem, *Rethinking German History* (London, 1987), Chapters 1–2; also J.C.G. Röhl (ed.), *From Bismarck to Hitler. The Problem of Continuity in German History* (London, 1970).

46 Gisela Bock, *Zwangssterilisation im Nationalsozialismus. Studien zur Rassenpolitik und Frauenpolitik* (Opladen, 1986), p. 28.

47 Ibid., p. 29.

48 Ibid., pp. 35–6.

49 Cornelie Usborne, *The Politics of the Body in Weimar Germany: Women's Reproductive Rights and Duties* (London, 1992), p. 4.

50 Wehler, 'Sozialdarwinismus', citing observations by Engels.

51 See Adrian Desmond and James Moore, *Darwin* (London, 1991), for a general account of Darwin's life and ideas.

52 David McLelland, *Marxism after Marx* (2nd edn., London, 1979).

53 Richard Weikart, 'The Origins of Social Darwinism in Germany, 1859–1895', *Journal of the History of Ideas*, 54 (1993), pp. 469–88, here p. 471 (italics in original).

54 See Larry Eugene Jones and Konrad H. Jarausch, *In Search of a Liberal Germany* (Oxford, 1992), for a summary; Dan H. White, *The Splintered Party. National Liberalism in Hessen and the Reich 1867–1918* (Cambridge, Mass., 1976) is an important regional study.

55 David Bellomy, 'Social Darwinism Revisited', *Perspectives in American History*, New Series 1 (1984), pp. 1–129, esp. pp. 1, 100.

56 Weikart, 'Origins', p. 471.

57 It is a different matter when Weikart argues that nineteenth-century German liberals in general had an 'organic conception of society' (p. 472). Weikart provides no evidence in support of this view, however, and in fact, virtually all varieties of German liberals in the mid-century decades (roughly from the 1840s to the 1870s) were more inclined to favour a contractual than an organic view of society.

58 Kelly, *The Descent of Darwin*, pp. 101–22.

59 Britta Rupp-Eisenreich, 'Le darwinisme social en Allemagne', in Patrick Tort (ed.), *Darwinisme et Société* (Paris, 1992), pp. 169–236.

60 Kelly, *The Descent of Darwin*, pp. 100–1.

61 Tim Mason, *Social Policy in the Third Reich. The Working Class and the 'National Community'* (Providence and Oxford, 1993). See especially the 'General Introduction' by Ursula Vogel (pp. vii–xv), and Mason's own Introduction and Epilogue (pp. 1–18 and 275–369).

62 Tim Mason, 'Intention and Explanation: A Current Controversy about the Interpretation of National Socialism', in Gerhard Hirschfeld and Lothar Kettenacker, *The 'Führer State': Myth and Reality. Studies on the Structure and Politics of the Third Reich* (Stuttgart, 1981), pp. 23–42, here pp. 37, 39.

63 This seems an appropriate point to note that the attempt to equate Social Darwinism with eugenics by R.J. Halliday ('Social Darwinism is defined as that discourse arguing for eugenic population control') is historically unconvincing and conceptually unduly restrictive (R.J. Halliday, 'Social Darwinism: A Definition', *Victorian Studies*, 14 (1971), pp. 389–406, here p. 401).

64 Hans-Josef Steinberg, *Sozialismus und deutsche Sozialdemokratie. Zur Ideologie der Partei vor dem Ersten Weltkrieg* (2nd edn., Bonn, 1972). The most widely read of all Social Democratic texts, August Bebel's *Die Frau und der Sozialismus*, first published in 1878, contained a substantial section on Darwinism, in which he portrayed class struggle as a version of the Darwinian struggle for survival of the fittest and the eventual triumph of socialism as a natural historical process (60th edn., Berlin, 1929), p. 550.

65 Roger Chickering, *We Men Who Feel Most German. A Cultural Study of the Pan-German League 1886–1914* (London, 1984), p. 239.

66 See also the account of Woltmann's ideas in George L. Mosse, *The Crisis of German Ideology. Intellectual Origins of the Third Reich* (London. 1964), pp. 99–104.

67 Chickering, *We Men*, pp. 240–5.

68 Quoted in Crook, *Darwinism, War and History*, p. 83.

69 Quoted in Imanuel Geiss (ed.), *July 1914. The Outbreak of the First World War: Selected Documents* (London, 1967), p. 22.

70 H. Pogge-von Strandmann and Imanuel Geiss, *Die Erforderlichkeit des Unmöglichen: Deutschland am Vorabend des ersten Weltkrieges* (Frankfurt, 1965).

71 Holger Afflerbach, *Falkenhayn. Politisches Denken und Handeln im Kaiserreich* (Munich, 1994).

72 Crook, *Darwinism, War and History*, p. 30.

73 James Joll, *The Origins of the First World War* (London, 1984) pp. 152–3, 184–91.

74 Evans, *The Feminist Movement*, Chapters 5–6.

75 Dieter Dölling, 'Kriminologie im "Dritten Reich"', in Ralf Dreier and Wolfgang Sellert (eds.), *Recht und Justiz im 'Dritten Reich'* (Frankfurt am Main, 1989), pp. 194–235, here p. 222; Gustav Aschaffenburg, *Das Verbrechen und seine Bekämpfung* (3rd edn, Heidelberg, 1923), pp. 196–201, 220–2, 226–7.

76 Aschaffenburg, *Das Verbrechen*, p. 223. There is a useful brief discussion of this subject in Robert Proctor, *Medicine under the Nazis* (Cambridge, Mass., 1988), pp. 202–5.

77 Alfred Hoche (ed.), *Handbuch der gerichtlichen Psychiatrie* (Berlin, 1901), pp. 414, 419.

78 Gustav Aschaffenburg (ed.), *Bericht über den VII. Internationalen Kongress für Kriminalanthropologie* (Heidelberg, 1912). See especially the articles by Graf Gleispach, 'Die unbestimmte Verurteilung' (pp. 226–43), Prof. Dannemann, 'Die Entmündigung chronisch Krimineller als Mittel zur Verbesserung der sozialen Hygiene' (pp. 313–21), Hans Maier, 'Erfahrungen über die Sterilisation Krimineller in der Schweiz und Nordamerika als Mittel der sozialen Hygiene' (pp. 322–31), and H. Klaatsch, 'Die Morphologie und Psychologie der niederen Menschenrassen in ihrer Bedeutung für die Probleme der Kriminalistik' (pp. 56–73).

79 See the account of these views, and the controversy they aroused when they were put forward in the *Archiv für Kriminal-Anthropologie und Kriminalistik*, in Peter Gay, *The Bourgeois Experience*, Vol. 3: *The Cultivation of Hatred* (Oxford, 1994), pp. 165–6.

80 Paul Nacke, cited in ibid., p. 165.

81 See the list of delegates in Aschaffenburg. *Bericht*.

82 Gustav Roscher, *Grossstadtpolizei* (Hamburg, 1906).

83 Hans von Hentig, *Strafrecht und Auslese* (Berlin, 1914), p. 216.

84 For a more extended treatment of this topic, see my *Rituals of Retribution*, Chapters 12–16.

85 For a balanced treatment of this topic, see Richard F. Wetzell, 'Criminal Law Reform in Imperial Germany' (Ph.D., Stanford University, 1991), and the same author's forthcoming book, which extends coverage through to the 1950s.

86 For the conflation of Social Darwinism, organicist biology and eugenics, see Weindling, *Darwinism*, p. 303, and Pietro Corsi and Paul J. Weindling, 'Darwinism in Germany, France, and Italy', in David Kohn (ed.), *The Darwinian Heritage* (Princeton, 1985), pp. 683, 698. In the same article, Weindling also confuses Social Darwinism with 'social factors in the propagation of Darwinism' (p. 697).

87 Benno Müller-Hill, *Murderous Science. Elimination by Scientific Selection of Jews, Gypsies and Others, Germany 1933–1945* (Oxford, 1988), takes this rather narrow approach; but Müller-Hill is a geneticist, not a historian.

88 Fritz K. Ringer, *The Decline of the German Mandarins* (Princeton, 1969); Michael H. Steinberg, *Sabers and Brown Shirts: The German Students' Path to National Socialism 1918–1935* (Princeton, 1977).

89 Jeremy Noakes, 'Nazism and Eugenics: the Background to the Nazi Sterilization Law of 14 July 1933', in R.J. Bullen *et al.* (eds), *Ideas into Politics. Aspects of European History 1880–1950* (London, 1984), pp. 75–94, here p. 78.

90 Quoted in Anne Bäumer, *NS-Biologie* (Stuttgart, 1990), p. 120.

91 Woodruff D. Smith, *The Ideological Origins of Nazi Imperialism* (Oxford, 1986), p. 144.

92 Peukert, 'Arbeitslager', quoting a draft law of February 1944.

12

FROM RACIAL HYGIENE TO AUSCHWITZ[1]

In the past few years, biotechnology, gene manipulation, *in vitro* fertilization, foetal tissue transplants and other, similar developments have given rise to an increasingly impassioned debate on the politics and morality of controlling human reproduction. Participants in the debate frequently raise the spectre of the racial, biological and medical policies carried out by the Nazis in the 1930s and during the Second World War. Hitler's Third Reich forcibly sterilized some 360,000 inhabitants of Germany thought to be suffering from hereditary complaints (often as vaguely described as 'feeble-mindedness' or 'alcoholism'). A programme was launched to kill off 'incurable' patients in mental hospitals. Five thousand children, many suffering from Down's syndrome, were selected for extermination by an official medical tribunal. X-ray units run by the SS toured occupied Poland and Russia and shot 100,000 of the inhabitants who were discovered to be tubercular. A medical statistician advocated a 'final solution' for the 1.6 million 'antisocials' he believed to be living in Germany.

Although Hitler was known for his personal susceptibility to quackery and alternative medicine, the medical killings and sterilizations of his Third Reich were carried out by mainstream scientists firmly anchored in the medical, biological and university establishments. Even Josef Mengele (1911–84), who became notorious for the human experimentation which he carried out while camp doctor at Auschwitz, had previously won international recognition for his work on the aetiology of cleft palates and harelips. Moreover, senior scientific figures such as Otmar von Verschuer (1886–1969), who had given powerful support to camp research and enthused about Mengele's work on eye-colour anomalies (for which the eyes of gypsies imprisoned in Auschwitz had apparently been used), were reinstated in university posts in West Germany during the 1950s, while the surviving victims of sterilization and experimentation went uncompensated and unrecognized.

The story of medicine and biology under Nazism has been told by a number of authors in recent years, including Robert Jay Lifton, Michael Kater, Gisela Bock, Ernst Klee, Götz Aly, Karl-Heinz Roth and others. What concerns Paul Weindling in this major new study (1989), however, is less the documentation of medical killing than the exploration of its longer-term roots in the rise of eugenics and racial hygiene and the development of the German medical profession since the late nineteenth century. In part he sees the story in sociological terms. Throughout the book he emphasizes, sometimes perhaps overemphasizes, the desire of all sections of the medical profession for money, power and status – even where, as in the case of the racial hygienists, they appeared to have sacrificed career prospects in the service of a theory that the medical establishment spurned for decades. He chronicles the varied struggles of medical scientists against competing groups such as feminists, sex reformers, nature therapists, Communists, and finally against the Nazi ideologues who considered the mass sterilization policies of the medical men misguided because they were not directed against 'inferior' races.

Weindling provides eloquent detail on the way in which scientists responded to the increasing control of research funding by the SS by trying to devise projects which would meet with the approval of Himmler and Heydrich. He rightly points out that by behaving in this way, scientists were entering into a Faustian pact with the regime. They might have been able to keep their research institutes and their university chairs, and even to extend their role in the formulation and execution of public policy. But it was only at the cost of adapting evermore cravenly to ideas and institutions – above all, as time went on, those of the SS – which they had initially rejected as unscientific.

The main concern of this book, however, is not to provide a social or political history of German medical science but to give a history of its ideas, principally in the area of eugenics. Basing his account on a large quantity of unpublished documentation in over forty public and private collections in East and West Germany, Britain, Switzerland and the United States, Weindling cautions strongly against oversimplifying the lines of descent from the eugenics of the founding fathers to the selection ramp at Auschwitz. The early eugenicists derived much of their inspiration from utopian socialism, wore Dr Jaeger's outlandish woollen clothing (favoured at the time in Britain by George Bernard Shaw, among others), took an interest in telepathy and were inclined to commune with nature on long moonlight walks. The democratic element in their thinking faded only gradually, and continued to inspire a number of socialist eugenicists long afterwards. Positive eugenics, which often involved a strong commitment to social reform, were for many years much more widely accepted than the negative eugenics of the kind which eventually triumphed under the Nazis.

Ernst Haeckel, who had a powerful influence on the early eugenics movement in Germany, drew up a hierarchical scale of thirty-two human races and declared that no woolly-haired people had ever been of historical significance; but he also regarded war as an act of racial suicide because it killed off the bravest and the best. Haeckel's Monist League was indeed an important element in the German pacifist movement during the First World

War. Under the Weimar Republic, eugenic ideas gained ground among the social hygienists, but a good number of these were close to the Social Democrats and rejected racism. The eugenicist and racial hygienist Rainer Fetscher (1895–1945) campaigned for eugenic sterilizations and actually carried some out himself during the Weimar years. He also compiled a vast index of people he thought were hereditarily inclined to criminality: like many other such databases drawn up under the Weimar welfare system, it was subsequently used by the Nazis to identify people for extermination. But in Hitler's Third Reich, Fetscher became a leading figure in a largely Communist resistance group. Similarly, physical anthropologists might declare that races with long heads and blond hair were superior to those with round heads and dark hair, but some of them found it hard to avoid consigning Hitler to the latter group, and he was classified by them as an un-Nordic East Slav.

The history of racial hygiene in Germany in fact exhibited a striking continuity in its leading personnel men such as Alfred Ploetz (1860–1940), who set up a League to Invigorate the Race as early as 1879, was the moving spirit behind the founding of the Racial Hygiene Society in 1905, and sent a letter to Hitler in 1933 acclaiming him as 'the man who had the will to implement racial hygiene'. The co-founder of the Racial Hygiene Society, Ploetz's sometime brother-in-law Ernst Rüdin (1874–1950) played a major role in drafting the Nazi sterilization law of 1933. Enthusiasts such as these were pushed in a more racist and authoritarian direction above all by Germany's defeat in the First World War, which undermined the value attached to individual life and shifted the emphasis to collective national survival. The triumphs of bacteriology in the era of Robert Koch in the 1880s and 1890s had already persuaded medical scientists of the legitimacy of human experimentation; war and revolution weakened their liberal commitment to the freedom of the individual. The shock of 1918 had a major effect on a number of eugenicists, although few went as far as the Lamarckian biologist Richard Simon, who shot himself, wrapped in the imperial flag, on hearing the news of Germany's defeat. Already in 1920 the nationalist professor of psychiatry at Freiburg University, Alfred Hoche (1865–1943), was demanding euthanasia for an estimated half a million 'idiots'; prudently, perhaps, he kept a loaded pistol in his consulting-room in case any of his patients should disagree with his diagnosis.

Ideas such as these were still rejected by the majority in the early 1920s, but the experience of the prolonged and deep economic Depression in Germany from 1929 to 1933, with its mass unemployment, poverty, destitution and disorder, converted many welfare eugenicists and social hygienists to the idea of compulsory sterilization. Weindling is surely going too far when he describes this as 'a brief age of scientific dictatorship': the Depression may have generated a sense of eugenic bankruptcy, but conditions were scarcely favourable for the doctors to solve it by their own efforts. Weindling seems undecided as to whether the Depression narrowed the gap between welfare eugenics and racial hygiene, but the detail he provides does show the racial hygienists beginning to move into more influential positions in the scientific community by this time. Finally, the coming to power of the Nazis shifted the views of many eugenicists still further in an authoritarian direction. Racial hygiene gained significantly in power and prestige: it was incorporated into the medical curriculum; and racial hygiene institutes were set up at almost half the universities in Germany.

Understandably, perhaps, in view of the sweeping and undifferentiated approach which is to be found in some of the recent literature, Weindling places greater emphasis on what divided eugenicists, racial biologists and social hygienists than on the factors that united them. He pays close attention to the political and academic feuds which rent the medical and scientific community in these fields, and relates them illuminatingly the 'polycratic' structure of the Third Reich, with its constant in-fighting between different agencies. Yet all this detail, especially when combined with the fact that Weindling writes in a flat, dull style, consisting of an endless sequence of very short sentences, each containing little more than a subject, a verb and an object, and making extensive use of the passive voice, does not make this an easy book to read.

Moreover, while the detailed account of medical theories and personalities is very impressive, Weindling's grasp of the more general historical background is sometimes rather less secure. There are some embarrassing slips in this area; thus, Imperial Germany did not have a restrictive franchise – it had universal manhood suffrage from the outset. Posadowsky-Wehner was not Chancellor in 1904 – Bernhard von Bülow was. Heinrich Brüning was not the 'Centre Party leader' in the Weimar Republic but only chairman of the party's Reichstag delegation, Weindling also appears to confuse the Allied occupation of the Rhineland in 1920 with the French occupation of the Ruhr in 1923. The book would have been improved by being embedded more firmly not only in a national political and social context, but also in an international comparison. Weindling alludes to the fact that eugenic sterilization was practised in Scandinavia and the United States, but he does not do enough to explore either the origins of the weaker resistance to eugenics in Britain, or the reasons why the abuse of medical power ultimately went so much further in Germany than anywhere else.

Nevertheless, despite these weaknesses, Weindling's book is a major contribution to an important subject. It brings a mass of fascinating and illuminating detail to bear on the medical origins of Nazi exterminism. And it will be required reading for all serious students of modern German history.

NOTES

1 Paul Weindling, *Health, Race and German Politics Between National Unification and Nazism, 1870–1945* (Cambridge, Cambridge University Press, 1989).

13

ANTI-SEMITISM

Ordinary Germans and the 'longest hatred'

Ever since the full horror of Hitler's death camps dawned upon the world, historians, sociologists, political scientists and philosophers from many countries have been trying to understand how and why it was in Germany rather than anywhere else that antisemitism, one of the longest-lasting and most widespread of ethnic and religious hatreds in European history, led to the deliberate mass murder of Europe's Jews. For what distinguished Hitler's so-called 'Final Solution of the Jewish Question' – in reality, as many observers have noted, not really a Jewish Question but a German one – was not so much its brutality, violence and fanaticism, though this was indeed extreme (similar cruelty and barbarism has been seen in more recent times, in Rwanda, Bosnia and Iraq), but two rather different factors. The first of these was its mechanized and bureaucratized character. In no other case of genocide has a state devoted such vast resources of central planning and administration to the total extermination of an ethnic minority. The second factor that made it unique was the fact that it was intended to eliminate the Jews not just of the country where the policy of extermination originated, but of the whole of Europe, indeed ultimately the world. The lists of prospective victims drawn up at the Wannsee Conference in January 1942, when the implementation of the extermination policy was organized, included many Jews in countries such as Britain and Ireland which had not yet fallen under Germany's sway. The sheer scale of the operation, and the fact that a major European state was prepared to devote massive resources to it at a time when it was fighting a major world war against powerful and well-resourced opponents, has posed a supreme challenge to the historical imagination. It has elicited many different responses, and provoked many fine, thoughtful, occasionally even inspiring works of history. Not only the specific policy of extermination but also its wider context of antisemitism is one of the most intensively studied, most written-about subjects in modern German, indeed European history.

It is a bold scholar, therefore, who claims, as Daniel Jonah Goldhagen does in his book *Hitler's Willing Executioners* (1996), to have found an entirely new answer to the question of how it was that Germans rather than some other European people turned antisemitic prejudice into mass murder.[1] Goldhagen's book has attracted widespread media attention, making its author, a junior professor of political science at Harvard, a celebrity overnight. It has made the best-seller lists in Britain and America and stayed there for some months, outselling in the process almost every other book that has been published on the Third Reich. Its arguments have thus in all probability become extremely influential, not just among students but above all among the wider reading public. For a book that originated in a Ph.D. thesis, this is no mean achievement. At the same time, it aroused a storm of criticism in Germany, provoking a title-page story and in-depth articles in the popular magazine *Der Spiegel*, a series of critical appraisals in the liberal weekly *Die Zeit*, numerous polemics in the daily press, and now a whole book devoted to the debate.[2] German commentators in particular felt aggrieved, even puzzled, that their country seemed to be in the dock again. Old gaps in historical understanding seemed to be opening up once more between the Germans and their former opponents in the Second World War, despite half a century of alliance and international accord.

In view of all this controversy, it is worth devoting close attention to Goldhagen's book, to subject the theses it advances to critical scrutiny, and to ask why it has achieved such a wide resonance above all in Britain and the United States and aroused such attention in Germany. Goldhagen's argument is essentially very simple, though it is disguised in a good deal of political-science jargon. It is that Germans killed millions of Jews during the Second World War not because they were forced to, nor because German traditions of obedience enabled a handful of fanatics at the top to do whatever they liked, nor because they were succumbing to peer-group pressure from their comrades-in-arms, nor because they were ambitious careerists, nor because they were acting automatically, like cogs in a machine. Least of all did they carry out the extermination of the Jews because they faced death themselves if they refused to obey the order to do so. Goldhagen argues that Germans killed Jews in their millions because they enjoyed doing it, and they enjoyed doing it because their minds and emotions were eaten up by a murderous, all-consuming hatred of Jews that had been pervasive in German political culture for decades, even centuries past (pp. 31–2). Ultimately, says Goldhagen, it is this history of genocidal antisemitism that explains the German mass murder of Europe's Jews, nothing else can.

This is a bold and arresting thesis, though it is not new: much the same was said during the Second World War by anti-German propagandists such as Robert Vansittart or Rohan Butler, who traced back German antisemitism – and much more – to Luther and beyond;[3] a similar argument was put forward by the proponents of the notion of a German 'mind' or 'character' in the 1960s,[4] and by William L. Shirer in his popular history of Nazism.[5] What evidence does Goldhagen offer in its support? The core of his book, and by far the best part, is a minutely detailed empirical study of aspects of the genocide which, he says, have been neglected by historians obsessed with studying mechanized death factories such as Auschwitz and Treblinka: the mass shootings of Jews in Eastern Europe by units under the command of the SS, the 'destruction by labour' of Jews in labour camps, and the 'death marches' which camp guards forced Jews to make at the very end of the war, as the Red Army closed in. Goldhagen shows in horrific detail the wanton, bestial cruelty of many of the perpetrators in these events, cruelty which went far beyond the mere indifference to suffering of which other historians have convicted them; far beyond, indeed, what their superiors had ordered (pp. 356–7). For many of those involved, there was clearly no question of simple 'obedience to orders', let alone reluctance or revulsion at what was going on. Goldhagen hypothesizes that the main purpose of the 'death marches', many of which were quite aimless in geographical terms, was really to inflict suffering and death on the Jews. They were 'the ambulatory analogue to the cattle car' (p. 328). And he demonstrates how 'extermination through labour' was thought by Nazis to be a particularly appropriate form of death for a group of people whom antisemitic propaganda had portrayed as incapable of doing any really productive work without being forced to.

Here too, most of what Goldhagen says is not really new, though some of the detail is and all of it certainly bears repeating many times over. A recent book published under the title *Those Were the Days* (1991), by Ernst Klee and others, is devoted in a similar way to documenting the enthusiasm with which many of the perpetrators went about their murderous business.[6] The Auschwitz trials of 1964, which generated a massive amount of media attention, even the Nuremberg trials of 1946–7, produced similar evidence, much of it brought before a wider public in books such as Lord Russell of Liverpool's *The Scourge of the Swastika* (1951).[7] Above all, however, Goldhagen's lengthy and detailed account of the activities of Reserve Police Battalion 101, a group of mostly older German men who moved through occupied Eastern Europe carrying out mass shootings of at least 38,000 Jews over a considerable period of time, was anticipated in 1992 by Christopher Browning's short but powerfully argued study *Ordinary Men*.[8] Browning argued that the police reservists were shocked and surprised by their orders to kill Jews when they first received them; their commander, Major Trapp, was openly dismayed and allowed any of his men who wanted to pull out of the operation to do so; another officer, Lieutenant Buchmann, objected and obtained a transfer. Many of the men, however, reluctant to abandon their comrades, carried out the shootings; offloading the fear and aggression they felt in a brutal and desperate wartime situation, they quickly became brutalized, dulled their sensibilities with drink, succumbed to a deep-seated feeling that they should obey the orders they were given as military men, lost contact with the realities of the situation, and were soon murdering Jews *en masse* as a matter of routine.

Goldhagen, however, asserts that these men were murderers because they were antisemites. He admits that he has no evidence of actual statements by the men to this effect, neither from the time before they enlisted, nor from the period when they carried out their campaign of mass extermination (p. 255), so he has to fall back on the circular argument that they were antisemites because they murdered Jews. Beyond this, he asserts that they were antisemites because they were Germans. This is where the real weaknesses of the book begin. Goldhagen asserts that German society as a whole had been deeply antisemitic since the Middle Ages. The tradition of Christian antisemitism was reinforced by Luther, and further strengthened in the nineteenth century by the rise of German nationalism, which defined Germanness from the outset against the 'otherness' of the Jew (pp. 44–5). By the late nineteenth century, antisemitism was not only all-pervasive but also exterminatory. To be antisemitic in Germany meant to will the physical annihilation of the Jews. It was a doctrine, Goldhagen claims, that was adhered to by the vast majority of Germans throughout modern history.

What is the evidence Goldhagen presents for this sweeping claim? It rests partly on his all-embracing definition of antisemitism, which he extends far beyond the conventional notion of a conspiracy theory alleging that the Jews wished to destroy civilization and therefore had to be restricted in their access to public goods, professional activities and civil rights. For Goldhagen, German liberals were antisemitic because they wanted to assimilate the Jews into German society instead of allowing them a separate culture and existence. All German liberals were racial antisemites by 1900, he claims (p. 59), while elsewhere he refers to 'Conservatives and Volkish nationalists in Germany, who formed the vast majority of the population' in the Imperial period (p. 56). In the Reichstag elections of 1893 openly antisemitic politics triumphed, 'the vast majority of the votes having been cast for the Conservative Party' (pp. 75–6). The pervasiveness and centrality of antisemitism to German political culture in the late nineteenth century was reflected in the fact that 'the "Jewish Problem" was written about in Germany with a passion and frequency unmatched by any other political subject' (p. 64).

But these arguments are open to many serious objections and are in a number of cases based on assertions that are simply factually incorrect. If German nationalism defined Germanness by opposing itself to the negative image of the Jews, how was it then that the civil equality and legal emancipation of the Jews was one of its demands from the outset, finally implemented in full in the unification of 1871? If the German population and German elites were so deeply antisemitic, why did Jews actually gain civil equality by legislative enactment all over Germany in the course of the nineteenth century? If German liberals of all hues were racial antisemites, how do we explain the fact that so many of their leaders, from Ludwig Bamberger and Eduard Lasker to Walther Rathenau, Hugo Preuss and Theodor Wolff, were Jewish? In any case, to equate the desire to assimilate the Jews into German society by giving them civil equality with the kind of racial antisemitism that demanded precisely the opposite – namely, their exclusion from civil society – is to blur crucial distinctions. Giving people civil rights, as liberals were well aware, meant giving them the ability to defend their cultural identity if they so wished, something which would be far more difficult if those rights were curtailed. German liberals were not so kind to Catholics, the abrogation of whose religious freedoms and civil rights they actively supported during the so-called *Kulturkampf* and whom they consistently regarded thereafter as primitive, backward and super-stitious, in sharp contrast to their much less negative attitude towards Jews. Goldhagen is simply wrong to claim that conservatives and volkish (or racial) nationalists formed the vast majority of the population in Imperial Germany. By most historians' definition, the Conservative Party espoused radical antisemitism in 1893 in a vain attempt to shore up its declining popularity, while many left-liberals rejected volkish nationalism, and the Catholic Centre Party went into an election in 1907 on the platform of criticizing the brutal behaviour of German colonial administrators towards subject races in Africa. The Conservative Party did not win a majority of the votes in the 1893 Reichstag election but just under 14 per cent; openly antisemitic parties scored another 3.5 per cent between them. There is no evidence that Jewish issues were written about with more frequency and passion than other issues of the day; on the contrary, religion, especially during the *Kulturkampf*, socialism and revolution, foreign and colonial policy, and many other issues, took up far more space in the newspapers and journals and generated a far more extensive and impassioned pamphlet literature in this period.

Richard S. Levy, author of an important book on antisemitism in Imperial Germany (1975), has argued in contrast to Goldhagen that antisemitism was not central to German political culture in the nineteenth century but marginal to it. Rejecting one of Goldhagen's major contentions as resting on a 'skewed' reading of a very limited number of sources (including an obscure 1963 Heidelberg dissertation which Levy must be one of the few scholars apart from Goldhagen to have read), Levy declared:

> I know of no case where genocide was proposed as a systematic solution to the Jewish question before 1914. Rare threats of physical violence came in the form of 'jokes' or fantasies or poorly veiled wishes, usually appeared as parenthetical remarks, and in almost every case were subject to denial, disavowal, and wide public disapproval.

Goldhagen neglected to mention the fact that the mad Count Pückler, who performed murderous charades with Jews as his victims, and was used by

Goldhagen's father, cited in the book, as an example of how nineteenth-century antisemitism presaged twentieth-century, was rejected as an embarrassment 'by almost every antisemitic politician and publicist'. Finally, Levy found Goldhagen's definition of antisemitism at fault. He began with an all-embracing concept ('negative beliefs and emotions about Jews *qua* Jews') and then blurred the distinction between ideas and action. Thus he implied, without any evidence, that anyone who held such beliefs and emotions was automatically committed to killing Jews on the largest possible scale.[9] Such a blurring, one may add, is itself a symptom of postmodernist intellectual trends in America, where pornography is now widely asserted to be indistinguishable from rape, and where reading about a murder is said to be the same as committing it. But without in any way wishing to trivialize these matters, it remains important that such distinctions should be upheld. They certainly would have been apparent to the victims of real acts of murder, torture and rape.

Goldhagen is unable, or unwilling, to engage in the international comparison that is necessary (whatever he says) to back up his explicitly comparative claim that the Germans were more antisemitic than other peoples, asserting that 'it is precisely because antisemitism alone did not produce the Holocaust that it is not essential to establish the differences between antisemitism in Germany and elsewhere'. The fact that the Germans rather than anybody else murdered millions of Jews means in Goldhagen's view 'that German antisemitism would have qualitatively different consequences from the antisemitisms of other countries'. This is what used to be called the *post hoc, ergo propter hoc* argument: but of course such kind of backward reasoning is no substitute for empirical proof, so Goldhagen repeats once more his view that 'no other country's antisemitism came close' to matching German antisemitism in the nineteenth century (p. 419).

In fact, around the turn of the century, at least two other major European powers witnessed prolonged outbreaks of antisemitism far in excess of anything seen in modern Germany up to that time. In France, the Dreyfus affair sparked a wave of antisemitic riots in over thirty towns and cities and the murderous obscenity of antisemitic pamphleteers such as Maurice Drumont exceeded anything found in Germany before the days of Julius Streicher.[10] In Tsarist Russia, the efforts of the regime to regain the initiative after the 1905 Revolution relied heavily on the encouragement of antisemitic pogroms. In the two weeks following the declaration of the Tsar's October Manifesto, which made major concessions to the idea of a constitutional monarchy, there were 690 documented pogroms in Russia, with over 3,000 reported murders. In the town of Odessa, 800 Jews were murdered, 5,000 wounded and over 100,000 made homeless. The antisemites had been actively supported by the Tsarist police, another branch of which had earlier been responsible for concocting the most notorious antisemitic document of modern times, *The Protocols of the Elders of Zion*.[11] Subsequently, during the Civil War that followed the Bolshevik Revolution, anti-Jewish pogroms were carried out by all sides, including the Reds. The counter-revolutionary 'Whites' were by far the most active perpetrators, and were accustomed to give their soldiers several days' freedom to rob, rape and kill the Jewish inhabitants of any town they took. Cossack troops burned the Jews of Chernobyl alive in the local synagogue. Ukrainian nationalists were not far behind in their antisemitic violence. Polish forces invading Russia during this chaotic period contributed their part. It has long been known that at least 50,000 Jews were killed in this way; a report made by Jewish organizations in Soviet Russia in 1920, recently released from the Russian archives, gives a total of more than 150,000 reported deaths and up to as many again wounded or badly mutilated.[12] The most widespread public antisemitic outbursts in modern German history up to the Third Reich, the 'Hep!-Hep!' disturbances of the pre-1848 years, though unpleasant, were seldom murderous, and could not stand comparison with this. Indeed, nothing on this scale was ever seen in modern Germany, not even in the Third Reich before the Second World War. There was only one pogrom in Germany in the Imperial period, in Neustettin, in a backward part of Pomerania in 1881.[13] In comparison with Russia or even France around the turn of the century, Germany was not a bad place for Jews to live.

Goldhagen also claims that no minority in Europe had experienced legal discrimination to the degree suffered by the Jews under Nazism during this time (p. 138). But this is not true either. In Tsarist Russia for most of the nineteenth century, Jews were denied even those few basic rights enjoyed by the majority of the Russian population; they were forced to live in a 'Pale of Settlement', and in the early 1890s they were summarily expelled from Moscow. During the interwar years, Poland and Hungary introduced a whole series of laws discriminating against Jews, very similar to those enacted in Nazi Germany. Anti-Jewish legislation was common throughout the states of Central Europe at this time. The difference in Germany was that it formed part of a much wider package of eugenic and racial measures including marriage loans, the sterilization of the 'unfit' and other policies which had few parallels elsewhere in Europe. Even a fairly brief exercise in comparative history, therefore, seriously undermines Goldhagen's thesis that German antisemitism was unique in its extent and its extremism in the nineteenth and early twentieth centuries.

II

No one has demonstrated, Goldhagen claims, that significant groups of Germans had any reservations about what he has identified as their cultural heritage of exterminatory antisemitism. But this is completely untrue. For he totally ignores the fact that the Social Democratic Party, by far the largest political organization in Wilhelmine Germany, with the largest number of votes and from 1912 the largest number of seats in the Reichstag, was opposed to antisemitism at every turn. Even those who have attempted, somewhat implausibly, to interpret Marx's early essay *On the Jewish Question* as antisemitic have been unable to show convincingly that the Social Democratic party harboured antisemitic views.[14]

As Rosemarie Leuschen-Seppel showed in her standard monograph on the Social Democrats' confrontation with the 'Jewish Question' and the Anti-semitic Parties in Imperial Germany (1978), the Party believed that Judaism would disappear along with other religions after the socialist revolution, and Jews would therefore be completely assimilated into German society. The alleged defects of the 'Jewish character', which Party literature conceded might have some substance in reality, were in its view the product of social influences and discrimination dating from the Middle Ages, and would vanish after the socialist revolution as well. After the publication of Engels's *Anti-Dühring*, the Party resisted the temptation of equating Jews with capitalists, and indeed devoted a great deal of attention to the plight of the poverty-stricken Jewish proletariat in Russia and in Congress Poland. The open expression of antisemitic views, allusions or phrases was never tolerated at Party Congresses or meetings. Even at the height of fierce debates involving controversial Jewish Party members such as Rosa Luxemburg, no-one ever used them: Luxemburg's Jewishness was simply not an issue. Indeed, in the 1880s, popular Social Democratic leaders of Jewish origin were treated to spontaneous demonstrations of public support from ordinary Party members when they came under attack from Adolf Stöcker's antisemites. At the end of a speech by Paul Singer in Berlin in the 1880s, for example, the working-class audience stormed the platform with cries of '*Bravo, Judenpaule!*' and carried the speaker in triumph from the hall.[15]

Nevertheless, although it did not tolerate open antisemitism within its ranks, the Social Democratic Party was less than completely perceptive when it came to accounting for the rise of antisemitic politics elsewhere. The official Social Democratic line on the emergence of the Antisemitic Parties in Germany during the 1880s and 1890s was that this was the temporary expression of the economic decline of 'medieval' social strata, a process which would end by bringing these social groups into the Social Democratic camp. The Party thought that antisemitic feeling was being manipulated by the Reich government in order to divert attention from the problems that beset it. The fact that the Antisemitic Parties scored some electoral successes in areas such as the Hessian countryside was attributed to the peasantry's resentment of the economic role of Jews in these areas. This rather complacent mixture of economic reductionism and political determinism prevented the Social Democrats from recognizing the psychological power of antisemitism, and contributed to the Party's failure to take advantage of the politicization of the peasantry which the rise of movements like Otto Böckel's Antisemitic Party in Hesse represented. Nevertheless, in Hesse itself the Social Democrats were vigorous in their opposition to the Antisemites, and fought a number of street battles against their more violent elements. The Party took the Antisemites' agitation seriously enough to mount a massive campaign of propaganda and recruitment in the area, though without much success: no peasant farmer was going to respond very positively, after all, to the message that he was a member of a declining 'medieval' social class which would eventually fuse economically, socially and politically with the revolutionary proletariat.

As the Antisemitic Parties went into decline from the mid-1890s onwards, so the Social Democrats began to pay less attention to them, although they always remained vigilant where there was competition for support, as among the unionized white-collar workers, many of whom belonged to the strongly antisemitic German-national Commercial Employees' Union. It was above all the outbreak of pogroms in Russia in the wake of the 1905 Revolution, as the Tsarist regime moved to re-establish its authority over the country, that occupied the German Social Democrats' attention in the years leading up to the outbreak of the First World War. Indeed, the violent antisemitism of the government-backed Black Hundreds, and the international publicity given to the Beiliss affair, in which a Jew was tried on a trumped-up charge of ritual murder in Kiev in 1912/13 with the full support of the Tsar and his ministers, convinced the German Social Democrats that the Russians were violent, backward and barbarous, and thus helped them decide to vote for war credits in 1914. In Germany itself, however, the Party's vigilance relaxed. The Social Democratic leadership did not ask itself why the supporters of the now-defunct Antisemitic Parties had failed to join them as predicted, nor where they had gone instead.

Moreover, as Leuschen-Seppel has shown, while the Social Democratic Party apparatus continued to criticize antisemitic ideas and practices at a political level, its efforts were progressively undermined by the growth of the Party's entertainment press, which largely failed to break free from socially current antisemitic stereotypes and portrayed Jews in caricature and verse not only as symbols of materialism and the profit motive but even as dirty, smelly, and sexually depraved. Antisemitic jokes and cartoons were commonplace in many Social Democratic weeklies by 1914. Leuschen-Seppel argues that the entertainment press was allowed to get away with this because the Social Democrats rigidly separated politics from culture, and regarded the latter, including all its cultural journals and magazines, as politically neutral. However, while this may have been true of some areas of 'high culture' it surely was not the case as far as the social observation and commentary which formed the staple diet of the magazines in question, such as *Der Wahre Jacob*, are concerned. It is more likely that the editors of these publications simply did not pause to think about the emotional and political resonances of the sterotypes they were using, nor of the longer-term effects of repeating them.

The extent to which the antisemitic cartoons and doggerel to be found in some of the Social Democrats' entertainment magazines actually influenced, or had an effect on, the Party rank-and-file is hard to gauge. Just as hard to answer is the question of how far the Socialists' formal hostility to antisemitism actually penetrated down the ranks and influenced ordinary Party members. Leuschen-Seppel took a gloomy view, asserting that antisemitic prejudices were 'virulent' among the rank-and-file, and that Social Democratic culture was 'delivered up helplessly to the dominant culture' in this, as in other, areas.[16] But a great deal of research carried out in the 1980s has done much to modify this view, showing that the Party's cultural apparatus and activities did in many respects offer a genuine and radical alternative to the bourgeois stuffiness and prejudices of official Wilhelmine culture,[17] though it is also clear that it was increasingly undermined, or sidelined, by the growth of commercial leisure and entertainment offerings for the masses, to which, indeed, the Party's entertainment press may well have been trying to adapt.[18] Ordinary workers got most of their information from the Party's daily press, rather than from glossy magazines like *Der Wahre Jacob*, which were designed to appeal to the better-educated and the better-off. A unique source which gives us some insight into the extent to which workers' views were affected by, or diverged from, those of the Party that claimed to represent them – the pub surveillance reports of the Hamburg Political Police – shows that there were virtually no antisemitic sentiments uttered by rank-and-file supporters of the Social Democrats during the Wilhelmine period.[19]

Under the Weimar Republic, the Social Democrats continued to combat antisemitism, while for the most part also continuing to underestimate its emotional and psychological power and reduce it instead to a manipulative tactic of right-wing demagogues. Fearful of giving credence to accusations that they were a 'Jewish' party themselves, Social Democrats in government did too little to bring violent antisemites to book or to defend the rights of Jewish immigrants from Eastern Europe. Antisemitism, as 'the socialism of fools', earned nothing but their contempt; and Social Democrats under Weimar continued to believe that it would disappear – as would the Nazi Party – when the petty-bourgeois groups who espoused it declined into the proletariat and became socialists themselves. The Nazis' antisemitism was interpreted mostly as part of a general assault on civil rights, and Social Democrats failed to see its centrality to the movement, or to recognize its murderous virulence. Most serious of all, perhaps, as in the Imperial period, and indeed in the writings of Marx himself, the Party accepted widespread social stereotypes of Jews without criticism, merely ascribing the 'Jewish character' to social rather than racial origins. Nevertheless, despite all these weaknesses, the fact remains that antisemitism was almost completely absent from Social Democratic and labour movement culture and politics right up to the end of the Weimar Republic, that the Party continued up to the end to devote considerable resources to combating the antisemitism of the Nazis and the far right, and that rank-and-file members remained almost free from antisemitic prejudice as far as it is possible to tell.[20]

What changed matters as far as the working class was concerned was the decay and then collapse of labour movement traditions in the 1920s and 1930s. This is particularly relevant to the participation of a substantial number of working-class men in the mass shootings of Jews by Police Battalion 101 on the Eastern Front in the early 1940s. For Christopher Browning, these were 'ordinary men' in an extraordinary situation. Given the same circumstances, he suggests chillingly, anybody else could have done the same. For Goldhagen, however, they were not 'ordinary men' but 'ordinary Germans', driven by fanatical hatred of the Jews. As both Browning and Goldhagen point out, the men were drafted into the police from the working population of Hamburg in the early Summer of 1941; they were mostly married, and they came from varied social backgrounds, with the lower middle class slightly over-represented and the working class slightly under-represented. Fewer than half of them were members of the Nazi Party, and hardly any of them belonged to the SS. But this does not make them merely 'ordinary' men or 'ordinary' Germans without further distinction. For the crucial factor in the composition of the battalion is one to which neither historian pays sufficient attention, and that is the age of the men who belonged to it.

The great majority of the police reservists were in their thirties; some were a little older. This means that most of them would have been born in the years leading up to the outbreak of the First World War. This particular generation of men grew to consciousness in the violence of war and revolution, between 1914 and 1923; they lived through the chaos of the great inflation, when money lost all value, and when poor and modestly off families begged, stole and fought for food and fuel. They came onto the labour market during the high unemployment of the years of post-inflationary industrial rationalization and the mass unemployment of the Depression from 1929 to 1933. Many of them would have been drafted into the Nazi Labour Service or served as conscripts in the army in the early years of Hitler's Third Reich. They would have been in their early-to-mid-twenties when Hitler came to power, and have known little except economic hardship, political violence and state coercion during their adult lives. None of this was a good recipe for the inculcation of civilized moral values in these men. Moreover, those who were working-class would have had little contact with the socializing traditions of the trade unions and other organizations of the labour movement, since they would not have been likely to have had permanent jobs in industry before 1933, and the labour

IDEOLOGICAL ORIGINS OF NAZISM

movement was decimated by the experience of mass unemployment then suppressed altogether by the Nazis. Theirs was a lost generation, morally adrift, and particularly susceptible therefore to the siren call of Nazism. It was also a generation that had grown up in a culture of violence, and which had far fewer scruples than its predecessors about using it. Finally, these men, like all Germans, had been subjected since 1933 to a ceaseless and unrestrained barrage of government and media propaganda against the Jews, portraying them at every level as parasites, bacilli, dangerous, verminous, dirty and scheming creatures who did not belong to the German race. This view clearly found its expression in the letters of the men of the police battalion, which, when they mentioned Jews, portrayed them in exaggerated terms as a threat to their own survival. Yet the main motivation was not a rabid but vague hatred of Jews as such, but the belief that the Jews of occupied Eastern Europe were a threat because of their support for or orchestration of 'partisan' and other subversive activities.[21]

Men of this kind may well have been among those working-class people who cast their votes for the Nazi Party in the elections of the early 1930s, though the Party's working-class constituency lay mostly in small towns and among unorganized rural and handicraft workers.[22] Remarkably in view of his general thesis, Goldhagen devotes no more than a single page to the Nazi seizure of power (p. 87). If his overall argument is correct, then we would expect this to be largely due to the popularity of the Nazis' antisemitic message. But even he is aware of the fact that modern research has overwhelmingly demonstrated that antisemitism was not an important factor in generating votes for the Nazis in the elections of 1930–3 when they became a mass party. At least, Goldhagen is forced to fall back on the argument that the Nazis' antisemitism did not put voters off (p. 497, n. 22). But even this is not true. As William Sheridan Allen showed long ago in his classic study of the small town of Northeim, Nazi propaganda deliberately played down the antisemitic aspects of the Party's ideology from 1928 onwards because they had been found to be unpopular with the electorate.[23] Despite all this, Goldhagen persists in asserting that in 1933 the vast majority of Germans subscribed to the Nazi view of the Jews – virulent, racist and murderous (pp. 87–8). Here it is necessary to recall, however, the well-known fact that no more than 37.4 per cent of the voters ever supported the Nazis in a free election, and that even in the elections of March 1933, when faced with massive intimidation by the recently installed Nazi government, the party still failed to win an overall majority.

III

It is necessary to make all these points because Goldhagen's erroneous and poorly researched arguments about the unique centrality of antisemitism to German political culture in the nineteenth century and early twentieth constitute the essential factor which he uses to explain the murderous activities of German police battalions, labour camp guards and death march squads during the 1940s. By the time we reach this period, indeed long before, Goldhagen has framed his account in language which in the absence of any real historical evidence becomes a substitute for rational argument. For throughout the book, he refers to the perpetrators as 'Germans' or even 'the Germans', as if every single German was directly involved. During the 1930s, he writes, 'the Germans began to exclude Jews from governmental service . . . the Germans removed Jews from the cultural spheres and the press' (p. 137). He refers not to the Nazis' anti-Jewish policy but to 'the Germans' anti-Jewish policy' (p. 141). 'Germans', he claims, 'were generally brutal and murderous in the use of other peoples' (p. 315). 'Every German was inquisitor, judge and executioner' (p. 194). The behaviour of the perpetrators reflected 'the German culture of cruelty . . . towards Jews' (p. 255). In places this linguistic convention becomes positively absurd, as when for example Goldhagen says 'the Germans' were forced to stop shooting Jews on the town square in Bialystok by objections of a bystander – who himself happened to be German (p. 189). This endless repetition of the sweeping phrase 'the Germans' instead of more precise terms such as 'the police battalion', 'the SS camp guards', and so on, gives the book an unmistakeable flavour of reverse racism, attributing to a whole people the characteristics of a minority.[24] This flavour is strengthened by Goldhagen's refusal to distinguish between Germans and Austrians (whom he claims, quite wrongly, were overwhelmingly in favour of the *Anschluss* in 1938 (p. 286)). Thus in claiming that twelve ritual murder trials were held in Germany and the Austrian Empire before 1914, he neglects to mention that only one of them was held in Germany (and there is much evidence to show that it aroused strong disapproval amongst ordinary working-class Germans), and does not remind his readers either of the fact that the Austrian Empire included all or part of present-day Hungary, Poland and Romania, where antisemitism was notoriously strong, or of the fact that in none of the trials did the jury uphold the charge.[25] No wonder the book has been described by a neutral observer, the Hungarian-born journalist Gitta Sereny, as 'a hymn of hate to the Germans'.[26]

Goldhagen's linguistic usage becomes positively distasteful when he states (pp. 170–1) that 'the Germans established, maintained and staffed' the concentration and extermination camps, ignoring the fact that many of them were in fact staffed by guards of other nationalities – above all, Lithuanians and Ukrainians – whose cruelty towards the Jews was sometimes even more marked than that of their German fellow-guards, and whose countries had a long-term record of virulent antisemitism which also found its expression in murderous pogroms carried out by local people at the instigation of the SS immediately after the German invasion in 1941. Goldhagen justifies his linguistic procedure by claiming that the perpetrators were 'Germans first and SS men, policemen, or camp guards second'. They were 'Germans pursuing German national political goals' (pp. 6–7). But this again is wrong: those of them who were Germans were Germans in specific historical, political and institutional circumstances which conditioned them to commit genocide. Their behaviour cannot in itself be taken as evidence that all Germans were keen to do the same thing if only they had the chance, and the argument that it was only Germany's international weakness which prevented the Nazis from starting the extermination programme as soon as they came to power has no evidence to support it whatsoever (p. 419). Germans in general were deeply divided over national political goals, as the Nazis' failure to win any free election had demonstrated.

In a curious way, what Goldhagen is doing is endorsing the view relentlessly propagated by Hitler and Goebbels that the German people were deeply antisemitic from the outset; indeed he explicitly praises Hitler for his insight into the depth of the Germans' feelings on this matter (p. 443). His book constitutes a craven surrender to the Nazi view of German history. Whether the Nazi leaders actually believed their own propaganda is another matter. They knew, for example, that their campaign of boycotting Jewish shops on 1 April 1933 and the public destruction of Jewish property, the mass arrests, maltreatment and murder of Jews in the pogrom of 9–10 November 1938, the so-called 'Night of Broken Glass', had not only failed to arouse public enthusiasm among ordinary Germans but had even led to visible disquiet. A British journalist reported that many people in Hamburg, Cologne and Berlin had spoken to him of their anger and shame at these events. The American consul in Leipzig said the vast majority of ordinary Germans in the town were 'benumbed' and 'aghast' at the destruction, and 'nauseated' and 'horror-stricken' at the physical violence meted out to the Jews on the streets and the zoo by the Nazis.[27] It was not merely outrage at the destruction of property which upset them, therefore. The Nazis thus went to considerable lengths to keep the mass extermination of the 'Final Solution' secret. Spreading 'rumours' about what went on in the camps was a criminal offence. The extermination took place outside Germany, not within its borders. Talking to SS leaders in Posen on 4 October 1943, Himmler said of the extermination programme that

> we will never speak about it publicly . . . This is a glorious page in our history, and one that has never been written and can never be written . . . Later perhaps we can consider whether the German people should be told about this. But I think it is better that we – we together – carry for our people the responsibility . . . and then take the secret with us to our graves.[28]

The reason for this secrecy was clearly that Himmler and the other leading figures who devised and implemented the extermination programme feared it would arouse controversy within Germany if it became widely known.[29]

Goldhagen argues that because there was no overt opposition to any of these antisemitic acts within Germany – no demonstrations, no mass protests, no uprisings against the Nazis – therefore all Germans must have been strongly in favour of them (p. 418). In fact, of course, the absence of overt opposition demonstrates nothing of the kind, however else one may wish to explain it.

As David Bankier and others have shown, and as the Jewish philologist Viktor Klemperer chronicled in minute detail in his recently published diaries of the Third Reich (a best-seller in Germany), German Jews in the Third Reich encountered many small gestures of sympathy, solidarity and guilt from Germans, not least after they were forced to wear the yellow star in September 1941, an event signalled by Goldhagen simply as another step in the progressive isolation of the Jews from the rest of the population.[30] Even the Nazi propaganda chief Josef Goebbels complained to Albert Speer that the introduction of the yellow star had only prompted people to show sympathy for the Jews. 'This people', he raved, 'simply hasn't grown up, it's full of idiotic sentimentality.'[31] Fear of denunciation kept them from doing anything more open, and again, recent research, notably by Robert Gellately, has demonstrated the key role played by denunciations sent in to the Gestapo by the public – often for reasons that had little to do with politics or ideology or even with anti-Semtism – in maintaining the regime in power and in stifling protest and dissent. There was enough sympathy among ordinary Germans to keep several thousand Jews alive in hiding in Germany until 1945, including Klemperer himself.[32]

In arguing that Hitler, the leading Nazis and indeed by implication the Germans as a whole, intended to exterminate the Jews from the very beginning of the Nazi movement, Goldhagen ignores a mass of empirical evidence and scholarly research which demonstrates the contrary. During the 1930s, for example, not only were Jews allowed to emigrate from Germany – and hundreds of thousands did – but the SS actually encouraged many to do so, and urged young German Zionists to learn basic agricultural techniques so that they could take up farming when they got to Palestine. The emigration of Jews from Germany, indeed, was not stopped by the regime until October 1941, while there is no evidence of any planning for death camps before about the same time. For Goldhagen simply to assert that the decision to exterminate the Jews was taken at the beginning of the year (p. 147) flies in the face of all this evidence, and ignores the conclusions of a great deal of careful and minute scholarship carried out over the past few decades which puts the probable date for the decision in July or August.[33] He also seems unaware of the fact that the order given to the SS *Einsatzgruppen* before the invasion of Russia in June 1941 to kill Jews where they found them does not amount to the same thing as an order to the SS as a whole to kill the entire Jewish population of Europe.

Although the central, empirical chapters of the book are based on a good deal of archival research, they are not free from error. Goldhagen misrepresents significant details about Police Battalion 101. For example, he claims that Captain Hoffmann objected in writing to being ordered to sign a declaration that he would not steal from Poles because to suppose that he required an order not to do so impugned his sense of honour as a military man. This, says Goldhagen, shows that he considered stealing from Poles a far greater crime than killing Jewish women and children (pp. 3–4). In fact there is nothing in the document to say that it applied to Poles. It is more than likely that it applied to Jews, since Himmler in fact explicitly and repeatedly told his SS men (of whom Hoffmann was one, though Goldhagen does not mention this fact) that they had to remain 'decent', honest and incorruptible in the execution of his genocidal policies.[34] In noting that only a third of the men in the battalion were members of the Nazi Party too, Goldhagen neglects to mention that the actual proportion of Party members in the adult population as a whole was not one in three but one in eight.[35] These are small examples of the way in which he constantly selects evidence which suits his argument, and neglects facts which do not. The same may be said of his treatment of secondary work too.

Goldhagen's case is not strengthened by the vehemence of his condemnation of those historians whose views differ from his. To write off other people's arguments, often without much evidence, as 'absurd', 'specious', 'self-evidently false', 'erroneous', 'untenable', 'mistakes', and to adorn his own arguments repeatedly with adjectives such as 'incontestable', is no substitute for reasoned argument, and does not convince. This is the language of dogmatism, not scholarship. It betrays a disturbing arrogance that is of a piece with the exaggerated claims for novelty which Goldhagen makes in the Introduction. Moreover, Goldhagen's obsessive denigration of the work of Christopher Browning, the one scholar who has previously worked on the material about Police Battalion 101, is completely unnecessary. In order to establish that his own interpretation of the policemen as fanatical antisemites is right, and Browning's view that they were 'ordinary men' who became mass murderers as a result of circumstances and pressures which could apply to anyone, whether German or not, Goldhagen accuses Browning variously of presenting evidence 'improperly' (p. 550), of misportrayal of facts (p. 551), and (repeatedly) of making claims for which there is no factual basis – an ironic charge in view of Goldhagen's persistent practice of doing the same. The vehemence of Goldhagen's attacks on Browning is so great that it detracts from rather than adds to the plausibility of his own case.

In a review that was remarkable above all for its moderate and restrained tone, Browning noted that Oswald Rufeisen, a Jewish translator for the murderous police battalion (naturally he kept his Jewish identity secret from them, giving himself out to be a Pole), did not remark in his memoirs on any particularly antisemitic atmosphere in the unit. On the contrary, while recording a variety of reactions to the task of mass murder that ranged from enthusiasm for it at one extreme to a determination to be excused from taking part in it at the other, Rufeisen thought that the predominant feeling was that the shootings – in contrast to military operations against partisans – were 'dirty' and somehow tainting for the unit and its members, and that it was best if possible not to mention them. In arguing that it was deep-rooted antisemitism that drove such men to burn down Jewish villages and massacre their inhabitants, Goldhagen ignored the fact that the German army did the same to thousands of Russian and Ukrainian villages in the occupied territories, and killed three to four million defenceless Slavs (most notably prisoners of war), not to mention similar massacres in Italy, Greece and Yugoslavia.[36]

What remains therefore is the evidence he presents for the sadism and gratuitous brutality of many of those who carried out the extermination programme. This is a salutary reminder to those who may still think that the perpetrators were merely obeying orders, or were no more than indifferent to suffering instead of (as Goldhagen shows) actively promoting it. It is also a reminder of the very considerable numbers of people, Germans and others, who were involved in maintaining Hitler's system of terror, coercion and extermination. There were thousands of camps in the Nazi Empire, and millions passed through them. Recent research has thrown up evidence not only of numerous small sub-camps set up by the major German labour and concentration camps all over Germany, but also – using documents newly accessible since the fall of Communism and the collapse of the Soviet Union – of massive numbers of killings, which, though individually on a smaller scale than what went on in Auschwitz or Treblinka, none the less added up to a considerable number overall. Work on the German army, once thought to have been uninvolved in the genocide, has demonstrated its deep complicity in the killing of Jews and the mass murder of members of other ethnic groups as well. Altogether, Goldhagen himself estimates that there were about half a million people directly involved in carrying out and administering the extermination programme.

Yet that makes up well under 1 per cent of the population of 'Greater Germans' including Austria, the Sudetenland and other conquered areas, in the early 1940s. What about the other 79.5 million? For many years, historians have known that the number of Germans who were informed about these actions, through brothers or husbands in the army, through friends and acquaintances in the SS, through personal involvement on the fringes, as railway employees shuffling cattle-trains about on the timetable or along the tracks, as factory workers manufacturing and supplying poison gas capsules and other requisites to the extermination camps, or in any one of a number of capacities, was very large indeed. While the regime made every effort to keep details of what went on at Auschwitz and Treblinka and camps like them as secret as possible, details about the mass shootings which accounted for two million or more victims were much more difficult to suppress. Those who heard about them may even have constituted a majority of the German population. Moreover, many ordinary Germans witnessed Jews being driven out of their homes in Hamburg, Heidelberg and elsewhere and herded through the streets, while the disappearance of Jewish neighbours from German residential districts cannot have gone unnoticed. But all this is one thing: claiming that they were all positively enthusiastic about the extermination programme rather than merely indifferent towards it, or passively complicit in its implementation, is quite another, and Goldhagen has not provided any convincing evidence that they were. By contrast, there is a good deal of evidence to show that there was widespread disquiet about the programme among ordinary Germans, as Martin Bormann warned local Party bosses in 1942.[37] Himmler complained in his Posen speech in 1943 that every German had a Jew they wished to protect, while the German-Jewish *émigré* Franz Neumann noted that antisemitism, for so long prominent in the ideas of German intellectuals, had failed to strike root amongst the mass of the people. 'Spontaneous, popular antisemitism', he wrote in 1942, 'is still weak in Germany . . . It is significant that despite the incessant propaganda to which the German people have been subjected, there is no record of a single spontaneous anti-Jewish attack committed by persons not belonging to the Nazi Party.'[38]

IV

How can we explain this startling failure of scholarship in a book which after all began its life as a Harvard dissertation? It is surely relevant to note that it was supervised and examined not by historians but by political scientists, whose knowledge of the empirical aspects of the subject was clearly limited. It is significant that the prize it was given in 1994 was the Gabriel Almond Award of the American Political Science Association; it was not given any prizes by historians. Beyond this, the book also reflects one of the most disturbing and damaging aspects of contemporary American academic culture – the emphasis it places on new interpretations at the expense of solid research. Reputations are made less by major pieces of historical scholarship than by startling reinterpretations of what is already known, and in the hands of the over-ambitious and under-prepared this all too often leads to disaster.[39] Goldhagen is also clearly emotionally committed to his extreme views, and this commitment equally clearly owes a good deal to his father Erich Goldhagen, a survivor of the death camps, to whose 'many conversations' the author declares himself deeply indebted (p. 480), and who is the dedicatee of the book.[40] A powerful emotional commitment to a subject can be the source of good history if it is allied to a degree of scholarly detachment, but when it overcomes reason, as it too often does in this book, then it can be deeply damaging to scholarly standards.

More interesting than the reasons why this is, taken as a whole, such a bad book, are the reasons why it has aroused such widespread attention, and why it has sold so many copies. It certainly does not owe its success to any particular merits of its style; far from being written in an accessible or journalistic manner, it is heavily burdened with pretentious political-science jargon and often clumsily expressed. There can be no doubt that the publishers have marketed the book intelligently, and the subject is rightly one of widespread interest, which ensures a large readership for many books that are less sensational than this one. Moreover, one of the undeniable advantages of the author's strong emotional commitment to the subject is the way in which this conveys itself to the reader, above all in the central chapters. Academic historians of Nazi Germany have on the whole chosen a sober, analytical approach and eschewed the repetition of the more horrific aspects of the Third Reich's crimes. By contrast, Goldhagen describes murder, torture, cruelty and sadism in almost loving detail, producing what one commentator has called 'an aesthetics of horror'. Evil acquires a face and often indeed a name. Thus the book packs a powerful punch, and has the ability to shock even those who are familiar with these matters.[41] But the attention it has attracted in Britain, the USA and Germany clearly requires an explanation beyond this as well. In all three cases it has struck a nerve. In many ways it has been fortunate in its timing.

For the British, Goldhagen's book came at a time when a national debate about the United Kingdom's relationship with the European Union moved to the centre of the political arena, above all within the Conservative Party. The 'Eurosceptics' who wish Britain to leave the Union (not for economic reasons, but in order to restore national sovereignty) regard Germany as the Union's dominant power and therefore use the German past as a way of attacking it. For them, Britain's finest hour was in 1940, when the country stood alone against a hostile European Continent dominated by Hitler's Third Reich, and a straight line runs from Churchill's rhetoric of the time through Margaret Thatcher's notorious 'Chequers seminar' at which a group of experts were enlisted in reluctant support of the then Prime Minister's view that German reunification posed a threat to British liberties, to the post-Thatcherite Euroscepticism of the present-day Conservative Right. Thus it is not surprising that a leading Conservative newspaper, the *Daily Telegraph*, greeted Goldhagen's book (which even its reviewer found 'sometimes too impassioned to be convincing') with the conclusion that it showed that 'Germany has not . . . completely civilised itself':

There is an underlying paranoia in German policy, an unstated fear that makes their leaders demand ever-greater European unity in order

167

to protect their nation from the beast within. German failure to confront beastliness, and our cowardly reluctance to raise it with them, has fenced European discussions with a string of . . . unmentionables. Those inhibitions do nothing to enhance mutual trust or enrich our faith in Germany's good intentions.[42]

Thus Goldhagen's book was enlisted in the service of the Eurosceptic belief that the Germans had failed to confront the Nazi past and therefore risked repeating it in a new form through their dominance of the European Union. Of course, far from having failed to confront the Nazi past, German political and intellectual culture has been dominated by it since the late 1960s, and the idea that it has taken Goldhagen's book to 'put German guilt back on the agenda' is patently absurd: it has never been off it. Not surprisingly, for all its resonance in the press, serious British specialists in German history, including Ian Kershaw and Arnold Paucker, condemned the book as ignorant and simplistic at a symposium held at the German Historical Institute in London on 21 May 1996.

Yet similar comments have also greeted the book's appearance in the United States, where the book became an instant best-seller and was the subject of a laudatory review by the eminent specialist Gordon A. Craig in the *New York Review of Books*. Protests from those who were worried that Craig would be seen to be speaking for the profession – he is, after all, a former President of the American Historical Association – prompted him to publish what amounted to a recantation of his views in the liberal German weekly *Die Zeit*, where he again welcomed Goldhagen's book as a provocation to think again about the subject, but added that he found its arguments undifferentiated and exaggerated.[43] These are precisely the qualities, however, which are most likely to have contributed to its success among the general public. History as a simple story of heroes and villains has always played a major role in American popular culture, whether in depictions of shoot-outs in the Wild West or fantasy conflict set in the intergalactic future. Moreover, as Robert Hughes remarked in his brilliant polemic *The Culture of Complaint*, victimhood has now become a major source of legitimacy in American society, as different groups – blacks, Hispanics, women, gays, even white Anglo-Saxon males who are now claiming to be the victims of political correctness imposed by the others – use it as a means of shoring up their own claims for equal rights or even preferential treatment in education, employment and other areas of social competition.[44] The supreme symbol of victimhood is the 'Holocaust', and it is no accident that recent years have seen a number of 'Holocaust Memorial Museums' founded in various American cities, nor that they have been extremely popular with visitors, nor that the great majority of those visitors have been non-Jewish. The view of the Germans purveyed by the Washington, DC museum – all the more powerful because of the museum's superb and moving construction and presentation of its materials – is uniformly negative. There is, for instance, only one small panel on the German resistance to Hitler, focusing on the students of the 'White Rose' movement in Munich: nothing on liberal, socialist or Communist resisters, nothing on the conservative nationalists of 20 July 1944, many of whom found what was going on in Auschwitz morally repugnant, nothing on the many German victims of Nazism. The visitor is almost bound to come out of the exhibition regarding 'the Germans' as the perpetrators in a collective sense. Goldhagen's book too is a kind of memorial to them, a museum of words. To some extent this is necessary, just as the museums are, at a time when the neo-Nazi literature of 'Holocaust denial', the vast majority of which originates in and is distributed through America, is reaching new audiences through pseudo-academic journals and magazines and through the internet.[45] But it is surely not necessary to carry out this project in so simplistic and undifferentiated a fashion, even if this does contribute to its popularity and accessiblity.

In this sense, the debate over the book has opened up yet again the gulf between academic and popular history. The most popular general history of Nazi Germany is still William L. Shirer's *The Rise and Fall of the Third Reich* (1960), which takes a similar line to that of Goldhagen, and repeats wartime propaganda about the pervasiveness of antisemitism, racism, militarism and authoritarianism in nineteenth- and early twentieth-century German culture.[46] For all its academic trappings, its political-science jargon and its modish postmodernist insistence on the primacy of ideas and beliefs in history, Goldhagen's book, which is said to have sold some 40,000 copies within a couple of months of its publication, falls very much into the same category.[47] Hence the agonized objections of so many American academics, amongst whom the book's theses have been overwhelmingly rejected. In a seminar discussion on the Internet German History List,[48] Eric D. Weitz, for instance, found the book's claims to originality 'largely hyperbolic' and undifferentiated. Most seriously, Weitz charged that the book shamefully neglected the history of Nazism's other victims. Michael Allen found the book 'tendentious' and 'specious'. Similarly, as we have seen, Richard S. Levy, author of a standard work on the antisemitic parties in Imperial Germany, also rejected Goldhagen's theses about the place of antisemitism in the political culture of the day, while Christopher Browning was also deeply critical of Goldhagen's views. With the exception of a few non-specialists like Simon Schama, professional historians in America too, on the whole rejected the book and its arguments.

Among the wider public, Goldhagen's book not only benefited from intellectual and political trends current at the time of its appearance, it also came out at a time of crisis in world Jewish politics and identity following the assassination of Israel's Prime Minister Rabin. Identifying the experience of suffering and mass murder under the Nazis, and constructing 'the

Germans' as a symbolic enemy to remind Jews that the threat of annihilation still existed and had to be combated, suddenly became important again as a way of overcoming political divisions and reaffirming Jewish identity, above all in the USA. Yet Jewish and Israeli scholars have also been highly critical of Goldhagen's book. Moshe Zimmermann, for example, director of the Richard Koebner Centre for German History at the Hebrew University of Jerusalem, noted that Goldhagen's views were the same as those of the Israeli general public, and therefore failed to stir up any controversy there. In this sense they could not be called startlingly original or new. From the point of view of the specialist historian, however, the book constructed 'an erroneous collective guilt' thesis which was not borne out by the German people's indifferent or critical attitude to the 1938 *Kristallnacht* pogrom. Zimmermann pointed out that even Hitler, in his *Table-Talk* on 15 May 1942, complained bitterly that the German 'bourgeoisie now sheds tears when we ship them (i.e. the Jews) off somewhere to the east'.[49] There was no evidence that the vast majority of Germans were 'eliminationist antisemites', and all too frequently Goldhagen offered assertion instead of proof, ignoring scholars whose arguments ran against his. Finding the book's theses 'distorting and tendentious', Zimmermann even convicted it of adopting a 'mythological or even quasi-racist definition of the concept of "Germans"', not least in its denial that German Jews, most of whom in the nineteenth century considered themselves German patriots, and many of whom fought in the German army in the First World War, were in any sense German.[50] Similarly, Saul Friedländer, while pleading for a fair debate based on a careful reading of the book, admitted he could not subscribe to Goldhagen's thesis that German society was already permeated by antisemitism before 1933. It was 'much too sweeping', blurred crucial distinctions between different types and degrees of antisemitism, and ignored the effects of events such as the First World War, the collapse of the German Empire, and the world economic crisis of 1929–33, in radicalizing and spreading antisemitic views. As a political scientist, said Friedländer, Goldhagen ignored the discontinuities and changes in German history over the period in question. The book ran the risk of encouraging anti-German prejudice.[51]

This fear was echoed by comments from younger historians such as Gulie Ne'eman-Arad of Tel Aviv University, who accused the book of painting history in black and white, and thereby pandering to commercialism. It portrayed 'the Germans' as culturally completely different from other peoples, a position, she wrote, which 'is reminiscent of the Nazis' position towards the Jews'. Ne'eman-Arad, like many others, regretted the absence of a comparative perspective in Goldhagen's work, and criticized the tone of his attacks on Christopher Browning. She considered that his demonization of the Germans testified to the central role played by the 'Holocaust' in the construction of American Jewish identity, which required the constant suggestion of an external threat in order to hold itself together. Another young Israeli historian, Oded Heilbronner, also criticized the book's over-simplifications as 'populist'.[52] As elsewhere, therefore, so too in Israel, the reaction of professional historians was overwhelmingly negative.

Reactions to the book were strongest of all in Germany.[53] After the reunification of the country in 1989/90 and the passing of the fiftieth anniversary of the end of the Second World War in 1995, many Germans hoped that a line could be drawn under the postwar era and a fresh start made, unencumbered by the weight of historical responsibility for the Third Reich. Some commentators saw in Goldhagen's book a new 'collective guilt thesis' that threatened to accompany the Germans for the rest of time.[54] One felt like Sisyphus: every time the Germans felt they had managed to remove the stone of collective guilt from their shoulders, someone put it back there again.[55] Another feared that Goldhagen's hypothesis that German antisemitism sometimes took on a 'latent', silent and inactive form, only to erupt above the surface again a few decades later on, could apply to the post-1945 period just as much as to the centuries before. 'If one believes the book's theses, then the Germans' path into the twenty-first century can only be contemplated with scepticism and fear . . . The American reader who knows little about modern German history will find here the ethnology of a people that has never completely left the Middle Ages.'[56]

But it would be quite wrong to see in such comments 'the German' reaction to Goldhagen's book. German reactions on this, as on every other political or historical issue, were divided. Right-wing newspapers such as the *Frankfurter Allgemeine* and *Die Welt*, from which the comments quoted above are taken, had been arguing for some time that it was time for Germany to cast off the burdens of the past and assume a self-confident and independent role on the world stage once more. But as the liberal daily the *Süddeutsche Zeitung* pointed out, such a hope was illusory from the start, 'for Germany's past under National Socialism is so monstrous that it will not be forgotten even centuries hence',[57] and it was bound therefore to have a long-term, even permanent effect in limiting the ways in which Germany could pursue its foreign policy and regulate its relations with other states. The left-wing weekly *Freitag*, which addresses itself particularly to citizens of the former German Democratic Republic in the East, criticized the sharp condemnation of Goldhagen's book in other parts of the press, and chose instead to condemn the fact that the German Federal Parliament had so far refused to vote a retrospective amnesty for deserters from Hitler's army and denied compensation to homosexuals and handicapped people persecuted by the Third Reich. This, the newspaper claimed, could only happen because Germany had refused to accept the verdict of the Nuremberg trials, now revived by Goldhagen. If it had, then neo-fascist extremists would not be allowed to roam the streets beating up members of racial minorities.[58] Similarly, Kurt Pätzold, a distinguished specialist in the history of Nazi

Germany who had held a senior academic post in the former German Democratic Republic, accused Goldhagen's critics of 'wounded vanity' because his book had been more successful than theirs. They had responded first as Germans, he suggested, and only secondly as specialists.[59]

But in Germany too, professional historians reacted to the book with dismay. Specialists such as Eberhard Jäckel and Norbert Frei made clear their view that the book was simply based on inadequate research.[60] Hans Mommsen similarly found the book well behind the current state of research.[61] Hans-Ulrich Wehler saw the book as engaging in a 'demonization' of the Germans which reproduced the Nazi mentality itself, merely reversing the signs. This was a 'pseudo-scholarly resurrection of quasi-racism, camouflaged as the history of mentalities'. Goldhagen's subsequent declaration that the Germans had changed since the coming of democracy after 1945 lacked all credibility in view of his overall stress on the unique depth of German antisemitism, the more so since he took the view in the book that it could go underground for half a century or more and adopt a 'latent' form that was at any time liable to become manifest once again. Wehler obviously thought it something of an insult that Goldhagen should explicitly approach the Germans rather like an anthropologist approached a Stone-Age tribe in New Guinea. Why this should be objectionable is not entirely clear. He was on safer ground when, like many others, he criticized Goldhagen for his failure to engage in proper international comparisons. Goldhagen, he concluded, was turning back the scholarly clock to the early 1950s, ignoring all the research that had been carried out in Germany and elsewhere since then. In his book, and in his appearances in the American media, he was pandering irresponsibly to American resentments and prejudices against the Germans.[62]

V

Goldhagen himself replied to his critics at length in a voluminous article in *Die Zeit* on 2 August 1996. He modified or withdrew some of his most extreme arguments. Thus he now claimed for example, that 'most Germans would never have had the idea themselves of drawing the most radical consequences from their opinion of the Jews and carrying them out'. He agreed that it took historical developments such as the world economic crisis of 1929–33 for Hitler to come to power, and conceded that without Hitler there would have been no extermination of the Jews. His stress on the breadth and depth of German antisemitism, he now said, was designed to explain how the regime obtained the willing *help* of hundreds of thousands of Germans in carrying out its exterminatory programme. But for the most part he repaid his critics' arguments with rhetorical abuse, accusing them of failing to read his book properly, misrepresenting its arguments and ignoring the material it presented. He disputed, though far from convincingly, the charge that the book lacked a comparative dimension and insisted, though again without any concrete details, that it had brought a new social-scientific methodology to bear on the subject with which it dealt. He insisted that his critics had no right to make their criticisms unless they could put forward a better alternative themselves (a view that, if widely accepted, would bring an end to criticism altogether, and which in any case ignored, once more, the work of scholars such as Christopher Browning, which had been devoted precisely to putting forward alternative explanations of Nazi barbarism and brutality on the Eastern Front).[63] Repeating what he had already written in the book itself, Goldhagen underlined the gratuitous brutality of the perpetrators – a fact which no-one has disputed – and claimed once more that this could only be explained by a long-term and unique history of exterminatory antisemitism in German political culture. But apart from one or two very minor points, he did not reply to any of the detailed factual objections which critics had made to his account of German antisemitism. He simply insisted, without going into any detail at all, that his arguments were 'empirically supported' by the evidence he had presented.

Goldhagen had a point when he now remarked that whatever the degree or uniqueness of German antisemitism, the really important fact was that only Germany in the 1940s was in a position to carry out the extermination of Europe's Jewish population, and in this sense, comparison with other countries was irrelevant. Yet this was not how it seemed in the book. Similarly, he was correct enough in denying that his definition of 'Germans' was explicitly racial or biological or that he had used the concept of an 'eternal German character'. Yet 'political culture' as it is used in *Hitler's Willing Executioners* often seems little more than a modish and ill-defined euphemism for such terms. He denied, reasonably enough, any intention of impugning the present-day Germans, who he said had developed a political culture based on democratic values. Yet this was not how his book was read by a good number of its supporters as well as by some of its more nationalistic German critics, and the concept of 'latent' antisemitism which it employed made such a reading, to say the least, as Wehler had pointed out, perfectly plausible. He denied correctly that he had ever used the words 'collective guilt' and reminded his readers of his insistence throughout the book on individual responsibility. Yet many individuals make up a collectivity, and when all of those individuals are German, and all of them are said to have imbibed murderous antisemitism with their mother's milk, then the end effect is little different.

He accused his critics of defamation when they pointed to the influence Goldhagen said his father had on his views, and asked whether anybody would ever criticize a German historian by pointing to the past of his relatives. The implication was that the critics who pointed to his Jewish origins were closet antisemites. Two points need to be made here. The first is that it is perfectly in order to point to historians' origins, upbringing or personal circumstances to explain how they have reached the conclusions they have. That, after all, was E.H. Carr's advice long ago: 'Study the historian, before you study his facts.'[64] And indeed, contrary to Goldhagen's assertion, this has been done many times with German historians, from the polemics surrounding the Fischer controversy in the 1960s, to the *Historikerstreit* of the 1980s, when many critics pointed out that the late Andreas Hillgruber's defence of German troops allegedly defending civilization against the Red Army on the Eastern Front from 1944–5 clearly had something to do with the fact that he had been one of them himself. Secondly, however (and here Goldhagen is perfectly right), engaging in this exercise does nothing in itself to tell us whether the arguments the historian in question puts forward are right or wrong. They have to be taken on their own terms. In this sense, Goldhagen successfully defends his argument that more than 'bureaucratic perfectionism' was involved (the thesis of Hans Mommsen) by citing reports from some of the perpetrators who presented the burning of hundreds of Jews in a synagogue, and similar sadistic acts of murder and humiliation, as 'fun'. But this is a long way from proving that all, or even a majority, of the perpetrators felt a sense of positive enjoyment in their work. Surely here the account of Christopher Browning is inherently more convincing – that there was a wide range of motives, a whole gamut of emotions, among those directly involved. Amongst them there was undoubtedly, as Goldhagen pointed out in his reply to the critics, a quite widespread view that the Jews they killed did not deserve to live. But again, that is a long way from proving that the perpetrators were all positively desperate to kill them, or that their views reflected a deep-rooted antisemitic culture amongst the entire German people that went back to Luther and beyond.

Against those who have cited accounts by Viktor Klemperer and others of kindnesses shown to persecuted Jews by ordinary Germans under the Third Reich, Goldhagen cited the many letters written to him by survivors of the experience indicating the contrary. But without wishing to question the veracity of this testimony, it is clear that this is a biased sample, and, moreover, contemporary documents must have greater credibility than memories composed more than sixty years after the event. In his reply, Goldhagen also accused his critics of never citing the voices of the victims in their own work. But whether this was true or not, it had no bearing on the points they made about his. Similarly, in suspecting historians of reacting allergically because he was importing social-science methods into their area of competence and demonstrating them to be superior, Goldhagen was committing the same sin that he accused them of when he castigated their interest in the fact that he was Jewish and that his father was a survivor of the death camps. What relevance did the fact that they were from a different discipline from his own have to the validity or otherwise of their arguments? Finally, it was noticeable that he addressed himself in his reply exclusively to his *German* critics: not once did he mention the fact that Moshe Zimmermann, Saul Friedländer, Gordon Craig, Christopher Browning and other non-Germans had also appeared in the German-language press as critics of his book. The inevitable, but wholly false, implication, was that the critics he attacked in his reply were critical of his work not least because they were German.[65]

This was the view taken too by another American political scientist, Andrei Markovits, who claimed that 'because Goldhagen's message discomfits the Germans, some have gone to work to discredit the messenger and his work as quickly and permanently as possible'. Markovits went on to attack Goldhagen's critics for mentioning the author's father (though the author himself does this so often, and so prominently in the book, that it is scarcely possible to avoid it). As a political scientist, Markovits too saw in the reaction of German historians an allergic defensive mechanism against an interloper from another discipline. If its theses about German antisemitism rested mainly on secondary literature, so what? But of course, as we have seen, they rested only on a very small and partial selection of it. There would be nothing wrong with the book if it had summarized the existing state of knowledge and taken it further by the application of new theories. The problem however, is that it falls far behind the existing state of knowledge. Markovits attacked Goldhagen's journalistic critics in Germany for criticizing Goldhagen's supporters in America because they too were journalists, which is fair enough; but to pillory them for pointing out that most of these American journalists were Jewish, when he himself repeatedly underlines the fact that they for their part were German and supposedly articulated widespread German attitudes, seems less than fair. The decisive point, surely, is not that journalists of any description are entitled to write about anything they like – of course they are – but that the most telling criticisms of Goldhagen's book have come from professional historians who have worked in the archives and on the history of the Third Reich, historians who, as we have seen, are not just German but American, British and Israeli as well. History has always been open to influences from the social sciences, and when – as for example in Jürgen Falter's work on who voted for the Nazis – these prove to be fruitful they are generally welcomed.[66]

The real cause of the historians' rage is surely a feeling of impotence and frustration, as they see a pretentious piece of bad scholarship hit the best-seller lists in several countries, while the media attention lavished on it completely ignored all the sound scholarship they had been engaged in themselves for so long. But this, surely, is only what can be expected from the mass media, who have already shown in the past that selling newspapers is more important than telling the truth: as Rupert Murdoch is said to have remarked after the 'Hitler diaries', for which he had paid $1.2 million for serialization rights in the *The Times* and *The Sunday Times*, had been exposed as forgeries in 1983, 'Circulation went up and it stayed up. We didn't lose money or anything like that . . . After all, we are in the entertainment business.'[67] Similar thoughts, perhaps, were in the minds of Simon and Schuster executives in 1996 as they paid £500,000 for the English-language rights to *OpJB*, a book written by John Ainsworth Davis, a retired TV director, who claimed that as an acting lieutenant in the Royal Navy, he had been sent by Ian Fleming, subsequently author of the James Bond spy novels, in May 1945 to capture Martin Bormann and force him to reveal the whereabouts of hidden Nazi gold. Described by the publishers as 'the last and greatest revelation from the Second World War . . . an astonishing story that will mean rewriting history', the book describes how Davis spirited Bormann back to England, where he continued to live in the Home Counties under an assumed name for another forty-four years, while 95 per cent of the money, stored in Swiss bank accounts, were restored to its former owners. No doubt the book will sell well, just as will books claiming that the 'Rudolf Hess' imprisoned in Spandau was not the real Hess, or that the bodies discovered outside the bunker in 1945 were not those of Hitler and Eva Braun.[68] Inconvenient facts, such as the postwar discovery of Bormann's remains, verified against his dental records, not far from the bunker in Berlin, do not really matter. This is a kind of fantasy-world, in which games of good and evil are played out for the entertainment of a readership that does not really care whether they are true or false.

But the facts recounted by Goldhagen in his description of the atrocities committed by Police Battalion 101 and other perpetrators are demonstrably and undeniably true. It is this recognition which was behind the extraordinary public response which greeted the publication of Gold-hagen's book in Germany in September 1996. As he toured the country debating his arguments with professional historians such as Hans Mommsen and Norbert Frei, he was greeted by crowds whose size was unprecedented for occasions such as these: 2,000 in the audience in Munich, 700 in Frankfurt, with over a thousand more pressing to get in, similar numbers in Hamburg and Berlin. Goldhagen's role was no more that of a scholar, for the level of debate was scarcely very elevated at these meetings: he now appeared as an old Testament prophet, pointing the finger at the Germans for their past sins. Far from articulating some putative German resentment at what he was saying, the crowds he addressed overwhelmingly applauded his stand and passed over or dismissed the objections of his critics. At one point, Hans Mommsen had noted in a review that serious scholarship on Nazi Germany, unlike Goldhagen's book, eschewed the voyeuristic recounting of the details of Nazi sadism. But this, it seemed, was what the German public really wanted. The largely young audiences at the meetings, hitherto fed on a diet of abstract and over-intellectualized treatments of the Third Reich, applauded Goldhagen because he was telling them, as no-one else had before, exactly to what depths of sadism and cruelty the perpetrators of the 'Final Solution' had sunk. Just such a shock had been administered to an earlier generation of Germans in the late 1970s by the American television series *Holocaust*, and subsequently in the early 1990s by Steven Spielberg's film *Schindler's List*. Each new generation of Germans, it seems, wishes to rediscover the horrors of Nazism anew. An event such as the publication of *Hitler's Willing Executioners* burns the knowledge of Nazi atrocities into the German public consciousness in a way that academic history has never been able to achieve. By doing this, perhaps, Goldhagen has performed a service to modern German political culture, helping to strengthen young Germans' resolve to distance themselves more clearly than ever from the political culture in which their grandparents and great-grandparents lived before 1945.[69]

NOTES

1 Daniel Jonah Goldhagen, *Hitler's Willing Executioners. Ordinary Germans and the Holocaust* (London, 1996).

2 Julius H. Schoeps (ed.), *Ein Volk von Mördern? Die Dokumentation zur Goldhagen-Kontroverse um die Rolle der Deutschen im Holocaust* (Hamburg, 1986).

3 Robert Vansittart, *Black Record* (London, 1940); Rohan Butler, *The Roots of National Socialism* (London, 1942).

4 Peter Viereck, *Metapolitics: The Roots of the Nazi Mind* (New York, 1965); George L. Mosse, *The Crisis of German Ideology: Intellectual Orgins of the Third Reich* (New York, 1964).

5 William L. Shirer, *The Rise and Fall of the Third Reich. A History of Nazi Germany* (New York, 1960).

6 Ernst Klee, Willi Dressen, Volker Riess, *Those Were the Days. The Holocaust as seen by the Perpetrators and Bystanders* (London, 1991).

7 Lord Russell of Liverpool, *The Scourge of the Swastika* (London, 1951).

8 Christopher Browning, *Ordinary Men. Reserve Police Battalion 101 and the Final Solution in Poland* (New York, 1992).

9 Richard S. Levy, contribution to Internet seminar on H-GERMAN@msu.edu. See also Richard S. Levy, *The Downfall of the Anti-Semitic Parties in Imperial Germany* (New Haven, 1975).

10 Stephen Wilson, *Ideology and Experience. Antisemitism in France at the Time of the Dreyfus Affair* (New York, 1982).

11 Orlando Figes, *A People's Tragedy: The Russian Revolution 1891–1924* (London, 1996), p. 197. See also J. Klier and D. Lambroza (eds), *Pogroms: Anti-Jewish Violence in Modern Russian History* (Cambrdge, 1992), and Norman Cohn, *Warrant for Genocide* (New York, 1966).

12 Figes, *People's Tragedy*, pp. 687–9.

13 Jeremy Noakes, 'No Ordinary People', *Times Literary Supplement*, 7 June 1996, pp. 9–10, here p. 9.

14 See Karl Marx, *Early Writings*, ed. L. Colletti (Harmondsworth, 1975); J. Carlebach, *Karl Marx and the Radical Critique of Judaism* (London, 1978) and Isaiah Berlin, 'Benjamin Disraeli, Karl Marx and the Search for Identity', in idem, *Against the Current* (London, 1979); Paul Lawrence Rose, *Revolutionary Antisemitism in Germany from Kant to Wagner* (Princeton, New Jersey, 1990), p. 304; Robert S. Wistrich, 'Socialism and the Jewish Question in Germany and Austria, 1880–1914' (Ph.D., London, 1974), pp. 10, 261; idem, 'German Social-

Democracy and the Berlin Movement', *Internationale Wissenschaftliche Korrespondenz zur Geschichte der deutschen Arbeiterbewegung*, Vol. XII (1976), pp. 433–42; Edmund Silberner, *Sozialisten zur Judenfrage* (Berlin, 1962), p. 290; Hans-Helmuth Knütter, *Die Juden und die deutsche Linke in der Weimarer Republik* (Düsseldorf, 1971), p. 133. See also M. Geltman, 'Socialist Antisemitism', *Encounter*, July 1975, pp. 18–23, and George Lichtheim, 'Socialism and the Jews', *Dissent*, July–August 1968, pp. 314–42; David McLelland, *Marx before Marxism* (London, 1970), pp. 141–2. For a comprehensive demolition of the theory that the party subscribed to something called 'socialist antisemitism', see Rosemarie Leuschen-Seppel, *Sozialdemokratie und Antisemitismus im Kaiserreich. Die Auseinandersetzungen der Partei mit den konservativen und völkischen Strömungen des Antisemitismus 1871–1914* (Bonn, 1978), esp. pp. 36, 96, 100, 153, 171.

15 Leuschen-Seppel, *Sozialdemokratie*, p. 108.

16 Ibid., pp. 236, 287.

17 Vernon Lidtke, *The Alternative Culture. Socialist Labor in Imperial Germany* (New York, 1985).

18 Lynn Abrams, *Workers' Culture in Imperial Germany: Leisure and Recreation in the Rhineland and Westphalia* (London, 1992).

19 Richard J. Evans, *Kneipengespräche im Kaiserreich. Die Stimmungsberichte der Hamburger Politischen Polizei 1892–1914* (Reinbek, 1989). The introduction has a full discussion of the origin, significance and reliability of this source. See also 'Proletarian Mentalities: Pub Conversations in Hamburg', in Richard J. Evans, *Proletarians and Politics: Socialism, Protest and the Working Class in Germany before the First World War* (London, 1990), pp. 124–90.

20 Donald L. Niewyk, *Socialist, Anti-Semite, and Jew. German Social Democracy Confronts the Problem of Anti-Semitism 1918–1933* (Baton Rouge, 1971); Wolfram Pyta, *Gegen Hitler und für die Republik: Die Auseinandersetzung der deutschen Sozialdemokraten mit der NSDAP in der Weimarer Republik* (Düsseldorf, 1989); Werner Jochmann, 'Die Ausbreitung des Antisemitismus', in Werner E. Mosse (ed.), *Deutsches Judentum in Krieg und Revolution 1916–1923* (Tübingen, 1971), pp. 409–510; Donna Harsch, *German Social Democracy and the Rise of Nazism* (Chapel Hill, 1993).

21 Browning, *Ordinary Men*, p. 55; Detlev J.K. Peukert, 'The Lost Generation: Youth Unemployment at the End of the Weimar Republic', in Richard J. Evans and Dick Geary (eds.), *The German Unemployed. Experiences and Consequences of Mass Unemployment from the Weimar Republic to the Third Reich* (London, 1987), pp. 172–93. See also Hans Mommsen, 'Schuld der Gleichgültigen', *Süddeutsche Zeitung*, 20 July 1996.

22 Jürgen W. Falter and Dirk Hänisch, 'Die Anfälligkeit von Arbeitern gegenüber der NSDAP 1928–1933', *Archiv für Sozialgeschichte*, Vol. 26 (1986), pp. 179–216; Thomas Schnabel, ' 'Wer wählte Hitler? Bemerkungen zu einigen Neuerscheinungen über de Endphase der Weimarer Republik', *Geschichte und Gesellschaft*, Vol. 8 (1982), pp. 116–33; Thomas Childers, *The Nazi Voter. The Social Foundations of Fascism, 1919–1933* (Chapel Hill, 1983), pp. 155–55, 180, 185–7, 265; Harsch, *German Social Democracy*, pp. 106–7.

23 William Sheridan Allen, *The Nazi Seizure of Power. The Experience of a Single German Town 1922–1945* (rev. edn., New York, 1984), p. 29. See also Sarah Gordon, *Hitler, Germans and the "Jewish Question"* (Princeton, 1984), esp. Chapter 2.

24 Eberhard Jäckel, 'Einfach ein schlechtes Buch', *Die Zeit*, 17 May 1996, makes this point too.

25 Ibid; Noakes, 'No Ordinary People'; and Evans, *Kneipengespräche im Kaiserreich*, pp. 318–19, for working-class attitudes to ritual murder accusations.

26 Gitta Sereny, 'Spin time for Hitler', *The Observer Review*, 21 April 1996, pp. 1–2.

27 'Ein Volk von Dämonen?', *Der Spiegel*, No. 21/1996 (20 May 1996), pp. 48–77, here p. 66; Jeremy Noakes and Geoffrey Pridham (eds.), *Nazism 1933–1945: A Documentary Reader*, (New York, 1991), pp. 554–6.

28 Noakes and Pridham, *Nazism,* p. 1,119; Noakes, 'No Ordinary People', p. 10. Also quoted in 'Ein Volk von Dämonen?', p. 52, and in Mommsen, 'Schuld der Gleichgültigen?'.

29 For these points, also with quotes from Himmler's Posen address, see Alfred de Zayas, 'Kein Stoff für Streit', *Frankfurter Allgemeine Zeitung*, 12 June 1996, p. 11.

30 David Bankier, *The Germans and the Final Solution. Public Opinion under Nazism* (Oxford, 1992), pp. 67–88.

31 'Ein Volk von Dämonen?', p. 71.

32 Norbert Frei, 'Ein Volk von "Endlösern"?', *Süddeutsche Zeitung*, 13/14 April 1996, p. 13; Robert Gellately, *The Gestapo and German Society. Enforcing Racial Policy, 1933–1945* (Oxford, 1990); Klaus-Michael Mallmann and Gerhard Paul, 'Omniscient, Omnipotent, Omnipresent? Gestapo, Society and Resistance', in David F. Crew (ed.), *Nazism and German Society, 1933–1945* (London, 1994), pp. 166–96.

33 For a conspectus of recent research, see David Cesarani (ed.), *The Final Solution. Origins and Implementation* (London, 1994), pp. 74–150.

34 Jäckel, 'Einfach', p. 14. In his response to his German critics, Goldhagen correctly rebukes Jäckel for mistakenly claiming that he says Hoffmann was not an SS man, but is silent on the other details. See Daniel Jonah Goldhagen, 'Das Versagen der Kritiker', *Die Zeit*, 2 August 1996, pp. 9–14.

35 'Ein Volk von Dämonen?', p. 49.

36 Christopher R. Browning, 'Dämonisierung erklärt nichts', *Die Zeit*, 19 April 1996, p. 7.

37 'Ein Volk von Dämonen?', p. 51.

38 Franz Neumann, *Behemoth. The Structure and Practice of National Socialism 1933–1944* (New York, 1933), p. 121.

39 Goldhagen's claims for the novelty of his work are overstated, not only in respect of its overall thesis but also in respect of much of its detailed empirical research. He declares, for example (without providing any evidence), that there is still a general view that the extermination of the Jews was carried out only by gassing, and that those who carried it out did so mainly because they felt they had to obey orders. But no serious historian has held these views for decades.

40 See the interview with Erich Goldhagen in Henryk M. Broder, '"Ich bin sehr stolz"', *Der Spiegel*, No. 21/19946 (20 May 1996), pp. 57–8.

41 Ulrich Rauff, 'Herz des Finsternis', *Frankfurter Allgemeine Zeitung*, 16 August 1996.

42 Norman Lebrecht, 'A round-up of killers puts German guilt back on the agenda', *Daily Telegraph*, 24 April 1996.

43 Gordon A. Craig, 'Ein Volk von Antisemiten?', *Die Zeit*, 10 May 1996, p. 5.

44 Robert Hughes, *The Culture of Complaint. The Fraying of America* (New York, 1993); also specifically on the reasons for the popularity of Goldhagen's book in the USA, Johannes Heil, 'Nicht die Kritiker, der Kritisierte hat versagt', *Süddeutsche Zeitung*, 19 August 1996, p. 9.

45 Deborah E. Lipstadt, *Denying the Holocaust: The Growing Assault on Truth and Memory* (New York, 1993).

46 William L. Shirer, *The Rise and Fall of the Third Reich: A History of Nazi Germany* (London, 1960). See the classic demolition of the book's credibility by Klaus

Epstein, 'Shirer's History of Nazi Germany', *The Review of Politics*, Vol. 23 (1961), No. 2, pp. 230–2.

47 Indeed, the revival of the old wartime collective guilt thesis in the book has been seen as a kind of postmodernist game, in which the purpose has been to see what effects this has on the public, a suspicion strengthened by the conscious manipulation of discussion by Goldhagen, his agent and his publishers, who for example cancelled a public debate on the book in New York because it would pre-empt the publication of the German edition: Heil, 'Nicht die Kritiker', p. 9.

48 H-GERMAN@msu.edu.

49 H. R. Trevor-Roper (ed.), *Hitler's Table Talk 1941–1944* (Oxford, 1988), pp. 484–5.

50 Moshe Zimmermann, 'Die Fussnote als Alibi', *Neue Zürcher Zeitung* (International edn), 29 April 1996, p. 23. Zimmermann added that Goldhagen's footnotes often served him as an alibi, qualifying or denying some of the sweeping assertions he made in the text but not really countering their influence, since one small note was of little weight compared to the endless repetition of the overall argument in the main body of the book.

51 'Zu grob gestrickte Antworten', *Focus*, No. 34/1996, pp. 94–5.

52 Reported in Joseph Croitoru, 'Gegen Kitsch und Kommerz', *Frankfurter Algemeine Zeitung*, 9 August 1996.

53 Only the German-Jewish historian Julius Schoeps and a young cultural historian, Ingrid Gilcher-Holthey, attempted to defend Goldhagen. Schoeps thought Goldhagen had aroused hostility because his views were radical, but did not really comment on the substance of the issue; Gilcher-Holthey thought that treating the history of antisemitism as an aspect of the history of mentalities was a useful innovation, but again did not really engage with the substantive issues at hand: Julius H. Schoeps, 'Vom Rufmord zum Massenmord', *Die Zeit*, 26 April 1996, p. 4; Ingrid Gilcher-Holthey, 'Was die Kritik verkennt', *Die Zeit*, 31 May 1996. The editor at *Die Zeit* who organized the series of articles promised a 'new *Historikerstreit*', but it never happened, since hardly anyone was prepared to write in Goldhagen's support.

54 'Ein Volk von Dämonen?', p. 58.

55 Josef Joffe, 'Sisyphus ist Deutscher', Leitartikel, *Die Welt*, 16 April 1996. See also Manfred Rowold, 'Das ganze deutsche Volk as Hitlers williger Scharfrichter?', *Die Welt*, 17 April 1996 (Auslandsausgabe).

56 Frank Schirrmacher, 'Hitlers Code', *Frankfurter Allgemeine Zeitung*, 15 April 1996.

57 Editorial comment, *Süddeutsche Zeitung*, 13–14 April 1996, p. 13.

58 Wolfgang Ullmann, 'Das unangenomme Urteil', *Freitag*, 16 August 1996, p. 3.

59 Kurt Pätzold, 'Auf der breiten Spur der deutschen Täter', *Neues Deutschland*, 18 August 1996, p. 12.

60 Jäckel, 'Einfach'; Frei, 'Ein Volk'.

61 Mommsen, 'Schuld der Gleichgültigen'.

62 Hans-Ulrich Wehler, 'Wie ein Stachel im Fleisch', *Die Zeit*, 24 May 1996, p. 40.

63 Goldhagen, 'Das Versagen'. For the Eastern Front, *see also* Omer Bartov, *Hitler's Army. Soldiers, Nazis and War in the Third Reich* (New York, 1991).

64 E. H. Carr, *What is History?* (London, 1961).

65 'Goldhagen, 'Das Versagen', pp. 9–14. By this time some German journalists at least were growing weary of the debate. Evidently having escaped the critical eye of the sub-editors, the caption below a picture of Goldhagen adorning Johannes Heil's comment on his reply reads not 'Daniel J. Goldhagen' but 'Daniel J. Goldhafgenuch', roughly 'Daniel J. Goldhadenough' (Heil, 'Nicht die Kritiker').

66 Andrei S. Markovits, 'Störfall im Endlager der Geschichte', *Blätter für deutsche und internationale Politik*, No. 6/96, pp. 667–74.
67 Quoted in Robert Harris, *Selling Hitler. The Story of the Hitler Diaries* (London, 1986), p. 368.
68 Hugh Thomas, *Doppelgängers* (London, 1994).
69 For an important discussion of Goldhagen's book, its reception in Germany, and its relation to academic research, *see* Dieter Pohl, 'Die Holocaust-forschung und Goldhagens Thesen', *Vierteljahreshefte für Zeitgeschichter*, vol. 45 (1997), pp. 1–48, published after the completion of this chapter.

Part IV

FACES OF
THE THIRD REICH

Part IV turns to biography. The individuals discussed here were not major ideologues of the Nazi regime; all were detached from it in one way or another; the last two, indeed, Claus von Stauffenberg and Winston Churchill, became its mortal enemies. Chapter 14 takes a close look at the conductor Wilhelm Furtwängler, whose conduct in staying in Germany for the duration of the Third Reich has aroused fierce controversy over the years. Steering a careful course between Furtwängler's partisans, who refuse to believe that a great musician could not be a great man, and his critics, who refuse to believe that anyone who occupied as prominent a position in the cultural life of Nazi Germany as he did could not be an out-and-out Nazi himself, the chapter argues that Furtwängler is best understood as a man whose political conservatism and German nationalism caused him to have deeply ambivalent though by no means wholly hostile feelings towards the regime. When it originally appeared in *The Times Literary Supplement* in 1992, the review article was violently attacked by Furtwängler fans, while the letters and articles published in its support by critics of the conductor such as Bernard Levin did it little service either by going much further than I had done in condemning his conduct. Steering a middle course in a debate that had become totally polarized over the years proved, in other words, to be no easy task.

Equally fierce controversy was aroused by Chapter 15 when it originally appeared in the same journal a few weeks before the article on Furtwängler. Here the debate was polarized between those who, like Britain's wartime government and many since, just dismiss the Bomb Plot of 20 July 1944 as an outbreak of internecine warfare within the Nazi regime at a time when Germany was obviously heading for total defeat, and those who, like the surviving relatives of some of the plotters who wrote objecting to the review, consider that the plotters should simply be celebrated as brave men to be remembered and admired without criticism. In fact, a man such as Claus von Stauffenberg, the soldier who planted the bomb, was far more interesting and complex than either of these views will allow, and the review tries to summarize a mass of recent research devoted to his motives and conduct and those who plotted with him. Two points are at issue here. The first is the extent to which postwar German democracy owes the plotters a debt. Admirers of Stauffenberg, Goerdeler and the other resisters argue that their example helped Germany recover a democratic identity after the war. Chapter 15, following much recent literature, casts doubt on this view. Secondly, a number of people who had known the plotters wrote arguing that an historian (seated, as one of them put it, 'comfortably in an armchair in a democratic country') could have no understanding of the difficulties faced by resisters living under a totalitarian dictatorship. But this, while an understandable reaction from contemporaries, is to mistake the whole nature and purpose of historical scholarship, which is precisely to gain an understanding of past events, not experienced by the historian personally, through the exercise of historical imagination and judgement. If only people who have lived through the past are in a position to understand it, then we might as well all give up the attempt to write about it altogether. It is for the reader to judge, of course, whether the attempts we make are successful; but to believe that they lack any kind of validity would be to make the profession of historian wholly impossible.

Chapter 16 explores another aspect of this problem – namely, the extent to which people who lived through the past remember it accurately. Memory has many agendas, and often subordinates past events to present purposes. There is no more fascinating example of this than the architect Albert Speer, who became one of Hitler's closest personal friends and served as his Minister of Munitions during the war. Like all the leading Nazis, Speer was a young man when he attained political power; unlike almost all the others, however, he survived the war, spending twenty years in Spandau prison for war crimes and living on until 1981. His memoirs, published after his release from gaol, paint a compelling picture of life at the top of the Nazi regime; they are also a subtle exercise in self-justification. Chapter 16 looks at the journalist Gitta Sereny's account of her documentary investigations of Speer's writings and of the interviews she conducted with him over a number of years in an attempt to get him to admit the truth about his involvement in the extermination of the Jews. Evidently a man of considerable intellectual power and personal charm, Speer, it is argued, succeeded in the end in pulling the wool over Sereny's eyes just as much as he had done over everyone else's.

Finally in Part IV, we turn to the Third Reich's most implacable opponent, the British statesman Winston Churchill. Written for a German newspaper in an attempt to explain the controversy which arose in the 1990s between neo-Thatcherite Eurosceptics and traditional Conservatives about the consequences of Churchill's refusal to make a separate peace with Hitler in 1940 or 1941, Chapter 17 argues that the thesis that Churchill betrayed the

British Empire by entering into a major European military commitment can only be sustained on the basis of a complete misunderstanding of the nature and dynamics of Nazi ideology and power-politics, not to mention a total failure to comprehend the radical character and ambitions of the Nazi leader Adolf Hitler. Here perhaps more than in most cases, the subordination of history to present politics has led to an unacceptable degree of distortion in the interpretation of past events.

14

PLAYING FOR THE DEVIL
Furtwängler and the Nazis

Wilhelm Furtwängler (1886–1954) was, alongside Toscanini, the most widely revered conductor of his time. Already by the early 1930s he dominated the musical scene in Central Europe. He was as familiar a figure in Leipzig and Vienna, where he served as resident conductor of the Gewandhaus and the Philharmonic orchestras at various times during the 1920s, as he was in Berlin, where he was made music director of the Philharmonic in 1922. His reputation was not just Austro-German but worldwide, and from 1925–6 he had two successful spells as guest conductor of the New York Philharmonic. When Toscanni resigned as the American orchestra's permanent conductor in 1936, Furtwängler was invited to succeed him.

But by this time he had become a controversial figure in the United States. His appointment was opposed by a vociferous lobby which regarded him as a 'prominent and active Nazi' and therefore unwelcome in a city full of German exiles. So Furtwängler stayed in Germany. Indeed, he remained there as a major cultural figure right up to 1945. He was filmed conducting a special performance of Beethoven's Ninth Symphony on Hitler's birthday in 1942, and shaking Goebbels's congratulatory hand. When German radio announced the dictator's death, it was Furtwängler's recording of the slow movement of Bruckner's Seventh that accompanied the news. All this made the conductor even more controversial outside Germany. Jewish hostility was particularly pronounced; when Furtwängler died in 1954, an obituary in a Jewish newspaper described him as 'the chosen Staatskapellmeister of Hitler, Göring and Goebbels . . . the idol of Nazi arsonists and murderers, the musical henchman of their blood-justice'.

In *Trial of Strength*[1] (first published in German in 1986) and *The Devil's Music Master* (1992),[2] Fred K. Prieberg and Sam H. Shirakawa set out to rescue the great conductor's reputation. Far from being a leading light of the Nazi cultural scene, Furtwängler, they argue, consistently opposed the racial and cultural policies of the Third Reich, devoting much of his time to rescuing Jewish musicians from the clutches of the SS at great risk to himself. Indeed, in 1943, according to Shirakawa, 'nobody else in the Third Reich at this point was taking any kind of stand against the Nazis except

Furtwängler'. If he compromised himself, then it was because of his political ignorance and naivety. Prieberg goes even further. The conductor, he says, was not politically naive at all. On the Nazi seizure of power in 1933, Furtwängler quickly became involved in a conspiracy to bring about a 'politico-cultural coup'. When this failed, he set himself the aim of 'reversing Nazi policy towards the Jews'. The gestures and statements of support for the regime which got the conductor into such trouble abroad were, according to Prieberg, a smokescreen designed to give him the freedom to work against the Nazis from the inside. Furtwängler was a kind of 'double agent', pretending to sympathize with Hitler and his ideology while actually doing everything he could to undermine them.

Furtwängler himself, both during and after the Third Reich, in correspondence and conversation with critics of his conduct such as Toscanini and Bruno Walter, maintained that his overriding purpose had been to keep spiritual and human values alive in a regime that had consistently tried to destroy them. 'Human beings', he told Toscanini, 'are free wherever Wagner and Beethoven are played . . . Music transports them to regions where the Gestapo can do them no harm.' This is what he meant when he told the denazification hearing to which he was subjected after the war that his aim had been nothing less than 'the maintenance of liberty, humanity and justice in human life'. He was, he insisted, a musician, not a politician; he believed passionately in the ennobling power of music, and everything he had done, including the minor compromises he had been forced to make with the regime, had been done for the sake of the higher artistic values of which he considered himself to be the supreme exponent.

Ardent Nazi, resistance hero, or 'unpolitical German'? The truth is that Furtwängler was none of these. He certainly was not a Nazi. Unlike Herbert von Karajan, he never joined the Nazi Party; unlike Karl Böhm, he never gave the Nazi salute at the beginning of a concert. Prieberg has no difficulty in showing that many of the accusations made against him – that he regularly conducted 'work-break' concerts in factories, for example, or that he performed the Horst Wessel Song, the Nazi party anthem, in front of Hitler – are legends. And there is no doubt that he did his best to protect the Jewish musicians in his orchestra, and to help those who approached him for assistance during the Third Reich. He insisted on his right to perform music by composers frowned on by the Nazis, such as Stravinsky and Hindemith, and indeed it was his championing of the latter's *Mathis der Maler* that brought about his enforced resignation from the Berlin Philharmonic and the Staatsoper in 1934. After this, he worked as a freelance, and when he conducted the orchestra in occupied countries during the war, he was always careful to do so as an independent artist rather than a paid functionary of the German state.

But none of this made him a hero of the resistance. He did not run any great personal risk by the actions he took; unlike ordinary Germans who tried to help Jews, Furtwängler was doing so from a position of privilege that protected him from the danger of arrest or prosecution until very near the end of the regime. When a threat did materialize in 1945, he was simply given a heavy hint by Albert Speer and disappeared over the Swiss border as fast as he could. Almost everyone in a position of power in the Third Reich protected a small number of individuals with Jewish connections for one reason or another. Even Hitler had a favourite singer whose wife was Jewish, despite which he kept them both unmolested until the end of the war. Goering looked after the interests of a few Jewish artists whose talents he valued, such as Leo Blech, until well into the second half of the 1930s. One half-Jewish musician, Heinrich Lindner, the Mannheim orchestra's harpist, was so persistent in his attempts to obtain employment that Goebbels issued him with a special permit to do so as late as 1940. Furtwängler certainly helped a number of individuals who got into difficulties with the authorities, especially in the early years of the Third Reich, when it was much less dangerous to do so than it became later, but to elevate this into a general form of resistance, as both Prieberg and Shirakawa do, is not very convincing.

Even the conduct which led to his enforced resignation in 1934 was no act of principled defiance. As Prieberg showed in his earlier, and rather better, book, *Music in the National Socialist State*, Hindemith wrote *Mathis der Maler* in an attempt to win favour with the Nazi cultural establishment; not only was the music more accessible than his previous output, but the 'German' subject and story were thoroughly consonant with Nazi ideology. Championed by Goebbels, Hindemith stood a good chance of becoming an establishment composer at the time that Furtwängler took up his cause. It was only the enmity of Hitler, who never forgave the composer for his earlier, more iconoclastic works, and Alfred Rosenberg, who was trying to wrest political hegemony from Goebbels in the cultural sphere, that brought about Hindemith's downfall, and Furtwängler's with it. As for Stravinsky, Prieberg's earlier book shows that his music continued to be performed in Germany by a number of conductors until September 1939, when the fact that he was a French citizen made him an enemy alien and so subject to a ban by the authorities.

Far-reaching claims that Furtwängler was engaged in some kind of unique or outright resistance against Nazism can only be made on the basis of ignorance of the enormous historical literature that now exists on almost every aspect of resistance and compliance under the Third Reich. Neither Prieberg nor Shirakawa seems to be familiar with any of this work. Shirakawa, indeed, appears to know nothing at all about German history, and his book is full of howlers that would be a disgrace in a first year examination script, let alone a book published by Oxford University Press, Hitler was not, whatever Shirakawa might think, an 'unemployed house painter' in 1923, nor was Gustav Stresemann 'President of the Weimar

Republic', any more than Konrad Adenauer was 'President of West Germany'. To claim, as he does, that 'after the election of November 1932, Hitler wasted no time in restoring economic order' is absurd, since Hitler did not become Chancellor until the end of January 1933. Not that Shirakawa's account of that particular event is any more accurate. According to *The Devil's Music Master*, Hitler 'simply seized control of the government', being invested with power by 'none other than old Chancellor Hindenburg'; in fact, he was made Chancellor of a coalition government, in which the Nazis were in a minority; and Hindenburg, of course, was President, not Chancellor. 'Half the country – 51 per cent' did not vote Nazi in the March 1933 elections. 'Most Germans' were not won over to Hitler's cause by the appeal of antiseminitism. The Wannsee Conference was not held in September 1941. Denazification tribunals did not sentence people to death. And so on, and so forth.

Prieberg, as one might expect, does not make such elementary mistakes. But his book is full of special pleading, tendentious judgements and gross over-interpretation. His claim that Furtwängler conducted a special birthday concert for Hitler in 1942 under 'blackmail', 'threats' and 'force' is supported by no evidence at all. His assertion that the conductor only stated his support for the Third Reich as a cover for his real purpose of undermining it is mere conjecture And his attempts to explain away as a normal guest concert Furtwängler's performance of German music with the Berlin Philharmonic in Oslo a week before the German invasion of Norway in April 1940, an event described by the German embassy, which of course was fully cognizant of the invasion plans, as 'very suited to awaken and animate sympathy for German art and for Germany', completely fails to carry conviction.

A particularly distasteful feature of both books, is the authors' evident need to indulge in personal abuse and denigration of Furtwängler's critics. People who have judged the great man harshly, says Prieberg, have done so only in order 'to enhance their own reputations'. But is it really necessary to defend Furtwängler by claiming that German artists and writers exiled from the Third Reich needed to criticize him in order to compensate for their own political impotence, or their failure to stand up to Hitler as Furtwängler did? Do we really need to be won over to sympathy for Furtwängler's plight by being told that anti-fascist speeches in America and elsewhere were 'fashionable' in 1933 and delivered mainly by 'attention-seekers'? Does Furtwängler's cause need championing with the argument that those who left Germany, as Shirakawa claims, were taking 'the easy way out'? And do we have to be regaled with scurrilous gossip about Toscanini just because he disagreed openly with his great rival's stance during the Third Reich?

Most unpleasant of all is Prieberg's attempt to explain Furtwängler's anti-semitism. In 1933, the conductor noted privately his view that Jews should not be given organizational responsibilities in the cultural sphere and expressed his desire for 'tendentious Jewish pen-pushers' in the 'Jewish press' to be removed from their positions. He thought that most Jewish musicians lacked 'a genuine inner affinity with German music'. And he reviled 'Jewish-Bolshevist success' in the Weimar Republic. Prieberg tries to deal with these statements by claiming that many if not most Jewish musicians were 'good businessmen with few scruples', 'lacking roots', and that, under the Weimar Republic, they really 'did have the *goyim* up against the wall'. Hostility to them was thus 'not a case of simple "anti-Semitism"'. Does such a mode of argument really serve Furtwängler's cause? Is it necessary to describe Ira Hirschmann, the leader of the campaign against him in the United States, as 'a Jew from Baltimore, a climber by nature'?

Prieberg is reduced to such arguments because like Shirakawa, he does not have the necessary historical knowledge to be able to place Furtwängler's attitude towards the Third Reich in its proper context. It is to his credit, however, that he has been honest and scrupulous enough in his research to present the informed reader with the raw material with which the conductor's position can be assessed. Furtwängler belonged essentially to the conservative-nationalist elite that did so much to undermine the Weimar Republic and bring Hitler to power in 1933. In 1929, he wrote privately that threats to what he considered 'normality' included not only 'Bolshevism, that fashionable religion of hatred' – no mention here of Nazism as a religion of hatred – but also politics, democracy and progress. In the political language of the day, 'normality' meant the situation that had obtained under the last Kaiser, while 'politics' meant party-politics of the sort that flourished under Weimar. Later on, in 1939, Furtwängler underscored this fundamentally authoritarian attitude by contrasting what he saw as the orderliness of the Third Reich with the 'lawless, libertine Republic' of the 1920s. 'Why will Germany win in this war?' he asked himself. 'Because it is a feature of human nature that individuals cannot cope with limitless or even with just too much freedom.' That is obviously what he thought the situation was in Britain and France, the democracies with which Germany was going to war, and that is why he thought they would lose.

A German nationalist, he regarded music as primarily a German achievement. 'A genuine symphony', he declared, 'has never been written by a non-German.' Among the Germans he included, of course, the Austrians, and there is no reason to doubt his sincerity when he welcomed the *Anschluss* in 1938 as 'the immutable historical deed of Adolf Hitler'. In August 1934, he joined with Richard Strauss and other artists in publicly declaring that 'We believe in the Führer . . . We trust his work', and two years later, in his private notes, he betrayed a common reluctance to accept that Hitler was the driving force behind Nazi barbarism when he scribbled despairingly: 'Hitler! You do not know the things which are being done in your name!' His antisemitism was of a common, unreflective and

191

generalized type shared by most conservatives in Germany at the time, and fell far short of the fanatical hatred shown by the Nazis; but it was anti-semitism all the same.

When conservative nationalists described themselves as 'unpolitical' after the war, this was the kind of highly political set of attitudes they generally meant. Such people were close enough to Nazism for them to feel highly ambivalent about the policies and ideologies of the Third Reich, Disillusion, and the realization that Hitler was dragging Germany down into the abyss, eventually, very late in the day, led some of them to oppose the regime outright. But not Furtwängler. German histories have for some time conventionally distinguished between *Widerstand*, or general resistance on principle, and *Resistenz*, or partial resistance to the regime when it seriously interfered with the way people carried on their everyday lives. Furtwängler's activities, on the whole, belong to the latter category; he bitterly resented the Third Reich's interference in musical life, and did his best to retain as much control over it as he could. But he never engaged in principled opposition to those in power.

Like other conservative nationalists, Furtwängler welcomed the 'national revolution' in 1933, saw it as an opportunity to return to 'normality', and co-operated willingly in the establishment of the Third Reich. But like them too, he grossly underestimated the energy, fanaticism and ruthlessness of the Nazis, arrogantly assuming that he could harness them to his own purposes. Instead, he found himself comprehensively outmanoeuvred by Goebbels and Rosenberg in 1934 and 1935, just as the conservative cabinet majority found itself outmanoeuvred by Hitler and Goering in 1933. It was not because he was 'unpolitical', but because he shared many of the Nazis' basic political and cultural assumptions, that it was easy for Goebbels to manipulate him. The great conductor frequently made difficulties for the authorities. But, said Goebbels, 'he is worth the trouble. He may not be a political official, but he must give us a façade.'

The Nazis tolerated Furtwängler's self-importance, and the little gestures with which he distanced himself from the regime, because they knew that the presence of one of the world's leading conductors in the Third Reich gave them cultural respectability. Furtwängler's presence in Germany throughout the Third Reich helped convince the world and the Germans themselves that Germany was still a great, cultured nation despite the book-burnings and the concentration camps. One only has to imagine the sensation that would have been created had he left Germany in protest (as Prieberg suggested in his earlier book he should have done), say, at the beginning of 1935 to get some idea of the effect he created by staying. As Bruno Walter told Furtwängler after the war, he had to consider the fact that

> your art was used as a conspicuously effective means of propaganda
> for the Regime of the Devil . . . that the presence and performance of

an artist of your stature abetted every horrible crime against culture and morality, or at least, gave considerable support to them. Consider too that you ultimately have lived for twelve years in the Nazi Empire without terror, or fear of it, of what was happening there, and you were never forced into extremity, and that you carried your title and positions during this time. In the light of all that, of what significance is your assistance in the isolated cases of a few Jews?

NOTES

1 Fred K. Prieberg, *Trial of Strength: Wilhelm Furtwängler and the Third Reich*, trans. by Christopher Dolan (London, Quartet, 1992).
2 Sam H. Shirakawa, *The Devil's Music Master: The Controversial Life and Career of Wilhelm Furtwängler* (New York, Oxford University Press, 1992).

15

CLAUS VON STAUFFENBERG AND THE BOMB THAT FAILED

When Count Claus von Stauffenberg placed the briefcase containing his bomb in Hitler's field headquarters on 20 July 1944, he and those associated with him knew that their chances of success were slim. Ever since 1938, they had been plotting, on and off, to remove Hitler by one means or another. But until now, nobody had been found who was both willing to do the deed and had the necessary access to Hitler's person. Stauffenberg himself was hardly a promising candidate. Badly maimed in the North African campaign, he had only one eye, was missing half an arm, and had only two fingers left on his remaining hand. Under these circumstances, priming a bomb under the watchful eyes of Hitler's entourage cannot have been easy, and it is not surprising that he only managed to set half the charge before people began to cast suspicious glances at him. Unable to leave his briefcase too close to the Führer without attracting even more attention, he placed it on the other side of a massive table, made his excuses, and left.

When the bomb went off, the force of the blast was dissipated as the flimsy walls of the wooden hut blew out, and deflected from Hitler's body by the bulk of the table. However, convinced that Hitler could not have survived the explosion, Stauffenberg bluffed his way on to a plane to Berlin and set the *coup* in motion. It was already doomed to failure. Too few generals were willing to support it; Goebbels was able to secure command of the airways and bring on a shaken but still recognizable Hitler to prove that the plot had miscarried; the SS and Gestapo swung rapidly into action; loyal army leaders moved quickly to arrest the conspirators; and within a few hours the plot had fizzled out. Stauffenberg was summarily shot; and in the following months, hundreds of the plotters, their families and associates, sympathizers and waverers, were arrested, and brought before Nazi courts. Large numbers of them were executed, often with great cruelty. A few survived to tell the tale after the war.

Such is the story of the German Resistance, told innumerable times since the early post-war narratives of Hans Rothfels and Gerhard Ritter. In essence, it is a simple story. But it has been the source of seemingly endless fascination and controversy ever since. The four books under review supply yet further evidence of the Resistance's enduring appeal for historians. And they provide a wealth of detail, some of it new, much of it already well known, with which to attempt a reassessment of the plotters, their motives, their intentions and their ideas about what should happen if their *coup* succeeded.

Stauffenberg, himself, as Peter Hoffmann makes clear in his meticulously researched family chronicle (1992),[1] was a romantic conservative who derived much of his political inspiration from his youthful experience as a member of the close-knit circle that gathered around the poet Stefan George. Stauffenberg welcomed the coming of Hitler's Third Reich and looked forward to the creation of a new German legal and racial order after 1933. As late as 1938, he was advocating the removal of the Jews from German cultural life. What turned him against the regime was its conduct of the war on the Eastern Front from June 1941 on. A disciple of Clausewitz, he believed that war was politics by other means. The deliberate alienation and maltreatment of the occupied population in the East appalled him, and he became outraged by the mass murder of Jews and Soviet civilians and prisoners of war. He decided that the Nazi leadership had betrayed the fine ideals of 1933. Well before the plot was finally hatched, he was thinking in terms of removing Hitler, so that the army could take over the leadership of the country and establish a corporate state along lines worked out in Fascist Italy, with the aristocracy guaranteed a special place and the peasantry protected against the encroachments of industrialism.

Had Stauffenberg succeeded, the President envisaged by the plotters to head the new regime was General Ludwig Beck, former Chief of the General Staff. Beck was antisemitic, monarchist at heart and profoundly anti-democratic in his political thinking. A number of the other generals involved in the plot were deeply implicated in the policies of racial extermination carried out by the army on the Eastern Front from 1941 onwards. Admiral Canaris, who as head of military intelligence continued to operate against the Allies while joining in the conspiracy, was another monarchist. A sympathizer with the proto-fascist *Freikorps* in the early years of the Weimar Republic, he supported the Nationalist side in the Spanish Civil War and idolized General Franco, whose portrait he kept in a prominent place on his wall.

These men stood in a long tradition of Prussian, later German, military resistance to civilian rule, a tradition which included the furious, though ultimately abortive attempts of the generals to go beyond Bismarck's war aims in 1866 and 1870/1 and the army's ousting of Chancellor Bethmann Hollweg and sidelining of the Kaiser during the First World War. Like Stauffenberg, many of the generals involved in the plot of 1944 regarded Hitler as an amateur, an upstart who had to be removed because he did not know his place. The tradition in which they acted was not one noted for its kindness to occupied populations. Fanatical anti-Bolshevists to a man, they

195

did not, on the evidence of their conduct up to 1944, seem likely to do much for the defence of 'Western civilization' and 'German culture' against barbarism if they came to power.

The civilians involved in the plot were equally unpromising in their political outlook. The man nominated as Chancellor of the new, post-*coup* government, Carl Goerdeler, had served under the Nazis as Mayor of Leipzig and only broke with them in 1937. A strong monarchist, he believed in the separation of 'non-assimilated' Jews from the German community. His political vision, like that of many of his fellow-conspirators, did not involve going back to the party politics of the Weimar Republic, which they all despised, but was oriented instead on the authoritarian model of the Bismarckian Empire. The proposed Foreign Minister, Ulrich von Hassell, was an admirer of Mussolini, whom he had got to know during his time as German ambassador in Rome, from 1932 to 1938. The idealistic, mainly aristocratic members of the Kreisau Circle, heavily involved in the Resistance in its later stages, could only think of rebuilding politics on an individualistic, localized basis, and were equally hostile to the idea of political parties. The trade union leaders such as Wilhelm Leuschner, whom they managed to win over, shared many of these views and had welcomed the merging of the unions in the Nazi Labour Front in 1933. The Social Democrats involved, such as Haubach, Leber and Mierendorff, were in no way representative of the mainstream traditions or leadership of the Social Democratic labour movement.

Above all, virtually every one of these groups and individuals was a believer in a Greater Germany, including Austria, the Sudetenland, a large part of Poland, and Alsace-Lorraine, fully kitted out with the complete panoply of overseas colonies taken away from Germany by the League of Nations at the end of the First World War. As late as 1943, Goerdeler was still thinking of suing for peace on the basis of the German frontiers of 1914. In time, he and some of his co-conspirators began to enlarge their vision to encompass the creation of a unified Europe. But it was to be a Europe under German hegemony. Goerdeler's model was the British Commonwealth of Nations, transplanted onto European soil, with Germany as the Imperial power. It was not a Europe of equal sovereign states.

Given such views about the ordering of national and international politics after the removal of Hitler, it is hardly surprising that the conspirators were consistently rebuffed by the Western Allies. Klemens von Klemperer, in his exhaustive account of their increasingly desperate attempts to get the West to support them, *German Resistance Against Hitler* (1992),[2] rightly scotches the legend that Chamberlain 'saved' Hitler from an internal *putsch* in 1938 by conceding the Munich agreement; the generals' preparations were far too amateurish, and their foreign policy aims far too close to those of Hitler, for them to have succeeded. It was not until 1944 that the conspirators seriously began to scale down their Greater German ambitions in a desperate attempt to make meaningful concessions to the Allies. By the time of Stauffenberg's bomb, they were thoroughly disoriented, oscillating helplessly between the forlorn hope that they could preserve German hegemony in Europe by concluding a separate peace with the West, and the dawning realization that all their efforts were likely to achieve was an acceleration of Germany's plunge into total defeat. The crucial, inescapable fact about the plot is that it only came about when it had become clear to those in the inner circles of the government and the armed forces that Hitler was losing the war. As the late Martin Broszat notes in his contribution to the excellent, though rather brief volume of conference papers edited by David Clay Large, *Contending with Hitler* (1992),[3] the plot was

> in part a rebellion of those conservative elites who had initially been incorporated into the Nazi power structure but had subsequently lost influence and office to ardent party members and subservient newcomers. The conservative elites' disenchantment with the regime was caused not only by their loss of influence but also by their access to information about the war.

The same arrogance that had made German conservatives think they could manage Hitler in 1933 deluded them into thinking they could overthrow him eleven years later. On both occasions, they fatally underestimated the energy and determination of the leading Nazis and their fanatical adherents.

There was, to be sure, as Hoffmann and von Klemperer both insist, a moral dimension to their actions, which moved them to light a beacon of resistance against Nazi crimes, regardless of its prospects of success, so that at least some of the historical guilt they thought would attach to Germany's name in the future might be burned away. But the Germany that eventually emerged was very far removed from the one they envisaged. Their political ideas had no future, least of all in the internationally unambitious, party-political democracy of the post-war Federal Republic. It was the tradition of German political Catholicism, not German military conservatism, that won out in the end. If the bomb plot had succeeded, it might have saved lives by shortening the war. But it would have stored up trouble for the future by providing Nazis and German nationalists with another 'stab-in-the-back' legend with which to explain their defeat.

Hoffmann is surely wide of the mark when he claims that the Resistance gave Germany a moral perspective through which it could face up to its recent history. Belated attempts by Konrad Adenauer to claim the legacy of the Resistance as a legitimating force for the Federal Republic (and especially for German rearmament) in the 1950s had little public resonance. Popular interest was only awakened in the late 1960s, as the Social Democrats rediscovered, through the work of a new generation of critical historians, their own, much more widespread and committed contribution to resisting Hitler, from a position of far less privilege and power, and with far fewer prospects of immediate success. Ironically, therefore, the legacy of resistance in all its diverse forms and degrees only became manifest with the emergence of a new, critical distance from the plotters of 1944, some twenty to thirty years later.

Of the four books under review, only *Germans Against Nazism* (1992), a *Festschrift* for Peter Hoffmann which, like all good *Festschriften*, demonstrates the limitations of the dedicatee's work as well as paying tribute to it, really explores that legacy in all its aspects. It makes it clear that the conspiracy around Stauffenberg was only one part of a much wider, more fragmented process of resistance, dissent, and non-compliance in the Third Reich. Its ideas and ambitions offer little to those Germans who are trying to stop the growth of racism and violence in their newly reunited country. If there is any inspiration that they can draw from the past, then it is surely from the Social Democrats, Communists and others whose acts of civil disobedience and ideological solidarity offered the best hope of keeping some semblance of decency going in the much bleaker circumstances of the Third Reich.

NOTES

1 Peter Hoffmann, *Claus Schenk, Graf von Stauffenberg und Seine Brüder* (Stuttgart, DVA, 1992).
2 Klemens von Klemperer, *German Resistance Against Hitler: The Search for Allies Abroad*, (Oxford, Clarendon Press, 1992).
3 David Clay Large (ed.), *Contending with Hitler: Varieties of German Resistance in the Third Reich* (New York, Cambridge University Press, 1992).
4 Francis R. Nicosia and Lawrence D. Stokes (eds), *Germans Against Nazism* (Oxford, Berg, 1992).

16

THE DECEPTIONS OF ALBERT
SPEER[1]

'Albert Speer', wrote Hugh Trevor-Roper in the conclusion to his classic study of *The Last Days of Hitler*, 'was the real criminal of the Third Reich.' Not because he was a brutal murderer, like Hitler, or a vulgar antisemite, like Streicher, or a fanatical ideologue, like Goebbels, but because he was a sophisticated, intelligent and civilized man who personified the willingness of educated Germans to collaborate with, work for and in the end do everything they could to sustain the most destructive regime in history. Speer was an architect whose connections led him into Hitler's inner circle by the mid-1930s. Soon Speer counted among Hitler's small group of personal friends, and was preparing for him grandiose plans for rebuilding Berlin as the capital of a world empire after the war. On the chance death of Hitler's Armaments Minister Fritz Todt in an air crash early in 1942, Hitler appointed Speer his successor. Armed with wide-ranging powers, Speer organized Germany's war production with ruthless efficiency, bringing it to its peak output as late as 1944, when the war was already being lost. At the very end of the war, when Hitler ordered a scorched-earth policy and the destruction of German industry, Speer secretly countermanded his orders, thus preserving much of the country's economic base for the future. Brought to trial at Nuremberg, Speer did not try to justify what he had done, but delivered a sober and reasoned confession of where he had gone wrong. He had been seduced, he said, by the possibilities of technology, and led astray by the charismatic spell of his leader. Many of his former associates found it hard to forgive him for what they saw as this betrayal of everything they had stood for. The court found him guilty of using slave labour on a massive scale and sentenced him to twenty years' imprisonment in Spandau. He was still only forty years old.

Speer occupied his time in prison with gardening, going for a physically real but geographically imaginary walk round the world, writing letters, keeping his secret *Spandau Diaries*, which were published in English in 1977, and composing his memoirs, which appeared in this country in 1970 under the title *Inside the Third Reich*. The memoirs are by far the most perceptive and illuminating account we possess of the inner workings of the

199

top Nazi leadership written by an insider; Goebbels's voluminous diaries may be more detailed and more immediate, but they entirely lack the reflective and descriptive qualities of Speer's remarkable book.

Speer's memoirs, like his defence at Nuremberg, do not try to make any excuses. Speer was perceptive enough to see that this would have alienated readers. Much of their fascination comes from the spectacle they present of a cool, rational, and in many ways thoroughly decent man falling under the spell of a charismatic dictator and finding himself despite everything unable to escape it. Ever since the book's publication, however, historians have pondered not upon what Speer confessed in his book, but on what he did not confess. Was it really believable, many have asked, that someone as close to Hitler as Speer was, someone who had overall command of the whole of wartime production, someone who counted among the few close personal friends Hitler had, could have remained ignorant of Auschwitz and the 'Final Solution', when so many other studies have shown that the great majority of ordinary Germans, living in most cases infinitely further from the centre of power than Speer did, were well aware of what was going on by the middle of 1942 at the latest?

In his memoirs, Speer himself told the story of how his friend Karl Hanke, the Nazi party boss in Lower Silesia, warned him in 1944 not to go to Auschwitz, where things were going on that were too terrible to describe. Speer blamed himelf for not troubling to investigate the matter further. 'I had closed my eyes', he wrote, and evaded responsibility. Thus, he concluded, 'I still feel, to this day, responsible for Auschwitz in a wholly personal sense.' How much more strongly, he later said, could he put it? Yet some historians have seen this admission as a clever evasion, a means of drawing attention away from the fact that Speer knew very well what was going on in Auschwitz all along. In his book *Albert Speer: End of a Myth*, published in English in 1984, the German historian Matthias Schmidt presented concrete evidence of Speer's dishonesty. Before publishing his memoirs, Speer checked them through with a copy of the daily work record kept by his Ministry from 1941 to 1944, placed by Speer's associates in the German Federal Archives at Koblenz. Schmidt discovered from another copy kept at the Imperial War Museum in London that crucial passages had been cut out of the Koblenz copy before it had been deposited. They related in particular to the evacuation of Jews from Berlin, knowledge of which, Schmidt concluded, Speer had therefore been attempting dishonestly to conceal from posterity.

In fact, Speer had not been a party to the deception, and subsequently tried to put it right. But this was not the only point at which his memoirs were challenged. In 1971, the American historian Erich Goldhagen alleged that Speer had been present at a meeting held in Posen early in October 1943, where Himmler had spoken to the assembled senior leadership of the Reich on the extermination ('meaning kill or order to have killed', he said, to leave no room for doubt) of the Jews. The meeting was Hitler's idea, an attempt to bind the leadership closer together by creating a shared complicity in his crimes. At the end of his speech, according to Goldhagen, Himmler said: 'Speer is not one of the pro-Jewish obstructionists of the Final Solution. He and I together will tear the last Jew alive on Polish ground out of the hands of the army generals, send them to their death and thereby close the chapter of Polish Jewry.' Speer himself never mentioned this occasion in his published writing, and even went to the trouble of obtaining two sworn affidavits from associates certifying that he had not been there. Moreover, extant versions of the speech do not include the sentence quoted by Goldhagen, who later privately admitted that he had made it up, claiming that it had been put in inverted commas by mistake. Another attempt to prove Speer's knowledge of the 'Final Solution' had failed.

How much Speer knew, and from what point in time, and what, if anything, he did about it, are the central questions of Gitta Sereny's new book (1995). A Hungarian-Austrian journalist domiciled in London, Sereny, now in her seventies, is best known in this field for her book of interviews with the former commandant of Treblinka, Franz Stangl, *Into that Darkness*, published in 1983. Contacted by Speer after an article she had published on Hitler's own part in the 'Final Solution' in 1977, Sereny found herself gripped by his personality, rather as Speer had found himself gripped by Hitler's, and struck up what seems to have been a close but uneasy relationship with him over a series of lengthy interviews conducted with him until his death in 1981. So persistent does her questioning appear to have been, indeed, that an appropriate alternative title for this book might have been 'Albert Speer: His Battle with Gitta Sereny'. Through Speer and his former associates, she gained access to a great deal of fresh documentation, including early drafts of his memoirs, as well as thousands of letters written by him in Spandau prison and smuggled out by a friendly gaoler. In the years since Speer's death she has interviewed many of his friends, family members and former colleagues and examined the documentary evidence in a number of archives.

The results of this investigation, published here, make gripping reading, as Sereny delivers a biographical account of Speer's life interwoven with numerous interviews and documentary extracts which gradually but inexorably move closer to the central question of the real extent of Speer's complicity in the 'Final Solution'. On one point after another, Sereny shows Speer's published memoirs to have been inaccurate or misleading, and no-one can now afford to consult them without checking their account against this one at the same time. The book demonstrates, for example, that Speer joined the Nazi Party in 1931, much earlier than he claimed in his memoirs; that he was closely implicated in obtaining housing for his workers by removing Jews from Berlin in 1941; that his Ministry implemented orders to send Jewish slave labourers to 'disappear' in Treblinka in November 1942;

201

that he knew early in 1943 about the expulsion of Jews from the ghettos of Bialystok for 'resettlement'; that he was far more actively involved in the suppression of the Bomb Plot of July 1944 than he subsequently cared to admit in public; that he knew about the mass arrests of Hungarian Jews in 1944; that he was seriously considered as a candidate to succeed Hitler; and that the claim, advanced in his memoirs, to have confessed to Hitler in a dramatic last interview in the Berlin bunker in 1945 that he was disobeying his 'scorched-earth' policy is pure invention.

Above all, Sereny shows that Speer most definitely did attend the Posen meeting in October 1943, and that the affidavits he had signed to say he did not, were false. 'The more Speer tries to explain away awkward facts,' she says, 'the clearer it is that he is trying desperately to avoid facing the truth.' It is one of Sereny's great strengths, however, that she does not try to accuse Speer, as Matthias Schmidt did, of deliberately lying. A large part of the book's fascination lies in its revelation, through the author's repeated discussions of these topics with Speer himself, of the complex psychological processes by which Speer not only deceived others but also deceived himself. A remote, rather repressed man, brought up in a formal, loveless bourgeois German household, Speer evidently found in Hitler the kind of father-figure he had hitherto lacked; for his part, Speer offered Hitler, the failed artist, the possibility of acting out his personal architectural fantasies through the medium of a young and impressionable but undeniably competent professional. Their strange, intimate personal bond, a kind of platonic love-affair, kept Speer in Hitler's thrall even after he began to realize, as he told an intimate towards the end of the war, that his idol was nothing more than a 'criminal'.

It is Sereny's contention that the very fact of his widely known status as a close personal friend of Hitler prevented other people from talking to him about the extermination of the Jews. Highly placed officials were aware of the fact that Hitler wanted it kept secret, while ordinary people were afraid of saying the wrong thing. To his personal intimates such as Speer, Hitler himself preferred to avoid discussing matters of policy. And while many people knew about the mass shootings of Jews in Eastern Europe by the SS *Einsatzgruppen* from June 1941 onwards, far fewer were aware of the existence of the extermination camps. Speer, perhaps, had managed to turn a blind eye to earlier outbreaks of Nazi violence such as the 'Night of the Long Knives' in 1934 or the *Kristallnacht* pogrom of 9 November 1938, neither of which he mentions in the early drafts of his memoirs; but – Sereny argues – Himmler's speech in Posen in October 1943, coupled with a visit to the underground V2 rocket factory ('Dora'), where he was confronted with the brutal and murderous conditions in which the slave labourers who manned the plant were kept, made it impossible to avoid the truth any longer.

It was this realization of the brutal nature of Hitler's regime, argues Sereny, which brought on the mysterious illness which laid Speer low early in 1944. After this, his relations with Hitler were never the same again. Yet although he now knew about the extermination of the Jews, he was unable to extricate himself from Hitler's spell. Deceiving himself into believing that he had to continue working for Germany's sake, he found himself in effect actively shoring up a regime whose policies he knew to be morally abhorrent. Working to frustrate Hitler's orders to destroy Germany's economic infrastructure only partly salved his conscience, and in any case the policy was by no means as generally successful as Speer later claimed. All the ambiguities of his position, and that of many like him, were revealed by a bizarre incident on 12 April 1945, as the Red Army was already closing in on Berlin, and the Berlin Philharmonic held a last concert in which one of the main items was the final scene from Wagner's *Götterdämmerung*. Despite a desperate power shortage, Speer arranged for the concert hall to be fully supplied with electricity during the concert. As the audience emerged into the night afterwards, they were met with boys from the Hitler Youth offering them baskets filled with cyanide pills.

Unlike many other leading Nazis, Speer did not attempt to kill himself when all was finally lost. Still a young man at the time of his condemnation at Nuremberg, he had to lie to himself in order to live with himself. His evasions and repressions clearly made him uneasy, however. New relationships, with a Protestant chaplain at Spandau, a Catholic monk, and later a Jewish rabbi, encouraged him to come to terms with himself. He even, at last, discovered real sexual and emotional intimacy with a woman, a German more than thirty years his junior, living in London; she was with him in an hotel room in London when he suffered the stroke that killed him in 1981. Despite this upbeat ending to his life, however, it is difficult to share Sereny's optimism that he finally overcame the great lie he had lived with all those years. Sereny describes Speer showing her an affidavit written in 1977 in which he repeated his general responsibility for the actions of the Third Reich and his 'tacit acceptance of the persecution and the murder of millions of Jews'. Sereny regards this as Speer's final, direct confession of guilt, and places it at the end of the final chapter of her book. But in fact it amounted to no more than he had ever said, and he coupled it with the statement that his 'tacit acceptance' meant 'looking away, not by knowledge of an order or its execution'. Albert Speer lived his lie to the last.

NOTES

1 Gitta Sereny, *Albert Speer: His Battle with Truth* (London, Macmillan, 1995).

17

CHURCHILL
The end of glory?[1]

Many sacred icons of British society are being smashed in the white heat of the Thatcherite and post-Thatcherite late-bourgeois revolution, from the monarchy, sliding towards a state of apparently terminal crisis, to the red buses which have begun to disappear from London's streets in the process of privatization. Until recently, however, no-one has dared to lay a hand on the most sacred icon of all, the figure of Winston Churchill, the 'saviour of his country', as he was described in A.J.P. Taylor's standard *English History 1914–45*.

Even to breathe a word of criticism of the 'Greatest Englishman of All Time' was regarded as virtually treasonable in the 1950s and 1960s. In the 1970s and 1980s the multi-volume official biography by Martin Gilbert added massively researched detail in a further act of hero-worship. Such criticisms as there were tended to come from sources marginal to the mainstream of British intellectual life – the far left, who never forgave Churchill for his behaviour to the miners when he was Home Secretary before the First World War, or the far right, notably in the person of the Hitler-admirer David Irving, who portrayed Churchill as a drunken, egotistical warmonger who worked deliberately to bring the Second World War about. These criticisms were taken seriously by few people. During the 1980s, indeed, the Churchillian myth was actively exploited by Mrs Thatcher, who referred to the great man cosily as 'Winston', although he had hardly been an intimate acquaintance, and appropriated his rhetoric for that classic example of history repeating itself the first time as tragedy, the second time as bloody – the Falklands War of 1982.

Now, however, a new iconoclast has suddenly emerged, and a flurry of angry reviews, debates on radio and television, and – that most certain sign of ruffled feathers in the Establishment – outraged letters to *The Times*, shows that he has succeeded in hitting his target. In his *Churchill: The End of Glory*, the young historian John Charmley attacks Churchill's reputation head-on. Far from being the hero who rescued Britain from the humiliations of appeasement and led the country to victory over Hitler by his indomitable spirit, Churchill, says Charmley in the concluding passage of his book, was a failure:

Churchill stood for the British empire, for British independence, and for an 'anti-Socialist' vision of Britain. By July 1945 the first of these was on the skids, the second was dependent solely upon America, and the third had just vanished in a Labour election victory.

Churchill, says Charmley, threw away the Empire by squandering British resources on fighting Hitler, leaving the country too weak to hold on to its colonies. This was a mistake, for Third World countries such as India, Kenya or Uganda would have been far better off under continued British rule than they have been since independence. He mortaged British self-determination to the USA, and was comprehensively outmanoeuvred at the peace conference of Yalta by the wily and unscrupulous Roosevelt, who appears as one of the principal villains of the book, single-mindedly determined to bring down the British Empire and replace it with American hegemony. Finally, by allowing the Labour Party members of his wartime coalition government a free hand to pursue domestic reform while he himself concentrated obsessively on the military and diplomatic campaign against Hitler, he gave them a platform for their views, convinced the electorate that they could govern, and paved the way for their victory in the elections of 1945. The result in Charmley's view was the disastrous Attlee government of 1945 which created the rigid and wasteful bureaucratic state apparatus which crippled initiative and enterprise in Britain until Mrs Thatcher began the herculean task of dismantling it in 1979.

The man who has put forward these startling views is a classic historian of the 'yuppie generation', those 'young upwardly-mobile professionals' who were such a typical creation of the Thatcher years. Son of a docker from the decaying port of Liverpool, Charmley, in his thirties, and teaching at the University of East Anglia, disposed of his regional accent and his working-class background at Oxford and acquired the persona of a 'young fogey', complete with tweedy jackets, bow-tie and hearty, upper-class twit manner; a sort of Bertie Wooster of the ivory tower. But he is no fool. His book is massive, carefully researched and important. Amid the deliverately provocative statements and the flip judgements there is a lot of careful and sensible analysis. And a critical reassessment of Churchill is undoubtedly long overdue. On matters such as Churchill's role in the Norwegian campaign, Charmley's strictures are persuasive.

Much of the furore has in fact been created not by the book itself, but by an advance review in *The Times* written by the maverick part-time military historian and former Minister in Mrs Thatcher's government Alan Clark, who used it as a base from which to launch much wilder and more startling claims. In particular, Clark latches onto Charmley's suggestion that it was only because of Churchill's intransigence that the British government did not open exploratory peace talks with Hitler in the spring of 1940. Churchill's insistence on unconditional surrender robbed Britain of the chance of offering a compromise which 'would have detached Hitler from his chieftains'. But while Charmley is properly cautious in his analysis of the inconclusive discussions which took place in the cabinet on this subject at this time, Clark alleges that there were other occasions on which Churchill's obstinacy proved fatal, notably when Hitler's deputy Rudolf Hess brought 'excellent terms' with him when he flew to Scotland a year later. By rejecting these out of hand, says Clark, Churchill lost the opportunity to move enough forces to the Far East to save Malaya and Singapore from the Japanese and so preserve the British Empire. Nazi Germany and the Soviet Union would have been left to slug it out for supremacy on the Continent, and most probably would have fought each other to a standstill. At all events, Eastern Europe would have been saved from the blight of Stalinism which descended upon it in 1945.

It is these claims which have really caused the current storm. For they are part of the intellectual assault of the Tory Right on Britain's allegiance to Europe. Churchill's insistence on fighting Hitler undoubtedly involved committing Britain to a European future, and it is this to which the Thatcherite right wing of the Conservative Party objects. They would far rather have preserved a world in which British 'sovereignty' remained intact, in which British hegemony remained in place over the people of the Third World countries (to which Alan Clark once referred to collectively, in a notorious exchange with civil servants, as 'bongo-bongo land'), and in which the governance of Britain remained undisturbed by such inconveniences as the Social Chapter of the Maastricht Treaty or the European Court of Human Rights.

But this is historical and political fantasy. Leading British specialists on the 'Third Reich' have pointed out that the arguments of both Clark and Charmley are based on a considerable ignorance of the history of National Socialism. Conspiracy theorists of the far right in 1990s Britain believe that Churchill suppressed documentary evidence of the Hess mission because the deputy Führer flew to Britain at the invitation of British proponents of a separate peace. But there is no evidence that Hess was acting other than entirely on his own initiative. Nor is there any evidence of a cover-up. It is an absurd overestimation of British military strength in the 1940s to imagine either that it was pinning down German forces that could have stopped the Red Army conquering East-Central Europe had they been released, or that it would have saved the Empire had it been freed of European commitments. Indeed, without a corresponding invasion from the West, the Soviet forces might have made even more extensive conquests than they did.

Above all, it is a complete misreading both of Hitler's own personality and ambitions, and of the dynamic forces that drove his regime forward, to imagine either that a separate peace with Britain could have been concluded on terms acceptable to the 'Third Reich', or that it would have been a permanent peace. And it is a huge overestimation both of the strength of the internal opposition to Hitler, and of the extent to which its foreign policy aims differed from his, to suppose that a serious British offer of a separate peace in 1940 would have led to the Führer's overthrow from within.

There is little evidence to suggest that anything at all could have saved the British Empire in 1945. Indeed, Charmley's critics have pointed out that the British Empire was already doomed before 1939, and that victory in 1945 may well have preserved it a little longer, and given Britain an international status which she would not otherwise have had. Like other neo-conservative historians, Charmley, whose three books to date have all been biographies, believes that individuals are the moving forces in history; but most historians would take the view that the British Empire was destroyed by the same, more impersonal forces that have destroyed the other great empires of our time, not thrown away by the obstinate belligerence of one man. Hostility to a separate peace was no mere Churchillian idiosyncracy; it was widely shared in the British political elite and in the civil and military services in 1940 and 1941, and was never a serious political possibility. And the discrepancy between America's resources and those of the British was pointing towards the emergence of the USA as a superpower even without the Second World War.

There is little to suggest either that Africa or India would have fared better than they have done since 1945 had the British Empire not vanished into the mists of time. Religious massacres, famine, civil conflict and political disturbances afflicted these parts of the world before and during the colonial period as well as after it. In 1945, economic as well as political and geographical logic all pointed to closer ties between Britain and Europe, and there is a good case for saying that if Churchill is to blame for anything, it is for refusing to take Britain into the European Community in the early 1950s when he had the chance to do so.

Seen from the perspective of 1993, with Britain in the depths of economic depression, with businesses going bankrupt by the hour, millions seemingly permanently out of work, the country's industrial base in ruins, a massive balance of payments deficit, hordes of the homeless living in cardboard boxes or in doorways, homeowners being dispossessed at the rate of 70,000 a year because of unpaid mortgages, scenes of Dickensian squalor in the inner cities, the transport system falling apart, the National Health Service in a state of terminal decay, crime reaching unprecedented levels, gun law ruling on the streets of Manchester, and a government drifting helplessly in the face of events, there still seems a lot to be said for the Labour government that came to power in 1945 and instituted reforms that the majority of the electorate obviously considered long overdue.

NOTES

1 John Charmley, *Churchill: The End of Glory. A Political Biography.* (London, John Curtis/Hodder and Stoughton, 1992).

Part V

REUNIFICATION AND BEYOND

Memories of the Third Reich played a complex and contradictory part in German reunification and its aftermath, and the essays gathered together in Part V explore this from a number of different angles. Chapter 18 was written for the now-defunct magazine *Marxism Today* in the Spring of 1990, just as it had become clear that the process of reunification begun a few months before had become politically unstoppable. The magazine, originally an organ of the British Communist Party, had become by this time a forum for a whole range of political ideas very far removed from the encrusted ideologies of the traditional left, and its editor, Martin Jaques, was subsequently to found the non-party think-tank 'Demos', so it is no wonder that the magazine lost the support of its Communist financial backers and had to close down not long after this article was published. The invitation to write it provided a welcome opportunity to rethink the categories and ideas of the 1980s, when in common with virtually everyone else I had thought of German reunification as something that would only happen in the very distant future.

At the time it was written, voices were being raised on the right and the left in Britain warning against the revival of German nationalism and the creation of a 'Fourth Reich'. The British left had a long tradition of anti-Germanism, going back to the anti-fascist movement of the 1930s and the campaigns of Aneurin Bevan and the Labour Party left against German rearmament in the 1950s. It lived on in the sympathy of elements of the far left in Britain for the Serb side in the Bosnian civil war of the 1990s as a reaction against what were perceived as historic and political links of the Croats with German capitalism and imperialism. On the right, Conservative Eurosceptics, whether or not living off the Churchillian myth of 'Britain alone against Europe' in the Second World War, saw German reunification as reviving old demons of German militarism and world-power ambitions. Written in this atmosphere of suspicion and hostility, Chapter 18 tries to set reunification in its historical context and to argue that German nationalism has changed many times in its history, and has come in many different versions, of which the pan-German nationalism which reached its fateful apogee under the Third Reich was only one. Historical conditions, it argues, have changed to such an extent that a revival of this particular variant is no longer likely.

Chapter 19 turns to a historical dispute which raged during the 1980s about the uniqueness or otherwise of Auschwitz. Conservative neo-nationalist historians attempted to clear the historical ground for the re-emergence of a self-confident sense of German national identity by arguing that many other regimes at other times and in other places had committed similar crimes to those of the Nazis. These arguments were largely designed to bolster the old anti-Communist West German identity, and, as the chapter shows, have largely been superseded by the events of reunification. The problem of mastering the past now means confronting the forty years of the East German dictatorship as well as the twelve years of its Nazi predecessor. But the initial triumphalist offensive of the post-reunification 'new right' against the remnants of the former Communist regime and its erstwhile sympathizers in the West ran into increasing difficulties. Chapter 19 suggests why this was the case, and uncovers some of the problems of historical interpretation to which it gave rise.

Chapter 20 takes an extended look at the 'new right' on a broader front. Since reunification, it has become apparent that both left and right in Germany are having to rethink their fundamental positions on political and historical issues. Memories of the Third Reich are playing a crucial part in this process, but so too is the attempt to recapture an older history, dating back to the Bismarckian era and beyond. The attack on what the right regards as a self-flagellatory obsession of German historians with the Nazi era is balanced by the defence of a geopolitical mode of understanding German history and German politics. There are calls for a recovery of traditional feelings of *Heimat* and a Bismarckian sense of Germany's central position in a Europe of nation-states. Traditions of the German left in writing about, and justifying, national self-confidence and national self-determination, from Otto Bauer to Kurt Schumacher, are brought into play as well. The new right accuses the left of abusing the memory of the crimes (and victims) of Nazism in an attempt to provide an historical justification for the ideology of 'multiculturalism' and of politically motivated campaigns against an exaggerated German 'hostility to foreigners'. Yet overall, Chapter 20 argues, the new right is singularly bereft of positive ideas, obsessed with what it regards as the dominance of the left in the media and the academic establishment, and – with only a few (alarming) exceptions – crippled by its understandable concern to draw a clear line between itself and the right-wing extremism of the neo-Nazis. Here too, therefore, the legacy of the German past continues to shape the post-unification German present. Not only has there been no escape from the shadow of Hitler, it has been joined by the shades of Bismarck and the empire he created as well.

Finally, Chapter 21, which began life as a kind of afterword to a collection of essays discussing new trends in historical scholarship on Germany, but has been completely rewritten to take account of post-reunification developments, brings together some of the arguments put forward in this book and argues that readings and rereadings of German history since 1945 have reflected not merely conflicts of political ideology and changes in political circumstances, but also developments in the nature of history itself as a discipline. These two aspects of historical writing are not unconnected, of course, but they have also enjoyed a degree of relative autonomy from one another. Reunification did not imprint itself on people's understanding of the German past as on a blank sheet of paper, it impinged upon an already complex and sophisticated disciplinary context, in which, seen on a very broad front, modernist modes of appropriation and representation were giving way to postmodernist ones – fitfully and unevenly, as some of the other essays in this book have shown, but perceptibly none the less. Central postmodernist concerns such as identity, ethnicity, gender, the fragmentation of knowledge, the discursive mutability of seemingly fixed entities such as nations and nation-states, have been reinforced rather than thrust aside by German reunification. The German past has not gone away, nor are there any signs that it will do so; but the position in it of key events and problems is shifting after a long time of seeming immutability. Those who argue that this reflects a revival of nationalism in German historical writing, before which liberals and Social Democrats are largely capitulating, are, however, mistaken. What will happen in the future can only be a matter of conjecture; but historians should have no cause for worry or apprehension that their voice will be left unheard. Rereadings of German history will continue to provoke argument and debate as long as German history itself continues to be studied and written – and made.

18

GERMAN REUNIFICATION IN HISTORICAL PERSPECTIVE

German reunification in 1989/90 caused a lot of anxiety in the world. The sight of vast crowds in Leipzig waving the national flag and roaring for *'Deutschland, einig Vaterland!'* – 'Germany, united fatherland!' – awakened uncomfortable memories of the nationalist enthusiasms of the past. Chancellor Kohl's evident reluctance to acknowledge the validity of the present Polish–German border, the Oder–Neisse line, until forced to by his liberal coalition partners and by hostile international opinion aroused the suspicion that a united Germany might look for territorial gains in the East, at a time when an economically shattered country such as Poland hardly seemed in a position to resist whatever pressure the new colossus in Central Europe might bring to bear. National feeling was reviving all over Central and Eastern Europe, and the violence to which it has given rise in a number of areas, from Abkhazia and Azerbaijan to Bosnia and Bulgaria, is grimly suggestive of the emotive power which nationalism still possesses as the twentieth century draws to a close.

And there can surely be no doubt any more of the strength and resilience of feelings of national identity in Germany itself. Only a few years ago, before reunification, observers were proclaiming Germany to be a 'post-national' society, where local and regional identities and a general feeling of being European had largely superseded the national identification of the past. Opinion polls showed that only a minority of West Germans were proud of being German, in stark contrast to the strong feelings of national pride recorded by the pollsters in Britain or, still more, the USA. West German conservatives were lamenting the loss of national identity and orientation among the populace and trying to revive it by arguing for a more positive attitude towards the German past. The question of reunification figured well down the list of political issues which West Germans identified as urgent or important.

In the East, the Honecker regime was busy trying to create a separate sense of national identity through inventing a separate historical tradition for the regions which it occupied. Martin Luther, who was the subject of massive anniversary celebrations in 1983; Prussian heroes such as Frederick

213

the Great, whose statue was reinstated on East Berlin's main boulevard, the Unter den Linden; and even Bismarck, the subject of a major, and surprisingly conventional, biography by a leading East German a few years ago, were retrospectively turned into East Germans by virtue of the fact that they had lived or worked in areas subsequently occupied by the territory of the GDR. Popular identification with the country was supposed to be cemented by the massive investment in sporting prowess that earned East Germans so many Olympic medals in the Honecker years. And when the revolution began in October and November 1989, opposition groups such as the New Forum seemed clear that what they wanted was the democratization of their own country, not unification with another.

But such views were quickly revealed as illusory. All that Honecker's commemorations of historical figures like Luther seem to have done is to reinforce a sense of shared cultural heritage with the rest of Germany. And attitudes to the GDR's sporting heroes seem to have varied between sympathy at the regime of drug-taking to which so many of them were made to submit, to resentment at the extensive privileges which this enabled them to enjoy. Observers were not wholly wrong to recognize a sense of a separate identity among East Germans, but in retrospect it is clear that it ran no more than skin deep. Already in 1989 a third of a million East Germans left for the West; and in 1990 emigration was running at around 60,000 people a month, roughly a million people, or one-sixteenth of the entire population, crossed the border to settle in the Federal Republic in the space of twenty-four months. An even larger number of ethnic Germans – over 370,000 – emigrated to West Germany from other parts of Eastern Europe in 1989, and more followed. Clearly this showed a powerful sense of national identity at work; it is, after all, *Germany* they went to live in, not Austria or Switzerland or the European Community.

Yet it would be wrong to see this undoubted sense of national identity as a simple gut feeling of ethnicity. Far from being innate or unchanging, national feeling has been historically mutable and contingent. And of nowhere has this been more true than of Germany. Different variants and traditions of German nationalism have long existed side by side and come to the fore at various different conjectures. While they have always overlapped, they have seldom been identical. Cultural nationalism, economic nationalism and political nationalism have had widely varying implications in Germany over the past two centuries. Political nationalism itself has found many competing forms, varying from ultra-liberal to extreme reactionary. The Nazi or pan-German variant that reached its apogee under Hitler has been only one of these. Moreover, even the definition of who is German has changed over time and been a matter of frequent dispute among nationalists.

So it would be a mistake to regard those powerful images of German nationalism which the newsreel propaganda of the Nazi era has stamped on the international public memory as accurate representations of reality. After all, one of the most memorable of such images was that of the cheering crowds who greeted Hitler as he drove into Austria after the *Anschluss* of 1938. At that time, certainly, a great many Austrians did consider themselves German and welcomed their incorporation into the Reich, even if those who disagreed with this view stayed at home. Yet scarcely anyone would now suggest that German reunification should include Austria, despite the fact that, historically speaking, Austria did form part of the German Confederation from 1815 to 1866 and before that part of the Holy Roman Empire of the German Nation, as it was called. The long tradition of a 'big German' sense of national identity, including Austria, came to an end during and after the Second World War.

But the idea of German national identity has been historically contingent and mutable in other ways too. In literature, culture and the arts, for example, it may still be said to move rather freely across national political boundaries. A conductor like Herbert von Karajan was equally at home in Berlin and Salzburg, a writer like Peter Handke is not merely Austrian, any more that a playwright like Max Frisch is primarily Swiss. That is not to deny, of course, that the literary and artistic culture of a country such as Austria has its own individuality, especially when it turns, as for example in the work of Thomas Bernhard, in a political direction. But it is clearly the case that in a wider sense the German-speaking countries continue to share a common cultural heritage and a common cultural context, even where – as in East Germany until very recently – this has been grossly deformed by the pressures of political and ideological censorship and indoctrination. This has as few implications for a *political* sense of identity, however, as the common cultural heritage of the English-speaking nations does.

Yet the political resonances of a shared culture in this sense were of profound importance to the emergent nationalist movement of the early nineteenth century. As the culminating point of that movement showed, in the revolution of 1848, German nationalism was initially a radical and progressive phenomenon. Feudalism, serfdom, the denial of civil liberties to minorities such as the Jews, censorship, the police state, the refusal to contemplate free elections and parliamentary rule – all these were associated with the forty-odd individual and autonomous states, ranging from Austria and Prussia at one extreme to Mecklenburg and Schwarzburg-Rudolstadt at the other, into which the German Confederation was divided. Abolishing them all and creating a unitary national state with a single, sovereign Parliament seemed the quickest way to gain the classic freedoms which the men of 1848 were so committed to winning for the German people. Marx and Engels, too, saw a unified nation as the essential basis for historical progress at this time.

It was only with the political failure of the 1848 revolution and the unification of Germany under Prussian leadership, achieved by Bismarck's wars of 1864, 1866 and 1870–1, that German nationalism began to take on a different character. Of course, liberal nationalism did not die immediately; and the 1870s in particular saw a number of important liberal reforms which had been undoubtedly made easier by the achievement of unification. But as time went on, both Bismarck and the liberal nationalists began to look for the consolidation of national unity through the suppression of the alleged 'enemies of the Reich' within the new German Empire. In the 1870s Germany's large Catholic minority, mostly concentrated in parts of Germany which had fought on the Austrian side against Prussia in 1866, was subjected to harsh measures of discrimination during the so-called *Kulturkampf*. In 1878 it was the turn of the socialist labour movement, and even after the lifting of the formal ban on its organizations in 1890, it continued to be subject to police harrassment, prosecution and censorship. By this time the national minorities which lived within Germany's borders, most notably the Poles, were also falling victim to the Germanizing zeal of the authorities, backed up by the nationalist wings of the liberals.

German nationalism's move from left to right was completed around the turn of the century by the emergence of two new factors. First, the military might behind the creation of the German Empire under Bismarck was transformed into a bid for world-power status, backed by the construction of a big navy; and secondly, state nationalism began to be outflanked by a new, populist nationalism, fuelled by petty-bourgeois resentments and strongly coloured by antisemitism. The most radical of the new nationalists regarded the work of unification as incomplete, and pointed to the many millions of Germans living outside the boundaries of the Reich, in Eastern Europe. Here it was not so much cultural nationalism as racism that provided the impulse behind this 'pan-German' programme for the eastern extension of Germany's boundaries.

Pan-Germanism remained a minority current before 1914. It was after the war that the real radicalization of German nationalism took place. With the rise of the Nazi Party came the assertion of the view, held only by a tiny minority of pan-Germans before 1914, that the Germans were a superior race whose destiny lay in uniting themselves in a huge Central European empire where they would dominate and enslave millions of supposedly inferior races such as the Slavs. These beliefs, fed by a growing quantity of historical and scientific, or pseudo-historical and pseudo-scientific, publications on the historic mission of the Germans and the eugenic inferiority of Poles, Russians and Jews, found their most terrible expression in the war of conquest and extermination launched by Hitler against the East in June 1941.

It was the unfolding of this last and most radical transformation of political nationalism in Germany that provided the essential precondition for the dismemberment of the Reich after the war. The boundaries existing in 1937, before Hitler began his wars of conquest and annexation, were drastically revised and many areas of eastern Germany then inside the Reich were taken over by Poland and the Soviet Union. Some eleven million ethnic Germans fled to the West or were brutally expelled, with severe loss of life. In retrospect, this flood of German refugees and expellees was the first, and by far the most dramatic, act in a process of concentrating the Germans within a single set of state boundaries that has re-emerged in the last few years with the renewed influx of ethnic German refugees from Poland, Romania and the Soviet Union. Whereas pan-German and Nazi notions of national identity meant, among other things, *extending* Germany's state boundaries to cover major areas of German (and Slav) settlements in the East, the predominant post-war notion of national identity has meant the opposite: bringing Germans from those areas back into the much-diminished boundaries of the German state as it now exists.

Relatively few ethnic Germans now remain in the East. The thorough and long-established integration of the first, post-war wave of refugees and expellees into the West makes it seem unlikely that there would be much support for a revival of pan-German annexationism. But the reunification of East and West Germany is a rather different matter. Although, obviously, the division of Germany into zones of occupation in 1945 would never have happened but for the war started by Hitler in 1939, the hardening of the boundary between the Soviet zone and the three Western zones into a boundary between two separate states was above all the result of the Cold War. With the end of the Cold War, this legacy was liquidated. Despite Chancellor Kohl's hesitations about recognizing the Polish–German border established in 1945, the likelihood of a united Germany making claims on the territory given by international agreement to Poland seems relatively remote. Both internal and external political resistance to such an ambition is considerable. In the end, unlike the effects of the Cold War, the effects of the Second World War are simply too profound to be reversed.

This still leaves us with the question of what kind of national identity it is that the Germans are now forging for themselves. If radical, pan-German nationalism is now confined to fringe groups of the far Right such as Franz Schönhuber's Republicans, then what kind of nationalism are we dealing with? There is much to be said for taking an optimistic view, and for believing that what we are witnessing is a revival under modern auspices of the liberal nationalism of the nineteenth century, though largely shorn of its linkage to the idea of a shared literary and linguistic culture. This can be seen in the relinking of the idea of national unity to freedom, civil rights and democracy. It is important in this context to remember where the impulse for change has come from. It has been almost exclusively from the popular revolution in the East, led by young people whose political background is to be found in the opposition movements that were beginning to emerge in the last years of Honecker's rule: in movements centred on the Protestant Church, in demonstrations to change 'swords into ploughshares', in the campaign for non-military alternatives to conscription into the East German People's Army, in the growing protests against the appalling environmental pollution produced by the regime's reckless drive to increase industrial production. The moral outrage that overthrew the Krenz regime and destroyed the East German Communist Party when it was discovered that its leaders, such as Erich Honecker, had been leading a life of luxury while extolling to the people the virtues of socialist equality, derived its cutting edge from the moral, and sometimes religious, imperatives behind these opposition movements.

The idealism of the youthful revolutionaries in the East is indeed strikingly reminiscent of the idealism of the liberal nationalists of 1848. But as in 1848, this has its problems. For as West German big business muscled in on the East, and as the professional politicians from the Federal Republic moved in to dominate the course of events during the post-unification election campaign, it is hard not to see the idealists of the New Forum and the other home-grown movements that led the revolution of November and December 1989 as naive amateurs helpless before the realities of power. German unification, after all, is no marriage between equals. One of the two or three richest countries in the world has merged with one of the most crisis-ridden economies in Europe.

What is happening, in fact, is the re-emergence of yet another strand in the complex history of German national identity: economic nationalism. Back in the early nineteenth century, the emerging middle classes saw economic unification as the essential foundation for industrial growth and prosperity. The famous customs union or *Zollverein* brought the German states together in a single market long before they were politically united. And in the depths of the slump, in 1931, the German and Austrian governments once again saw economic union between the two countries as a way towards economic revival – a plan that was only stopped from becoming reality by the intervention of suspicious Western allies, who feared it would lead soon enough to political union as well.

Freedom and democracy were the political imperatives behind the political revolution in East Germany; a sense of national identity with Germans in the West drove on the crowds in Leipzig to raise the demand for reunification; but the real force undermining the viability of East Germany as an independent state was economic. The more people fled to the West in search of a better life, the more difficult became the situation of those who stayed behind. Factories lost their skilled workers; hospitals and schools found it more and more difficult to provide basic services in the absence of growing numbers of doctors, nurses and teachers; the service and supply sectors experienced evermore serious problems in coping. The East German people saw the affluent style of life available in the West, and they wanted it for themselves. As the situation in the East grew more dire by the week during 1989–90, so economic union with the West came to seem the only way out.

But the irony is that the drive for economic unification met with an increasingly hostile response from the people of the Federal Republic. It is all very well for people to support the idea of reunification in the abstract, as a principle, and the percentage of West Germans who did so, according to the opinion polls, increased from under half in the Autumn of 1989 to 75 per cent by the early spring of 1990. But as the real costs of reunification became steadily more apparent, so West Germans turned against the idea in practice. By February 1990, opinion surveys were showing massive majorities against raising West German taxes or cutting wages in order to help the East, while the proportion of those in favour of continuing to admit refugees from the East and paying them full social benefits had dropped to little more than a fifth.

National identity is all very well for the West Germans, in other words, as long as it does not mean having to accommodate millions of refugees in their towns and cities or pay out billions of marks to aid the recovery of the East German economy to an extent that people might actually want to stay there. Hostility to Easterners grew rapidly on the streets and in the pubs and bars of Hamburg, Munich and West Berlin in the course of 1990, and it was one of the many ironies of the situation that the far-right, ultra-nationalist Republicans were second to none in their condemnation of the influx.

All of this seems rather a long way from the rabid pan-Germanism that led to the Second World War. History, as everyone knows, seldom repeats itself, not even the first time as tragedy, the second time as farce. Nationalism and national identity are changeable, historically contingent, fractured and uneven phenomena. Being German means different things to different people at different times, just as being British or French does. Many of the social forces that nourished extreme German nationalism in the earlier parts of this century, from a large and resentful Protestant peasantry and urban petty bourgeoisie to a rigidly monarchist and authoritarian aristocracy and military elite, have now vanished or dwindled into insignificance. The seismic shock of total defeat in the Second World War has convinced the bulk of the middle classes that political adventurism and foreign expansionism are best avoided. Democracy has brought prosperity, and therefore seems a good thing to most people.

The real issues at stake in Germany during reunification were far removed from the kind of historically conditioned anxieties so often expressed outside. How was the exodus from the East to be stopped without serious infringements of human rights? How was the East's economy to be revived without lowering living standards or undermining the costly welfare state in East and West? How were latent antagonisms and social conflicts between Easterners and Westerners to be avoided? And were the millions of East Germans who supported Chancellor Kohl's line of immediate reunification by voting for the Conservative Alliance in the 18 March elections going to be disappointed if reunification failed to bring the rapid economic benefits that they were looking for? Aggressive nationalism has come to the fore in Germany at times of economic crisis and collapse, most notably in the early 1930s, and if the West German economy gets into serious trouble during the process of adjustment, then it may re-emerge. But it is very unlikely to take the kind of shape it had earlier in the century: much more likely, for example, would be a growth in anti-immigrant feeling directed against the large communities of Turks and others who have settled in Germany's major cities. There are no signs that German nationalism is likely to direct itself outwards again. On the contrary, there is a widespread feeling that reunification can only take place within the context of general European co-operation, above all in the European Community.

In the six or seven years since reunification, the process of adjustment and merging has at last begun. It will take a very long time to complete. East Germany may always remain a region of relative economic backwardness. Whatever the problems, however, it is clear that the anxieties felt in London, Paris and New York about a revival of German nationalism in 1989/90 have so far proved unfounded.

19

BEYOND THE
HISTORIKERSTREIT

The *Historikerstreit*, the historians' dispute of 1986–8 over the comparability of the crimes of Nazism and Stalinism, now seems to have taken place decades ago. Looking back at it is like looking back on another world. For this was in essence a political rather than a historical debate. It was not about the content of the past so much as about its exploitation for political purposes in the present.

The political context was set by US President Ronald Reagan's 'Second Cold War'. Reagan described the Soviet Union as an 'evil empire'. He sought to persuade the West Germans to accept a new generation of nuclear weapons and to back his ambitious Star Wars programme in which vastly expensive military hardware would be positioned in space, ready to shoot down any long-range missiles that America's enemies might launch against the West. In order to do this, Reagan naively attempted to suggest to the Germans that the horrors of the Third Reich had now been forgotten and forgiven. Conservative politicians and academics in West Germany supported Reagan's charm offensive. Some of them argued that Nazism's crimes had in any case been no different from those of other twentieth-century dictatorships. One historian, Ernst Nolte, went further and alleged that Hitler's antisemitism was in essence a legitimate response to the Communist threat to annihilate the European bourgeoisie, and that it had only taken on extreme dimensions when Hitler began to copy the example of Stalin's extermination of the kulaks, the property-owning class in the Russian countryside.

Those, such as myself, who challenged these arguments were outraged by what we saw as a series of wilful distortions of the evidence. In some cases, this came close to denying the reality of Nazism's crimes altogether; in others it presented them as being at least partly justified.[1] The historical record showed that Hitler's antisemitism predated his anti-Communism, and that his comprehensive, mechanized annihilation of an entire ethnic group, without exception, had no parallel in the annals even of twentieth-century mass murder. At the same time, there is no denying that the critics of Nolte and those who thought like him, led by the philosopher Jürgen Habermas, had their own political axes to grind as well. Reagan's extremism seemed a threat to world peace, while the encouragement of German national pride by means of generating a guilt-free attitude to the Nazi past seemed almost as disturbing in its own way.

This historical context has now disappeared. With the collapse of Soviet domination in Eastern Europe, the Cold War has come to an end. Star Wars have been replaced by disarmament. German reunification has brought not a massive resurgence of national pride but an outbreak of national self-examination and self-doubt, as the costs of modernizing the East German economy have spiralled out of control, and the cultural differences between West Germans and East Germans have turned out to be far greater than anyone expected.

The historians' debate thus suddenly belongs to a remote political past. That is the main reason why Imanuel Geiss's new contribution to it seems such a waste of time and effort. Geiss's earlier contribution, *Die Habermas-Kontroverse* (1988), a measured defence of the position of Nolte and his allies, is still worth reading – which is more than can be said for *Der Hysterikerstreit* (1992). Its author seems so embittered by his earlier book's failure to settle the dispute – as if that were ever possible – that he has lost all sense of balance or proportion. His new publication is one long howl of rage and frustration against those who disagree with him: a bizarre mixture of pedantry and paranoia, in places so incoherent as to be barely readable. Both title and subtitle are striking misnomers. In dubbing it 'the hysterics' dispute', Geiss has projected his own hysteria on to his opponents, whose treatment of the issues seems as sober as a telephone directory in comparison to his. And in calling it 'an unpolemical essay', he has done little more than draw attention to the excess of polemical overkill that is evident on almost every page.

Geiss's latest intervention is beside the point not only because of its lack of intellectual seriousness – indeed its lack of any kind of intellectual content at all – but also because the debate has now moved a long way beyond the issues with which it attempts to deal. One of the tragedies of Nolte's book, *Der europäische Bürgerkrieg*, which in retrospect emerges as the central text of the historians' debate, was that its author's thought-provoking comparisons of Nazism and Stalinism were obscured by his flirtation – above all in the footnotes – with Holocaust 'revisionism' and other pseudo-historical doctrines of the far right. It is gradually becoming clear that the issue that lay at the flawed heart of Nolte's book, namely the comparison between Hitlerism and Stalinism, has once more become a central preoccupation of political scientists and historians in Germany. For *Vergangenheitsbewältigung*, 'mastering the past', as Christa Hoffmann points out in *Stunden Null?* (1992), now means confronting not only the Nazi era, but the forty-year history of the German Democratic Republic in the East as well.

In both cases, the transition to democracy posed the problem of how to deal with the crimes of dictatorship. Most of Hoffmann's book is devoted to arguing that West Germany made a reasonable job of bringing Nazi criminals to book; or rather, it is devoted to defending the West German judicial establishment in this respect. She is right to point out that the prosecution of Nazi mass murderers was hampered by the restrictions placed on the jurisdiction of German courts by the Western Allies and by the necessity for a democratic judicial system to respect the rights of the accused. And in a lengthy and important foreword, the chief prosecutor of the official West German judicial authority charged with investigating Nazi crimes of violence, Alfred Streim, argues plausibly that the blame for the slow and hesitant progress of such prosecutions, particularly in the early years of the Federal Republic, lay chiefly with the politicians rather than with the lawyers.

Nevertheless, when all is said and done, it remains the case that no judge who sat on the People's Court or on the Special Courts in the Third Reich was ever prosecuted for the perversion of justice or any other crime. Despite the Auschwitz and other concentration camp trials of the 1960s, thousands of Nazi mass murderers still went unpunished. Many judges and senior jurists in West Germany after 1945 had held important judicial posts in the Third Reich, and, despite Hoffmann's disclaimer – asserted rather than argued – this surely bore some relevance to the failure of the legal system to deal adequately with the crimes of the Third Reich.

The political agenda behind Hoffmann's book seems plain. She argues that the East German Politbüro, and those of its servants responsible for crimes of violence such as the shooting of escapees on the border and at the Berlin Wall – should be tried for murder, and that the State Security Service (the Stasi) and its agents should be exposed and dismissed from their jobs. It would be a lot more difficult to do this if the legitimacy of the West German judicial system were compromised by its failure to prosecute the criminals of the Nazi regime.

But this compromised legitimacy is, of course, precisely the problem. And it is a problem because the crimes of Nazism were infinitely greater than those of the Ulbricht–Honecker regime. Hoffmann has to admit that the German Democratic Republic did not go in for mass murder. Nevertheless, she attempts to rescue the parallel by suggesting that Nazi genocide took place in the 'exceptional situation' of a world war. In peacetime, she says, Nazi justice was no more bloody than that of East Germany. Given the relative sizes of the populations of the two states, this is true enough. But Nazism existed for and through war: mass murder was its ultimate purpose. The war was not an 'exceptional' situation; it was where the regime found its true essence. The German Democratic Republic, on the other hand, was not made for war. On the contrary, it was a buffer-state erected by the Soviet Union out of fear of war. Terror and repression were instruments of a paranoid rather than a psychopathic ideology: it saw itself as beleaguered and beset by enemies rather than engaged on a career of world conquest.

The German Democratic Republic was not a home-grown regime: it was imposed by the Soviet Union. Hoffmann presents the whole development of state and society in East Germany not only as quintessentially German, but also as pre-planned from the very beginning: even the break-up of the big landed estates for example – which the Western Allies approved as part of the general dismantling of 'Prussianism' – is seen as a deliberate preparation for Stalinist collectivization. Post-war 'anti-fascist' measures such as these in fact enjoyed a degree of mass support in the Soviet zone. But when the Cold War began, towards the end of the 1940s, when the occupying power changed tack and created the German Democratic Republic as a carbon-copy of itself, this support melted away, culminating in the workers' uprising of 1953.

By contrast, the Nazi Party came to power in 1933 with the support of over a third of the electorate, and at times thereafter, notably in 1940, it seems to have generated a wide degree of consensus in support of its policies. Finally, although it only lasted twelve years, the Third Reich drew on much deeper traditions in German history, and could only function with the more or less willing collaboration of existing elites. A reckoning with the legacy of Nazism has thus been, ironically, even more difficult than a reckoning with the legacy of the Communist regime in East Germany which, although it lasted for over forty years, did not draw on deep-rooted sources of political culture, ideology or social attitudes in the German past.

Once more, in Hoffmann's book, we are faced with the instrumentalization of historical comparison for the purposes of present politics. The book disturbs because of its dogmatic and simplistic approach to complex historical problems, and its wearisomely repeated, almost fanatical insistence on the need to put the leadership of the former East Germany behind bars. Based on a very selective reading of the secondary literature, it makes no original contribution to the subject. Nevertheless, the issues it raises are important ones. It is certain that they will continue to be discussed for a good time to come.

NOTE

1 Imanuel Geiss, *Der Hysterikerstreit: Ein unpolemischer Essay*, Schriftenreihe Extremismus und Demokratie, (Bonn, Bouvier Verlag, 1992); Christa Hoffmann, *Stunden Null? Vergangenheitsbewältigung in Deutschland 1945 und 1989*, Schriftenreihe Extremismus und Demokratie, 2 (Bonn, Bouvier Verlag, 1992).

20

REBIRTH OF THE GERMAN RIGHT?[1]

The reunification of Germany in 1989/90 caught almost everyone on the intellectual scene in the Federal Republic by surprise. On the left, Germany's division had long been regarded as part of the price paid for the crimes of Nazism, and advocates of reunification as dangerous reactionaries who harked back to the days of the Bismarckian Empire if not the pan-Germanism of the Third Reich. Communist East Germany was depicted in neutral, even to some extent favourable, terms, often simply as a different kind of democracy, rather than a tyranny that had to be overthrown, or a part of Germany wrongfully under foreign occupation. Militant anti-Communism of the sort which became commonplace in the United States once more under the Reagan presidency appeared threatening because any serious attempt to conquer East Germany by force would inevitably lead to a war on German soil, with massive devastation caused by the use of tactical nuclear weapons. On the whole, therefore, reunification was opposed on the West German left because it raised old ghosts of German history and conjured up the nightmare of a nuclear holocaust.

When reunification actually happened, the left was completely wrong-footed. Some writers, most notably Günther Grass, openly opposed it from the outset, seeing in it a dangerous stimulus to the revival of old-style German nationalism. Most, however, were completely silent. The compromise position adopted by the Social Democratic Party – reunification was inevitable, but it ought to be accomplished more slowly and in a more cautious manner – may have been retrospectively defensible in the light of the problems which the pace of events, pushed on by Chancellor Kohl, subsequently brought, but to the German electorate it looked like curmudgeonly carping from the sidelines, and was judged as such. The elections of 18 March 1990 were a triumph for Kohl, whose vague but heady promises of prosperity and national unity won the day. Both politically and intellectually, the German left was in total disarray.

Reunification also disrupted existing ideologies of the right. Throughout the Federal Republic's existence, German conservatism had been built on anti-Communism. Germany, after all, was on the front line of the Cold War.

The threat of Soviet domination and the constant stream of political abuse emanating from East Berlin meant that conservatives saw the defence of Western values as their main task, and defined themselves *vis-à-vis* their opponents on the left principally by their greater distance from the politics and ideology of the German Democratic Republic. That Republic's collapse, therefore, took the ground from under their feet. For a short time, to be sure, German conservatives could bask in the enjoyment of what they saw, with some justification, as a definitive and historic triumph over their old enemy. Right and left argued over how far the reunited Germany should go in prosecuting the leaders of the former Communist regime in the East, in dismissing people in universities, state institutions and other walks of life who had worked for the regime, and in exposing writers, artists and others who had worked for, or collaborated with, the East German security police, the infamous Stasi. But all this replicated the old arguments between opponents and supporters of a compromise with the German Democratic Republic in the 1970s and early 1980s without really going beyond them. Even before these disputes began to die down in the mid-1990s, therefore, the German right found itself just as ideologically disoriented as did the left. With no serious threat of Communism remaining against which it could define itself, what was it now to do?

As the 1990s wore on, both right and left found themselves, perhaps surprisingly, still prisoners of the German past. Two major political issues revealed just how powerful the political and intellectual legacy of Hitler's Third Reich remained. First, German reactions to the Gulf War of 1991 were largely dictated by attitudes to the experience of Nazism. These attitudes to some extent cut across existing political divisions. The Iraqi dictator Saddam Hussein's invasion of the small Gulf state of Kuwait made him in the eyes of some on the left, such as the writer Hans Magnus Enzensberger, into a new Hitler, whose drive to dominate the Middle East and equip himself with a nuclear arsenal had to be stopped. Majority opinion on the left, however, was violently opposed to the war, seeing it principally as a threat to world peace. In no other European country were there such massive peace demonstrations on the streets. Everywhere, young people hung white sheets out of their apartment windows as a sign of opposition to the conflict. Yet at the same time, many were painfully aware of the fact that the targets of Saddam's rockets included locations in Israel, and that his long-term aims included the destruction of the Jewish state. Trying to stop the war could therefore easily be construed as evidence of a worrying disregard for the future of the Jewish people which historical experience should have led Germans above all others to defend. The pro-Israeli banners carried by some of the people demonstrating for the withdrawal of Allied troops from the Gulf only served to underline the political and moral confusion of the left.

On the right and centre of the political scene, by contrast, it seemed absurd that a reunited Germany should be barred by its constitution from sending troops and equipment to help the war against Saddam just because the appearance of German troops in foreign countries would awaken painful historical memories. Moreover, other countries in the Western Alliance were strongly critical of the Germans' reluctance to take part in the war. The Gulf War thus became the catalyst for an eventual revision of previous German policy, and subsequent conflicts, in Bosnia and Somalia for example, have seen German armed forces participating in military action under the aegis of NATO and the United Nations. The new willingness of Germany to involve its troops in foreign combat can be seen as part of a wider self-assertiveness which includes demands for a permanent seat for the Federal Republic on the United Nations' Security Council and found one of its earliest expressions in the German recognition of Croatia, a move which in retrospect appears to have been, to say the least, ill-advised. A willingness to send troops to defend Israel therefore served as the starting-point for a general drive for a resumption of Germany's independent status as a great power, a drive which itself has aroused some anxiety in its turn on the German left.

The second major political issue in which the shadow of Nazism has fallen over post-unification German politics has been that of immigration. Not only has there been a massive influx of people from the former East Germany into the former West, but the breakdown of Communism has also provided the stimulus and the opportunity for the migration of huge numbers of ethnic Germans into the Federal Republic from the former Soviet Union and other parts of Eastern Europe. Generous German asylum laws, established long ago in recognition of the refuge given in other countries to German exiles from the Third Reich, have opened the doors to political, or allegedly political refugees from all over the world. All this has aroused widespread popular anxiety in Germany itself. There are also millions of 'guest-workers' and their families living in the Federal Republic, from countries such as Turkey and the former Yugoslavia. Many of them are now second-generation immigrants with German as their first language. Yet German law, basing the right to citizenship on origin rather than domicile, has denied them equal civil rights with the rest of the population and still regards them as foreigners. Resentment against asylum-seekers and 'guest-workers', fuelled by youth unemployment, especially (though by no means exclusively) in the former East Germany, boiled over in the early 1990s into a series of organized, violent and murderous attacks on them by young neo-Nazi skinheads in towns such as Rostock, Solingen and Mölln. In some instances at least, these were openly tolerated by the police. All this raised the spectre of the open racism of the Third Reich and its appalling exterminatory consequences. Public reaction was swift. In many towns across Germany, millions of people joined in peaceful mass demonstrations, carrying candles and holding hands in a symbolic affirmation of solidarity with the victims.

These events indicated forcefully the continuing part played in German political culture by the memory of the Nazi dictatorship and its crimes. It is this memory from which the German right wants to escape in order to restore Germany's self-confidence as a nation and reap the full benefits of Germany's reintegration as a powerful, populous and prosperous nation-state in the middle of Europe. But how can this be done? The very concept of a German right has been discredited since the war. As the historian Rainer Zitelman points out in his contribution to *Die selbstbewusste Nation* (1995), it has hardly ever been used except in conjunction with the word 'extremism'. Helmut Kohl does not call himself 'right-wing', nor has he ever called for a coalition of political forces 'right of the Social Democrats' in the way that the late Willy Brandt called for a coalition of political forces 'left of the Christian Democrats'. Yet it is surely unjust to tar the right alone with the brush of Nazism, which, Zitelman suggests with some plausibility, combined elements of both traditional right and left in a new kind of political synthesis. The Christian Democrats describe themselves as centrist, and the absence of a 'democratic right wing' in German politics, says Zitelman, inevitably drives those people who do consider themselves on the right towards the extreme. It is this problem which the authors of *Die selbstbewusste Nation* are seeking to remedy.

Their starting-point for this attempt is a famous, or notorious article published in 1993 by the popular dramatist Botho Strauss in *Der Spiegel*. Written in an obscure, almost gnomic style, Strauss's essay was nevertheless umistakeable in its overall political thrust. It was time, he said, to break the intellectual tyranny of the post-1968 generation, time for Germans to dare to call themselves right-wing once more. Strauss's article ran into a great deal of criticism. The thirty essays collected in *Die selbstbewusste Nation* are all designed to defend it, and if possible to take its arguments further. The authors are journalists, academics and writers of various generations, ranging from the historian Ernst Nolte, born in 1923, to the part-time journalist Roland Bubik, born in 1970 and still a student. A few, such as Brigitte Seebacher-Brandt, widow of the former Social Democratic politician Willi Brandt, come from the left, but the overwhelming majority clearly wish to belong to the new democratic right which this book is intended to launch, at least in an intellectual sense.

There are many things to be said in favour of a democratic right wing in German politics, especially if, as Zitelman urges, it is careful to draw a sharp boundary between itself and the far right, and to oppose the violence, xenophobia and extreme hostility to immigrants which the extreme right encourages or condones. Other authors in this book, such as the journalist Ulrich Schacht, roundly condemn the extreme right for denying the Holocaust while so obviously being prepared to repeat it themselves if given a chance. Only one essay in this book, indeed, can be fairly described as extremist, a lengthy contribution by the journalist Peter Meier-Bergfeld, born in 1950, and Austrian correspondent of the *Rheinischer Merkur*. In this rather frightening article, Meier-Bergfeld sees Austria as a kind of conservative utopia, representing everything that Germany nowadays is not:

> The years without a sense of duty, the orgies of libertinism, the ceaseless hoisting of the white flag (with the cowardly slogan of fitting the means to the end), the toleration of no-go-areas for the law, the encouragement of revolutionary niches in the universities, the bringing of the state into contempt, the demonstrative mocking of its values and its representatives, the bacchanalia of self-hatred, the preliminary stages of civil war, the struggles of foreign gangs on German territory – Austria has never witnessed any of this and would never have tolerated it (p. 202).

Meier-Bergfeld praises what he sees as the lack of a market economy in Austria, its adherence to Christian ideals, and its rejection of individualism. The state comes first in Austria, he says, and he waxes enthusiastic about the fact that government Ministers are not responsible to the legislature there. Austrian prisons are no holiday homes. Crime rates are low. Austria in his view is a premodern society, which successfully avoided the excesses of 're-education' after the war. He attacks the campaign against former Austrian President Kurt Waldheim for concealing from the public his activities under the Third Reich, and he praises what he sees as Austria's rejection of 'aliens' and of the doctrine of multiculturalism.

Most worrying of all, Meier-Bergfeld sees Austrian neutrality as a model for a future German position in Europe, which prevents the country being sucked into the maw of 'Western' liberalism. He damns the Oder–Neisse line as Stalin's creation, and rejects Italian hegemony over the South Tyrol. His essay ends by expressing the hope that Austria will one day be reunited with Germany and exert its conservative influence over the resulting entity. 'For inside the German nation, like a Russian doll, another nation is hiding, and another and another' (p. 226). Theoretically, therefore, in his view, there is no end to German national aggrandisement. All this is frightening, but it is also extremely unrealistic. Meier-Bergfeld is simply wrong when he claims that virtually all Austrians (apart from a handful of Communists) regarded themselves as Germans before 1945: what evidence there is, suggests that at least half, if not more, would have voted for Austrian independence in the abortive referendum planned by Chancellor Schuschnigg on the eve of the *Anschluss* in 1938, not least because they rejected the authoritarian violence of the Nazis and rightly feared being subjected to German laws and institutions rather than being allowed to keep their own. Nowadays Austrian national identity seems firmly established, and the soul-searching that has occurred as a result of German reunification has been fairly muted. And even if there was another *Anschluss*, the likelihood of a nation of six million being able to impose its values on a nation of eighty million is so remote as to seem absurd.

Nevertheless, though Meier-Bergfeld's contribution is the only one even to toy with extremist ideas such as these, his advocacy of a strong, interventionist state and his hostility to the unfettered operation of market forces does tie in with one of the general themes of the book. Several of the contributors, most notably Ansgar Graw, Heimo Schwilk, Eberhard Straub and Rudolf Wassermann, reject what they see as the consumerism and hedonism of present-day German society, pillory the doctrine of individualism, and argue for a general strengthening of the collectivist ethos in society and an upgrading of the role of the state. Such views stand in stark contrast to the dominant ideology of the right in Britain and the USA, which over the last few years has argued overwhelmingly for a reduction of the state's role in society and the extension of market forces to every area of life. The privatization of public utilities (including the prisons and significant parts of the police force), the reduction of taxation, the introduction of business methods into the public sector, all these have been top priorities of the Anglo-American right. There is not a sign of them in any of the essays in this book. Nor is there any sign of the originality, the lateral thinking, the intellectual daring, which characterized, for good or ill, the British right during the 1980s, when it was making all the running in the market for political ideas. Instead, the tone of the overwhelming majority of the essays in this book is negative, querulous, pathetic. In a word, the book amounts to little more in the end than one long whinge about the current state of affairs in Germany, without any real attempt to offer a credible or practicable political alternative.

Four aspects of present-day German society arouse the pained protests of the authors. First, almost all of them, beginning with Botho Strauss himself, are obsessed with what they see as left-wing dominance of the media. Accusations abound of the 'intellectual terrorism' allegedly exerted by the dominant majority of the generation of 1968, of what Ulrich Schacht calls 'the block supervisor system of the West German PC-society and its PC-commissars' (p. 60), and of the Marxist 're-education' of the German people achieved by members of the Frankfurt school on their return from exile in the United States after the war. The practice of 'political correctness' arouses the pained resentment of many of the contributors, but the letters PC are used rhetorically, without anyone saying what they really mean in concrete terms. Indeed, the endlessly reiterated complaints in the book about what Roland Bubik calls the 'left-wing domination of opinion' in the Federal Republic are not backed up by any real examples at all, and nobody is able to demonstrate that the alleged hegemony of left-wing opinions has been created by anything other than their greater effectiveness and popularity in the free market of ideas. The very existence of a book such as this, and the fact that it has gone through three editions in less than six months, should be enough to refute any arguments to the contrary. And if it is true, as Rainer

Zitelman claims, that increasing numbers of intellectuals are crossing over from left to right in the wake of the collapse of Marxism, then what are they all complaining about?

The second aspect of present-day German society which repeatedly worries the authors of this book – who are, with one exception, men – is feminism. In a lengthy polemic on the subject, Felix Stern attacks the dominance of debate on women's place in society by 'a small, radical left-wing lesbian female elite'. He sees sexual harrassment legislation, as recently enacted in the state of Hesse, as part of a feminist plot to destroy heterosexuality. Feminism, says Rainer Zitelman, is the substitute ideology of the left now that Marxism is dead and buried. Ansgar Graw moans about feminism's spreading of the 'mad idea of human equality'. Unlike Stern, indeed, most authors in the book seem to think that the feminist movement is bent on more than the apartheid-like creation of a separate 'women's cultural sphere'. Heimo Schwilk declares grandiosely: 'The pacification of society in order to avoid any kind of pain has culminated today in its feminization, brought about by consumer hedonism and the cultural-revolutionary activities of feminism.' (p. 396). Predictably, Peter Meier-Bergfeld finds everything far better ordered in this respect in Austria: 'The emancipation of women has not yet degenerated into a permanent war of the sexes; Austrian women still flirt with men and still permit themselves to be assisted into their coats' (p. 206). Even the Social Democratic Party in Vienna is 'still a men's club' (p. 207). To regard the morality of the state as compatible with the moral standards of women and the family is, he says, fatal: 'In an extreme situation the state has to draw on the lives of its sons as soldiers; no female morality can tolerate this' (p. 209). In all this, however, the complaints of the authors must seem to anyone looking on from outside to be grotesquely exaggerated. In comparison with, say, the United States, the influence of feminism on society in Germany still has a very long way to go. And blaming the popularity of pacifism on the feminist movement is simply absurd.

The third object of the authors' protests is, perhaps more predictably, the continuing focus of German historians and public debate about history on the crimes of the Third Reich. Brigitte Seebacher-Brandt declares roundly that it is time to break free from a sense of national guilt about the Nazis and their deeds. Far from reunification having provided the opportunity for this, however, Rainer Zitelman considers that the idea of 'mastering the past' (*Vergangenheitsbewältigung*) gained a new lease of life in 1989. By concentrating on the struggle against violence towards immigrants and asylum-seekers in the early 1990s, the left was able to regain the initiative it had lost during reunification and perpetuate the feelings of German self-doubt and self-hatred which had become so widespread during the 1960s. A major contributor to this is what Ulrich Schacht calls 'post-German national-suicidal historical writing' (p. 62). Germans cannot, he says, forever be branded with the mark of Cain. Excessive use of the word 'Auschwitz' has become an obstacle to free thought, a claim echoed in the contribution to this book by the film director Hans-Jürgen Syberberg. But this too is surely exaggerated. To what kind of free thought, one wonders, is the memory of Auschwitz an obstacle? Since the authors of this volume are at such pains to distance themselves from the extreme right in German politics, it surely cannot be the thought of neo-Nazism. Moreover, as Ansgar Graw remarks, how can the right persuade people to remember the crimes of Stalin and Honecker if at the same time it is urging them to forget about the crimes of Hitler? Finally, Ulrich Schacht argues that the real legacy of Auschwitz ought to lie in the permanent support given by Germans to the state of Israel. This is all very well and good, but why then should it not lie in other areas as well, and in any case support for Israel demands the very kind of perpetuation of the memory of Auschwitz that Schacht and others wish to abandon, or at least play down, on a more general level. It is hard to escape the conclusion that the authors are caught here in a series of paradoxes from which they are unable in the end to find any way out.

The fourth area of contemporary German society and politics to which they direct their complaints is what they perceive as the lack of a properly developed national consciousness (the plea implied, indeed, in the book's very title). 'The self-confidence of our nation', declares Rainer Zitelman, 'has been broken.' Concentration on the Nazi past is of course the reason for this. Alfred Mechtersheimer warns that the 'vilification of anything nationalistic' can lead to the emergence of extreme and dangerous forms of nationalism, as in post-Communist Eastern Europe. He points to an honourable tradition of left-wing nationalism, begun by Kautsky and Bauer and continued in the postwar era by the Social Democrats' leader in the late 1940s and early 1950s, Kurt Schumacher. Other authors call for recovery of a German sense of belonging (*Heimatgefühl*), of the word 'fatherland', of an unbroken national identity. Reunification, remarks Karl-Eckhard Hahn, has suddenly made the Bismarckian Reich relevant again. 'The new Germany is beginning to reveal itself as a mixture of the tradition of Bismarck and the tradition of Adenauer.' This leads him into a lengthy history of geopolitical theories, but not, however, to any startling geopolitical conclusions. None of the authors of this volume wants Germany to leave the European Union, and several argue explicitly in favour of staying in. Hahn's main practical political argument, indeed, seems to be that Germany's central geographical position gives it a particular responsibility for integrating the Eastern European states into the Union. The furthest anybody goes in criticizing European integration is to argue, as does Manfred Brunner, against the single currency and to call for a confederal rather than a unitary European state. Of the extreme anti-Europeanism of the British 'Eurosceptic' right, however, there is no sign at all in this volume.

232

German national consciousness means for many of the authors an emphasis on German culture and a strong opposition to multiculturalism'. But none of them seems prepared to say what German national culture actually is. This is characteristic of the book as a whole, which is far more concerned to attack the left than it is to put forward any positive arguments or policies which might define the right. The authors are surely correct in their diagnosis of German national identity as fractured and contested. But the same is true of any national identity in the modern age, and indeed always has been from the very beginnings of nationalism. What one detects here is not only a strong sense of disorientation, but also a strong desire for order and certainty amidst the bewilderments of multicultural politics, feminist ideologies, critical history and free-wheeling debate about the future of the nation after the ending of that significant part of the old West German identity which was based on anti-Communism rather than, say, on prosperity or democracy. But amidst all the windy rhetoric, there are very few positive ideas for the future.

The problem for the new right in Germany, if indeed there is such a thing, is that the old right is doing very well, thank you; Helmut Kohl has now been in power for one-and-a-half decades, and if the media are as much dominated by the left as the authors of this book seem to think, then they have had so little effect on the direction of German politics that one wonders if they are worth all the ink spilled on them here. The new right emerged in Britain in the late 1970s as a response to a decade and a half of Labour Party electoral success under Harold Wilson, based on the feeling that radical new ideas were needed to recapture the political initiative. It has emerged in the USA in the 1990s as a response to the Clinton presidency, and for very similar reasons. Such stimuli are largely lacking in Germany. Reunification clearly demands some kind of rethinking for the German right, but given the continuing success of the Christian Democrats, the need for it does not really seem very urgent, and that lack of urgency is reflected in the general woolliness of the contributions to this book. Ultimately, one feels, *Die selbstbewusste Nation* will mainly be of interest to what are known in Britain as 'the chattering classes'. It testifies to a widespread sense of ill-defined resentment and disorientation on the German right following the end of anti-Communism as an integrating factor, but it has nothing very positive or persuasive to offer as an antidote to this condition.

NOTES

1 Heimo Schwilk and Ulrich Schacht (eds.), *Die selbstbewusste Nation. 'Anschwellender Bocksgesang' und weitere Beiträge zu einer deutschen Debatte* (3rd edn, Frankfurt am Main, Ullstein Verlag, 1995).

21

AFTER REUNIFICATION

What has been the overall effect of reunification on the writing of German history? Some, in particular the young, Cardiff-based historian Stefan Berger, have warned that reunification threatens the plurality of views on German history and poses the serious danger of a return to the narrow concern with national history and national identity which characterized German historiography for two centuries previously. Berger has argued that a 'renationalization' of German history is in progress. While some historians, like Gregor Schöllgen and Michael Stürmer, have revived the geopolitical interpretation of German history, according to which Imperial Germany got involved in a world war because it was 'surrounded' by hostile powers, others, like Rainer Zitelmann, Ernst Nolte and Christian Striefler, have urged a more positive interpretation of National Socalism as a consciously modernizing force which amounted to a rational and defensible response to the threat of Communism. This in Berger's view amounts to a 'torrent of Prussian calls for a revival of "national history"'. It has been aided and abetted by the emergence of a more negative assessment of the Federal Republic, now seen by historians like Karl Heinz Bohrer as a provincial deviation from the mainstream of German national history, created against the Germans' wishes by the Allies in 1949. German national identity, according to the young historian Karlheinz Weissmann, is based on collective memory and shared German ethnicity – the *Volk*, in fact: and Weissmann among others has been loud in his calls for Germans to reclaim it, just as others have accompanied this with the argument that the Federal Republic was too subservient to 'the West'.

The clamour for a revived German national identity also, in Berger's view, involved attacks on the legitimacy of the East German state and the wholesale denigration of its historians as Marxist hacks parroting the views of the Communist hierarchy. And not only East German historians. The new nationalists have also attacked the West German historical profession for failing to contribute significantly to the process of reunification. They were either silent in 1989/90, or hostile; and their main effect, through their consistently critical attitude to the German past and the history of German nationalism, has been in this view to weaken German national identity rather than strengthen it. The contrast with the Prussian historians of the nineteenth century, such as Droysen, Sybel and Treitschke, whose work was dedicated to preparing for and justifying the creation of a German nation-state under Prussian leadership, could not be more striking. While the Prussian historians wrote stirring political epics of national resurgence, their modern counterparts have produced jargon-ridden studies of social structure which no-one apart from their students is ever likely to read. To Berger's obvious dismay, 'critical' historians like Hans-Ulrich Wehler and Jürgen Kocka have responded to reunification by retreating from the *Sonderweg* paradigm, abandoning their previous view that Germany had entered a 'post-national' era after 1945, and surrendering key positions in the methodological battle between social history and political history to the advocates of a revived concentration on the political history of the nation-state.[1]

But work on German history which I have surveyed in the earlier chapters of this book show this view to be alarmist. Nationalist historical writing was around long before reunification. Thomas Nipperdey, for instance, wrote almost the entirety of his great history of nineteenth-century Germany, with its elaborate justification of German national unity, in the 1980s; similarly, Michael Stürmer was advocating his geopolitical interpretation of 1914, and Ernst Nolte and Rainer Zitelman were urging a more positive attitude to Nazism at a time when reunification was not even remotely considered a practical possibility.[2] Histories designed to revive pride in the past have been written at intervals all the way since 1945.[3] Calls for a return to the political history of the nation-state were already being issued by Klaus Hildebrand and others in the 1970s.[4] Attacks on the Federal Republic as a provincial state that had forgotten how to assert itself on the international scene began years before the fall of the Berlin Wall.[5] There has been no observable increase in the publication of such historical and methodological work since reunification. Indeed, there has been no long term increase in German nationalism since reunification. The radical right remains numerically insignificant and politically impotent. National identity remains divided and disputed, but insofar as one exists, it is the old 'post-national' identity of the Federal Republic rather than some neo-Bismarckian revival.[6] Moreover, it is mostly political scientists like Arnulf Baring and Hans-Peter Schwarz, rather than historians, who have been advocating a more positive attitude to the German past during these years. The overwhelming majority of German historians have rejected such calls or remained indifferent to them.

A great deal of concern was aroused in 1995, to be sure, by the publication of a new volume in the well-produced and widely read *Propyläen Geschichte Deutschlands* by Karlheinz Weissmann, one of the intellectuals of the 'new right'. The volume, covering the years 1933 to 1945, was originally supposed to have been written by Hans Mommsen, but years had passed without a manuscript having been delivered, and all the other volumes in the series had already been published. The publisher was taken over by a company led by the right-wing radical Herbert Fleissner, who made another right-wing radical, Rainer Zitelman, its editor-in-chief; Zitelman sacked Mommsen and commissioned his political associate Weissmann to write the volume without even informing the actual editor of the series, the historian Dieter Groh, that he had done this. Weissmann then wrote, in a remarkably short space of time, a history of the Third Reich from the point of view of the 'new right'. It ascribed the origins of Nazism to the socialist tradition, omitting all mention of ultra-nationalist, middle-class pressure groups such as the pan-Germans. It ignored the role of the old elites in bringing the Nazis to power. It blamed the appointment of Hitler as Reich Chancellor on the Social Democrats' refusal to support his predecessor Schleicher. It said much about the Germans under Nazism but next to nothing about the Jews. It made no mention of the regime's deliberate murder of millions of Eastern Europeans from 1941–4. It underplayed the 'Final Solution' to the extent that it only devoted ten pages to it, roughly the same as film and sport in the book's much longer section on the Third Reich in peacetime. It made little mention of the victims of the Third Reich at all, in fact; even in the sections devoted to murder and persecution, it concentrated largely on the description of the regime's policies, to the relative neglect of their actual effect. By contrast, it went into considerable detail on the atrocities committed by the Red Army on its march into Germany in 1944/5 and the sufferings of the victims.[7] All in all, it constituted a sustained attempt to downplay the horrors of the Third Reich on the one hand and uncouple them from the mainstream of German history on the other.

Alarmed critics asked how long it would be before such works as this would 'flood the book market' and become 'standard works'. 'Antiliberal intellectuals', they warned darkly, 'are being extremely successful in their march through educational institutions'.[8] But this was going too far. Zitelman, after all, is a relatively isolated figure, not only in the educational world, where he has been unable to make a career for himself, but also in journalism, where a mass revolt by journalists working for the conservative daily *Die Welt* secured his resignation from the editorial staff because even they were outraged by his extreme right-wing views. Moreover, the book met with an overwhelmingly negative response not only from the German press but also from subscribers to the Propyläen series, who returned their copies in droves. As a result of the scandal over his commissioning of Weissmann's book, Fleissner, the radical-right owner of Propyläen's parent company, the Ullstein Verlag, withdrew his stake in its ownership. So the affair ended with a substantial defeat for the 'new right' and the weakening of their position in the publishing world, rather than another step forward for the 'new right' in the 'long march through the institutions'.

It is not just the case that there are no more neo-nationalist historical works about in Germany after reunification than before. Equally important is the fact that the changes that have come about in the interpretation and methodology of German history in the last few years have had little or nothing to do with the reunification process and its consequences. In the first place, as we saw in Chapter 2, the demise of the *Sonderweg* theory, at least in its original form, has far more to do with the actual progress of historical research than with any putative reaction to contemporary political events. Here too the process began well before 1989.[9] Research and argument undermined it on several fronts during the 1980s, above all, of course, the great *Bürgertum* project in Bielefeld, which demonstrated not the social subservience and cultural weakness of the German bourgeoisie, but its tremendous resilience and power in German society in these respects. True, reunification has set the seal on the *Sonderweg* theory's demise by drawing attention to the multiple possibilities inherent in Bismarck's German Reich;[10] but its intellectual bankruptcy had been clear enough long before.[11]

As far as the revival of political history is concerned – notably evident in Wolfgang Mommsen's two-volume survey of Imperial Germany, discussed in Chapter 4 – here too German reunification is less important than other, more or less autonomous developments within academic history. For by the late 1980s, the great age of a social history that rested on overarching theories of social structure and social change – Marxism or modernization theory, for example – was coming to an end. Not just in Germany, but in other countries too, a 'revival of narrative' was taking place, restoring human agency and contingency to history, and refocusing attention on what social historians had long dismissed as the surface froth of events. Even among the leading figures of the *Annales* school of social historians in France, voices could be heard advocating a return to political history.[12] Far from making German historians isolated in the profession on an international level, the turn away from social-structural history is bringing them back into line.

Indeed, it is the persistence of social-scientific approaches to history in Germany well into the 1990s that is arguably exceptional. Traditionally, German historians had concentrated very much on political and diplomatic history, the narrative of the fortunes of the German state; economic history had established itself mainly in the medieval field, but even where it did intervene in the study of the nineteenth and twentieth centuries, it was predominantly under the primacy of politics, so that the Customs Union of the 1830s, the industrialization of the 1860s, or the inflation of the 1920s, were all viewed primarily in terms of their political significance. Attempts to introduce modern social history had made little impact, not least because of the centrality of explaining the Third Reich and its origins, for some decades after the Second World War. While British, French and American historians came increasingly under the influence of social sciences such as demography, sociology, statistics, geography and anthropology in the 1950s and early 1960s, this approach was overwhelmingly rejected by the majority of German historians, who continued to pay allegiance to traditional notions of understanding the past in its own terms, of so-called *Historismus*, a way of arriving at an objective truth through critical assessment of the documents, which had been the principal contribution of the Germans to historical methodology with the work of Leopold von Ranke in the nineteenth century.

The critical reinterpretation of modern German history that began in the late 1960s was based on a conscious rejection of this tradition and on the deliberate adoption of the theory and methodology of the social sciences. The task of history was not to understand the past in its own terms, but to tell us how we became what we were and thus help us find out what we were, or ought to be, in the process of becoming. Social science theory, quantitative methods and other innovations were mobilized in the service of a progressive and, on the whole, optimistic vision of history and its purposes. This vision often emphasized the negative aspects of the past, such as social inequality, structurally determined poverty, authoritarianism and injustice, and frequently tried to harness historical scholarship into the service of helping humanity escape from these evils. A critical under-standing of the German past could thus help people to grasp why Nazism had come to power, to eliminate its residues in the present, and to guard against its recurrence in the future.

History, in this view, was not just about politics, or society, or the economy, or culture, but had to take all these things into account and demonstrate how they related to one another. It needed social science theory to help it carry out this task. It was important to avoid giving absolute primacy to one particular aspect, whether the economy, as in 'vulgar Marxist' approaches, or high politics and diplomacy, as in traditional German historical scholarship. A theory that allowed historians to take account of the process of modernization without falling into anachronistic judgements of the past, a theory such as that of Max Weber, would facilitate a synthetic general account of the past that held all the disparate strands of political, social, economic and cultural history together and weave them into a common pattern leading to the present: a theory such as this was the only proper basis for understanding the German past.[13]

Thus, history became impossible without the social sciences; indeed, in the educational politics of West Germany in the 1970s, it came near to being replaced by the social sciences altogether, as it was pressed into the service of civic and political education. History, in this view, was an essential part of training for citizenship in a democratic society. And in carrying out this task, it had to make use of the latest sociological concepts, quantitative methods and conceptual innovations. History, indeed, was a social science; and the classic studies of modern Germany published during the 1970s and 1980s were characteristically filled with statistical tables and packed with terms borrowed from sociology, economics and political science. This was a modernist version of history, in which industrialization and economic growth were seen in positive terms as being linked with social mobility and civic freedom, and the task of German historians was primarily understood as lying in the explanation of why this conjuncture did not happen in the German case until the 1950s and 1960s. Here again, as German exceptionalism came to an end, so too did German history; everything that happened since 1945 was a postscript.

But the 1980s have undermined many of the sociopolitical assumptions which underlay this modernist vision of history. It was, for example, a vision which saw the past mainly in class terms, and explained German history through the concept of changing relations between the nobility, the bourgeoisie, the urban and rural petty bourgeoisie and the proletariat. Such a view was still by no means out of place in the 1950s. But by the 1980s it was becoming clear that the social antagonisms characteristic of classic industrial societies were yielding to more complex conflicts, as the industrial sector dwindled and post-industrial social structures came to the fore. Gender, ethnicity, generational identity, sexual orientation, all of which (even ethnicity) had been neglected by the modernist historians, began to attract historical research as they became more important in the present. Enthusiasm for modern industrial and scientific progress encountered widespread disillusion and criticism, as the environmental damage caused by unrestrained growth became evermore obvious. As the leading edge of research in the natural sciences shifted from chemistry and physics, space exploration and similar areas where the financial costs of technological gigantism were spiralling out of control, towards biology and medicine, where the practical returns were a good deal more obvious, criticism of unfettered scientific progress became increasingly vociferous, with protesters ranging from anti-vivisectionists and feminists at one extreme to religious fundamentalists and Catholic moralists at the other. Long-term mass unemployment added to these other factors to draw attention to the human costs of continued rapid economic and scientific expansion and growth.

By the middle of the 1980s, it was clear that the present from whose perspective the modernist historians were writing itself now lay in the past. Moreover, the conceptual and methodological tools they had used were being rapidly superseded. Quantitative history – 'cliometrics' – which had promised such gains in historical accuracy and certainty when it arrived with the age of the computer, had proved a disappointment. Studies of voting patterns in modern German history, for example, had reached an undreamt-of pitch of methodological sophistication, but they left the central question of what voters thought they were doing when they cast their ballot, of what voting actually meant, and of why voters supported the parties they did, as mysterious as ever.[14] Social-scientific concepts, like the modernist architecture of the 1960s, neglected the human dimension and reduced the people of the past to anonymous categories. It seemed more important to reinstate subjective experience at the centre of history than to continue the futile search for a conclusively scientific explanation of the objective factors thought to have determined people's behaviour in the past.[15]

The new history in Germany – *Alltagsgeschichte* or the 'history of everyday life' – focused on values, beliefs, mentalities and lifestyles rather than structures, class antagonisms, or economic fluctuations. It directed attention away from attempts to describe and analyse the structures of whole societies and towards the experience of the individual, the community, the small group, to the forgotten victims of history instead of the big battalions.[16] German historians proved unable to satisfy the new demand of readers and publishers for studies of values and feeling, the history of the senses and the emotions, and the 1980s saw, therefore, a flood of translations of works on these subjects from French, Italian and English into German, until a French medievalist such as Georges Duby or Emmanuel Le Roy Ladurie became more widely read in German than most German medievalists were. A book such as Alain Corbin's history of smell in eighteenth- and nineteenth-century France became a best-seller; there was no German equivalent.[17]

In pursuit of these new objectives in history, new methods and concepts began to be developed. Most obvious was perhaps the emergence of oral history as a means of recapturing the subjective experience of people in the past. But the way that values and feelings are expressed, through language, has also moved increasingly to the centre of historians' attention. The study of symbols, ceremonies and iconography has provided a new perspective on the meaning of political and social events and actions which the modernist historians took for granted as unproblematical. Literary analysis, poststructuralism, anthropology, semiotics, are taking the place of sociology and economics. Foucault has increasingly displaced Weber, though as Chapter 6 argued, this development is still partial and slow in Germany.[18]

Moreover, whereas it was commonplace in the 1960s and 1970s to speak of a decline in public historical consciousness, a 'crisis of history', expressed both in practical terms (old buildings were torn down, new shopping centres replaced old alleyways, and so on), and intellectually (social science was making the running and it often seemed difficult to justify the study of history at all, at least for its own sake), the 1980s have seen a dramatic revival of history. As we look around at the latest postmodern buildings or read the latest postmodern novels, it becomes clear that a central feature of postmodernism lies in the rediscovery of the past. Art, literature and architecture now make a point of abandoning the search for new forms so characteristic of modernism, and mix together pastiches of old styles and genres into a new synthesis instead. Conservative governments in Britain and the United States as well as West Germany preferred history to sociology, which itself entered a state of crisis in the 1980s. The notion of history as a foundation for a strengthened national consciousness in West Germany went well beyond the protagonists of the *Historikerstreit* and entered political discourse in events such as the ceremony at the Bitburg military cemetery in 1985, where Chancellor Kohl and US President Ronald Reagan honoured Germany's soldiers of the Second World War. The postmodern emphasis on mentalities has had a political counterpart in the positive reassessment by conservative historians of the supposed virtues of the Prussian Junkers. And the heritage industry, the fashion for historical exhibitions and the conversation of historical remains, has taken its place in Germany as well as in other Western countries.[19]

Modernist history was dominated not only by social science theory and methodology but also by the demand for relevance, and in pursuit of this objective, German historians, especially those in the younger generation, shifted their attention increasingly to periods near to the present: first of all to the Weimar Republic and the Third Reich, then finally to the post-war years. But the demand for relevance had its own perils. The Third Reich and its origins may have been the most relevant part of German history to the progressive historians of the 1960s and 1970s, who had either experienced the Nazi years themselves as children or had to confront the involvement in it of their parents, but this could no longer be assumed in the case of history students and graduate researchers born in the 1960s. For this generation, indeed, the origins of the Federal Republic were in many ways of more direct relevance, and this may help explain why so many of them turned to the post-war years for their research topics if they started work on a doctoral dissertation. It was precisely this worry – how to make the Nazi phenomenon relevant to a generation which had not experienced it even indirectly, through its parents – that underlay many of the attempts of proponents of *Alltagsgeschichte*, the 'history of everyday life', such as Martin Broszat and Detlev Peukert, to replace the tendency of so much historical writing on the Third Reich to create heroes and demons with an approach that recognized the people of the period as human beings, complex, divided, indecisive and often only dimly aware of the significance of their actions: as people, in other words, like us.[20]

By the 1980s, in other words, the relevance of the Third Reich could no longer be assumed, it had to be argued for. But in shifting the focus to problems such as the role of medicine and disease, sport and leisure, the media and entertainment, women and the family, homosexuality and deviance, religious belief, work, the treatment and experience of minorities, and so on, these historians were in fact accommodating the study of Nazi Germany to a much profounder shift in historical sensibility in which 'relevance' played no part at all. For the postmodern recovery of history, in addressing subjects such as identity, belief, experience and subjectivity, has

241

been a recovery of history as a whole, in which, indeed, the people of remote periods may be of more interest than those of the recent past, precisely because the otherness of the physical and emotional world in which they lived illuminates the limits and possibilities of the human condition in a richer and more varied way. Hence the popularity of books such as *Montaillou* and the revival of interest in the history of the Middle Ages, pioneered at first by the translation into German of the work of French historians but now being followed up actively by the Germans themselves.[21] To put it more concretely: for someone whose interest in history is inspired by feminist convictions, and perhaps also feminist doubts, a study of the female body, and ideas about it, in the early eighteenth century, may be just as 'relevant' as a study of women's place in the Third Reich, because the alien quality of the subject will provide a larger and richer understanding of what it is to be a woman, and what the relationship is, or might be, between the physical condition of femaleness and the social construction of gender at a general level.[22]

These shifts of focus in historical scholarship and consciousness during the 1980s have dramatically increased the fragmentation of history that began with the modernist historians of a generation earlier. Social science history created a whole new series of specialisms, some of them, such as demographic or econometric history, highly technical and often impenetrable to the uninitiated, others, such as urban history or family history, apparently unrelated to the central political problematic of German history as a whole. The result has been to undermine any consensus over what German history is about.[23] All this makes it difficult to accept the sweeping claim that reunification has led to a 'reorientation' of writing about German history as such. History as it is written in Germany today is simply too diverse to fit into neat generalizations like this.

What Berger and those few alarmists who think like him are essentially doing is to reduce the complexity and diversity of modern historical scholarship to an epiphenomenon of modern politics. Certainly, German historians have long played a role in public debate which has no equivalent in most other countries; but then, the crimes of Nazism make the history of Germany rather more politically sensitive than that of other countries. But politics is only one of a variety of influences on the way historians write and research. Academic disciplines also have their own dynamics, relatively independent of politics. Berger seems to be influenced here by the modish postmodernist argument that there is no discoverable truth about the past, merely competing points of view which reflect the political positions and power-aspirations of those historians who hold them.[24] Yet a history which includes Auschwitz and Treblinka, Hitler and Goebbels, cannot accept such a view, which opens the way to a total relativism that accords an unacceptable legitimacy to those who deny that Auschwitz ever happened.[25] Empirical discoveries about the past, achieved through research, really can alter our understanding of it, as the case of the *Bürgertum* project once again demonstrates.

And the same, surely, can be said of current events. It would be very strange indeed if German reunification had had no effect at all on the way historians view the German past. It seems quite obvious that it must set the problem of German identity back on the agenda, especially since it is proving such a contentious issue between inhabitants of the former East and the majority in the former West. Equally obvious is the fact that it calls 1945 into serious question as a turning-point in German history. For a long time, historians behaved as if German history had come to an end in 1945, when Germany reverted after a few short decades into the state of political division in which it had been for centuries before 1871. Now, suddenly, the postwar division of Germany turns out, with the exception of Austrian independence, not to have been permanent after all. German history did not come to an end in 1945. Rather, the events of 1989/90 suggest that changing boundaries and state forms have been a feature of German history all along. Bismarck's Reich, as Wolfgang Mommsen pointed out in the survey discussed in Chapter 4, acquires a new interest and a new significance as a result. Nor should it be surprising that those historians who believed that German identity as such had fragmented or disappeared by the 1980s have changed their minds since 1989. Reunification, after all, did demonstrate that they were wrong. The attempt by *Neues Forum* and other elements of the East German opposition to create a democratic but independent state foundered within weeks of the breaching of the Wall. In March 1990 East Germans voted overwhelmingly to join in a single state with the West. Whatever their concept of national identity may have been – economic, social, political, ethnic, linguistic, cultural – it clearly existed to some degree, even if it proved by the mid-1990s to be a little more problematical than many West Germans had initially thought.

It is doubtful whether the effective destruction of the East German historical profession in the process of reunification had much to do with the forging, or attempted forging, of a new German national identity. To begin with, the profession, like East German academia in general, was grossly inflated, with low staff–student ratios in the universities, and hundreds of academics in non-teaching institutions like the Academy of Sciences. Giving intellectuals well-paid jobs with little to do was the East German regime's way of ensuring they kept their mouths shut. Many East German historians worked in one capacity or another for the vast, bloated apparatus of the State Security Police, the infamous Stasi. State and party control over research and publication was as tight as it could possibly be. Cynics said that all East German historians needed to do was to write an orthodox Marxist-Leninist introduction and conclusion to their books, since that was all the Stasi would bother to read; they could put whatever research they liked into the middle. But if this was ever true, it only applied to monographs on more distant periods and subjects; as soon as sensitive areas like the labour movement or the Third Reich were dealt with, the vice of ideological control took the tightest possible grip.

In these circumstances it was amazing that historical studies of any value at all were published in the German Democratic Republic. Yet they were: East German contributions to agrarian history, above all in early modern and nineteenth-century Prussia, were far superior to their West German counterparts; studies such as Helga Schultz's structural social history of eighteenth-century Berlin or Hartmut Zwahr's pathbreaking work on the working class in nineteenth-century Leipzig received wide recognition outside East Germany itself. Handbooks on labour history such as those produced by Dieter Fricke were invaluable tools of research despite their impeccable ideological correctness.[26] History in the German Democratic Republic was not a 'desert', as some claimed in the wake of reunification.[27] Western appreciation of its best work did not change after reunification.[28] Of course the majority of East German historians, either because of their police or political connections or because of the poor quality or quantity of their work, were no longer able to find posts in German universities after reunification; but then, most of them had spent their careers propping up the regime or engaging in the political indoctrination of their students rather than in producing good-quality research. Of the minority who had managed in the face of tremendous difficulties to produce worthwhile historical work, a good number found employment.

In this process, West German historians' primary aim was not to resurrect German national consciousness by destroying the legitimacy of what their most competent East German colleagues had been doing; it was simply to reconstruct history teaching and research in East German universities after decades of ideological deformation. Undeniably, of course, judgements of value and quality were involved, as they always are when it comes to deciding on jobs in academic life or indeed any other area of life; but there is no real evidence that these judgements were being exercised significantly more harshly by West German historians after 1989 than they had been before. Moreover, as far as national consciousness was concerned, ironically enough, East German historians had been playing their part in its renaissance during the 1980s by following the regime's direction to concentrate on giving a positive image to figures such as Luther and Frederick the Great in an attempt to portray them as part of the 'heritage' of the geographical area in which the German Democratic Republic was located. Instead of being a more effective way of bolstering the separate identity of the East German state than the previous concentration on the history of the German labour movement had been, it is likely that this policy reconnected East Germany to the broader currents of German history and hence German national identity. In these circumstances, destroying the legitimacy of the East German historical profession simply was not necessary as an adjunct to the forging of a new sense of national consciousness after reunification.[29]

Similarly, it is difficult to see why denying the legitimacy of the East German state should be seen as evidence of a resurgent national consciousness in the West. The East German state had no legitimacy. Millions left it before the Berlin Wall was put up to stop them in 1961; millions more threatened to leave when the regime finally began to collapse in the Spring and Summer of 1989. It was, in truth, a foreign import, kept in being by Russian tanks and guns, as the fate of the attempted workers' uprising in 1953 so graphically demonstrated. And it fell almost as soon as the Soviet leader Mikhail Gorbachev announced that Russian tanks and guns would no longer be used to keep it going. Recognizing these facts in no way committed one to the politics of a revived German nationalism: it was simply a question of accepting the realities of the situation.

As far as historians in the reunited Germany are concerned, there seems to be no let-up in the continuing debate about national identity, no slackening in the furious arguments that rage about the German past and the place in it of the horrors of National Socialism. National identity remains as contested as does the historical interpretation of the Third Reich. It is clear, however, that reunification has not, contrary to what some outside observers have feared, so far brought about a resurgence of old-style German nationalism or a 'renationalization' of German historiography. Not only professional historians, but, as the extraordinary and overwhelmingly positive public reaction in Germany to Daniel Goldhagen's charge that the vast majority of Germans in the Third Reich were 'Hitler's willing executioners' has shown, ordinary Germans too remain as critical of Hitler's regime and as aware of the extent of its crimes as they were before reunification. Those who would have it otherwise remain in a minority; and, as the lachrymose complaints of the 'new right' surveyed in Chapter 20 suggest, even they do not seem to hold out much hope of changing things. German history thus remains a vital element in the constitution of German national identity after reunification: not in the sense of encouraging national self-assertion, however, but rather in the sense of encouraging reflection and debate on issues such as racism, nationalism, violence, war, and the oppression of minorities, to which the experience of the Third Reich has made public opinion in Germany a good deal more sensitive than it has in many other countries. The part historians have played and continue to play in this process of reflection is, as the gulf which opened up between the historical profession and the general public in the course of the Goldhagen affair showed, by no means a simple one: but it seems likely that it will continue to be greater and more politically charged in Germany than it is in most other parts of Europe.

NOTES

1 Stefan Berger, 'Historians and Nation-building in Germany after Reunification', *Past and Present*, 148 (1995), pp. 187–222.

2 Rainer Zitelman, *Hitler: Selbstverständnis eines Revolutionärs* (Hamburg, 1987); Ernst Nolte, *Der europäische Bürgerkrieg* (Berlin, 1988); and for Stürmer and the other participants in the *Historikerstreit*, Richard J. Evans, *In Hitler's Shadow. West German Historians and the Attempt to Escape from the Nazi Past* (New York, 1989). For Nipperdey, see Chapter 3, above. For geopolitics, see Hans-Ulrich Wehler, 'Renaissance der Geopolitik?', in idem, *Preussen ist wieder chic* (Frankfurt, 1983).

3 One of the most notorious, Hellmut Diwald's *Geschichte der Deutschen*, was published in Frankfurt in 1978.

4 For an account of this dispute, see Hans-Ulrich Wehler, 'Zur Lage der Geschichtswissenschaft in der Bundesrepublik 1949–1979', in idem, *Historische Sozialwissenschaft und Geschichtsschreibung. Studien zu Aufgaben und Traditionen deutscher Geschichtswissenschaft* (Göttingen, 1980), pp. 13–41.

5 See for example Hans-Peter Schwarz, *Die gezähmten Deutschen. Von der Machtbesessenheit zur Machtvergessenheit* (Stuttgart, 1985).

6 Konrad H. Jarausch, 'Die Postnationale Nation: Zum Identitätswandel der Deutschen 1945–1995', *Historicum. Zeitschrift für Geschichte* (Vienna), Spring 1995, pp. 30–5.

7 Karlheinz Weissmann, *Der Weg in den Abgrund. Deutschland unter Hitler 1933–1945*, Propyläen Deutsche Geschichte, Vol. 9 (Berlin, 1995). See the balanced critique by Ulrich Herbert, 'Die "selbstbewusste Nation" und der Nationalsozialismus', *Die Zeit*, 49 (1 December, 1995), p. 24.

8 Christian Jansen, 'Offener Angriff oder politische Mimikry?', *Die Tageszeitung*, 12 December 1995.

9 See Jürgen Kocka, 'Deutche Geschichte vor Hitler: Zur Diskussion über den "deutschen Sonderweg"', in idem, *Geschichte und Aufklärung* (Göttingen, 1989), pp. 101–13.

10 Jürgen Kocka, *Die Auswirkungen der deutschen Einigung auf die Geschichts- und Sozialwissenschaften* (Bonn, 1992), p. 18.

11 David Blackbourn and Geoff Eley, *The Peculiarities of German History* (Oxford, 1984).

12 Lawrence Stone, 'The Revival of Narrative: Reflections on a New Old History', *Past and Present*, 85 (1979), pp. 3–24.

13 Hans-Ulrich Wehler, *Aus der Geschichte lernen?* (Munich, 1988), esp. pp. 115–30.

14 For a guide to this situation, see Elizabeth Harvey, 'Elections, Mass Politics and Social Change in Germany 1890–1945: New Perspectives', Conference report in *German History*, Vol. 8 (1990), pp. 325–33.

15 See the debate in Franz-Josef Brüggemeier and Jürgen Kocka (eds), *Geschichte von unten – Geschichte von innen'. Kontroversen um die Alltagsgeschichte* (Hagen, 1985).

16 Gert Zang, *Die unaufhaltsame Annäherung an das Einzelne* (Konstanz, 1985).

17 Alain Corbin, *Pesthauch und Blütenduft* (Berlin, 1984).

18 See in general Lynn Hunt (ed.), *The New Cultural History* (Berkeley, Calif., 1989).

19 For a useful general discussion in the British context, see Raphael Samuel, 'The Return of History', *London Review of Books*, 14 June 1900, pp. 9–12. See also the discussion of exhibitions in *German History*, Vol. 1 (1984), and the account of Bitburg in Evans, *In Hitler's Shadow*, pp. 16–17.

20 Martin Broszat, *Nach Hitler. Der schwierige Urngang mit unserer Geschichte*, eds. Hermann Graml and Klaus-Dietmar Henke (Munich, 1986).

21 For a significant pointer in these directions, see Hans Medick and David Sabean (eds), *Emotion and Material Interest* (Cambridge, 1985).

22 Barbara Duden, *Geschichte unter der Haut* (Munich, 1987).

23 See for example the very heterogeneous contributions to Gordon Martel (ed.), *Modern Germany Reconsidered* (London, 1991).

24 Keith Jenkins, *Re-thinking History* (London, 1994).

25 Richard J. Evans, *In Defence of History* (London, 1997).

26 See for example Hartmut Harnisch, *Kapitalistische Agrarreform und Industrielle Revolution: Agrarhistorische Untersuchungen über das ostelbische Preussen zwischen Spätfeudalismus und bürgerlich-demokratisher Revolution von 1848/ 49 unter besonderer Berücksichtigung der Provinz Brandenburg* (Weimar, 1984); Helga Schultz, *Berlin 1650–1800: Sozialgeschichte einer Residenz* (Berlin, 1987); Hartmut Zwahr, *Zur Konstituierung des Proletariats als Klasse. Strukturuntersuchung über das Leipziger Proletariat während der industriellen Revolution* (Berlin, 1978); Dieter Fricke, *Die deutsche Arbeiterbewegung 1869 bis 1914: Ein Handbuch über ihre Organisation und Tätigkeit im Klassenkampf* (Berlin, 1976).

27 'Im Mittelmass Weltspitze', *Der Spiegel*, 23 July 1990, pp. 136–41.

28 Günther Heydemann, *Geschichtswissenschaft im geteilten Deutschland* (Frankfurt am Main, 1980); Andreas Dorpalen, *German History in Marxist Perspective: The East German Approach* (Detroit, 1985); Georg Verbeek, 'Kontinuität und Wandel im DDR-Geschichtsbild', *Aus Politik und Zeitgeschichte*, 9 March 1990, pp. 30–42; Georg Iggers (ed.), *Marxist Historiography in Transition: East German Social History in the 1980s* (Oxford, 1991).

29 Wolfgang J. Mommsen, 'Hilfe statt Beckmesserei. Die deutschen Historiker zur Lage der Geschichtswissenschaft in der DDR', *Frankfurter Allgemeine Zeitung*, 13 July 1990.

INDEX